# BOOK OF THE YEAR

## Punk Rock Tour Diaries: Volume 5

**T V SMITH**

ⓐ

Published 2014 by arima publishing

www.arimapublishing.com

ISBN 978 1 84549 633 3

© T V Smith 2014

Printed and bound in the United Kingdom

arima publishing
ASK House, Northgate Avenue
Bury St Edmunds, Suffolk IP32 6BB
t: (+44) 01284 700321

www.arimapublishing.com

Special thanks to George Mackie for the front cover photo and to everyone else who let me use their photos in this book:

Klaus Fleischer, Page 1(a)

Jean-Paul Stotjin, 1(b)

Sponge, 2(a)

Jaroslav Vancata, 2(b)

Jet Storm, 2(b)

Mariano Asch, 3(a,b), 87, 88, 89, and back cover

Patricia Reith, 3(c)

Lynne Blackburn, 4(a)

Micha Macando, 4(b)

Doug Haig, 5(c)

JGA-Crew Christian 6(a), 139, and back cover

Tommi Tornivaara, 6(c)

Paula Bailey, 6(d)

Uli Schmid, 7(a)

Gaye Black, 7(b), 169

Fishbones Glover, 8(a)

Jeff Moh, 8(b), 227

Yuko Morinaga, 58

Marc Carrey, 160

Denis Alekseev, 194

The rest were taken by me!

You never know where you might end up performing. In the year this book covers, as well as the usual clubs I played gigs on the floor, in a living room, on a table, in the street, in a garden, in a conference centre, in a tent, and once in a stadium in front of 30,000 people - for one song. And of course there were all the stages in between. So here's a glimpse of...

## A YEAR IN STAGES

Well, Anyway...
The year starts here
(Essen, Germany)

Gaffa to the rescue!
(Rotterdam, Holland)

Onstage in Berlin…
(Germany)

Onstage in Prague…
(Czech Republic)

…offstage in Vernouillet
(France)

Guesting with Duncan Reid
(Tandil, Argentina)

On the table at Clash City
Rockers (Montevideo, Uruguay)

Meg'n'Jez'n'me'n'Vom
(Düsseldorf, Germany)

Behind the Red Door
(Red Door Studios, London)

Strumming at Strummercamp
(Manchester, UK)

Best stage location ever.
Between those potted palms
(La Roche-Bernard, France)

Keeping it street (Outside La Mer Bière, Pénestin, France)

Preparations for Timfest (Robertsbridge, UK)

Full house at Rebellion acoustic stage (Blackpool, UK)

In tent
(Biskirchen, Germany)

In house (Jukka's unbirthday
party, Tampere, Finland)

Bored Teenagers at the Sidecar
(Barcelona, Spain)

The fans went wild
(Augsburg, Germany)

With Neil Gaiman, Tom Robinson,
Lenny Henry et al...
(Westminster Central Hall, London)

Kicking off with the Toy Dolls
(Glasgow)

Packed to the rafters at the
historic 12 Bar Club (London)

What happens on stage is only part of the story....

## 2nd January ESSEN

Ten years ago today a guy called Kalle got in contact and asked if I would play a gig in Essen to celebrate his wife Annette's fortieth birthday. I said yes. I always do.

My website manager Klaus drove me there, and since then we've all become friends, meeting up regularly at my gigs in the area. Kalle and Annette have even hosted some of my fan club concerts in a bar they now manage called the Anyway, and I've occasionally spent the night in their apartment upstairs. As it's now Annette's fiftieth, Kalle decided to hold a party at the Anyway with a surprise guest. Guess who the surprise guest is.

Annette looks suitably surprised when Klaus and I walk in. 'I'd hoped,' she says, 'but I didn't know...'

While Kalle sets up the small P.A. ready for the gig, the staff of the bar present Annette with a large birthday gift, which turns out to be a new monitor for her computer. 'This is great,' she says, 'the old one still works so I'd never think of buying a new one.'

'Now you will have to go upstairs and get on the computer,' I tell her, 'otherwise your guests will think you don't like your present.'

That's exactly what I accuse her of having done when I can't see her in the audience when I start my set, but in fact she is there in amongst the crowd and objects loudly. A lot of the people here have seen me before at the fan club gigs, and the relaxed atmosphere and party mood leads to a very enjoyable show. Afterwards there's a lot of drinking to be done, with trays full of murky-looking chilli-laced schnapps being passed around the room. 'That stuff makes you go blind,' says Klaus after the first couple. 'We'd better have tequila.'

Eventually one of the barmen walks with me up the road to his flat, where I'll be staying the night on a fold-out bed in the living room while he goes off to sleep at his girlfriend's place.

'That's my bedroom,' he says pointing at the door across the hall. 'I haven't tidied up for a while. You really *don't* need to look in there.'

I don't, but after he's left I go to get a glass of water from the kitchen and open the door to find every surface piled precariously with beer bottles, dirty glasses and plates. I close the door carefully hoping not to cause a landslide: I have a vision of it all toppling slowly to the floor and smashing item by item. Might be hard to explain in the morning.

## 3rd January ESSEN

I have time for a leisurely breakfast in Kalle and Annette's flat before Kalle drives me over to Dusseldorf airport. I still have a few hours free when I get to the Departure gate and realise it would be a good time to write a diary for yesterday. I've been so busy lately that I haven't been able to find time to keep up my tour diaries regularly and I want to make up for that this year. Then a ridiculous idea comes to me: how about not just writing up last night but also trying to write up every gig over the course of the coming year...?

Ridiculous. Here goes.

## 11th January MAIDSTONE

It's thirty five years since I last played Maidstone. That was with the Adverts at the art college in 1978. Now I've been invited to play a room behind a pub called the Style & Winch. The money's not great but I'm intrigued to find out what's going in this town which has slipped off my touring map somehow. The tight financial aspect threw me into alarm a couple of days ago when I realised I'd never had an email confirmation from the hotel which I booked over the internet months ago. It was already expensive back then, but when I phone them up and discover that they never received my booking but, yes, they still have a room free, I find the price has risen to just six pounds less than my fee. I tell them, 'You're out of my league.'

Luckily I've been following some talk about the gig on my website forum and spotted that one of the fans coming had found a room in a hotel nearer and cheaper, so I booked there instead—and as there's still an hour to go before soundcheck that's where I go as soon as I get off the train. They put me in Room 2, the *Wise Old Owl* room.

The guy who takes me up there hands over the key and points out that I should ignore the fact that the key fob says Room 12, but they lost the one for Room 2. As I take the key from him I have a worrying vision of me surprising the occupants of Room 12 as I attempt to force my way in with the wrong key in the middle of the night after a few drinks.

The venue is a ten minute walk away. I attempt to get into the pub through the wrong, locked, door and some of the people inside take pity on me and open the other one for me. 'Over here!' they shout.

Right next to the poster with a big photo of me on it.

'I'm off to a good start,' I say, as I negotiate my way through the door with my guitar and two bags, trying not to knock over anyone's drinks. Someone having a beer at the bar says, 'It's a pity they don't *ADVERT*ise which is the right door.'

'It's going to be one of those nights is it?' I say.

He says, 'I'm here all week.'

Behind the pub there's a large beer garden with a room that could hold around sixty people. At the moment it's empty except for Clive, the guy who invited me here, and who is currently setting up the P.A. system. Everything sounds great and soundcheck takes about two minutes. 'That was easy,' I say. 'What are we going to do now?'

Help is at hand with the arrival of the support act, two guys called John and Andy, who I'm surprised to see have a mate of mine Steven Cooper with them. I usually see Steven when he's playing in Blyth Power or his own band The Charlies. I last saw him two weeks ago at a gig I played at the other end of the country in Scotland. He claimed he was on holiday.

We have a beer to pass the time, and soon there's a decent crowd in the room, including another mate of mine, Shane, who has driven down from South London and got here in 35 minutes, straight down the A21, faster than he can get to a gig in London. We get talking about the problem I have remembering names when I meet so many people on the road. 'I'm usually very good with names,' he says, 'but I do have problems with some particular names. For example, I have a blank spot with Sigourney Weaver. If you was to ask me, what's the name of that bird who plays Ripley in Alien, usually I wouldn't be able to remember.'

'Would it help if I asked you the name of that bird who plays Ripley in *Aliens*, the sequel?' I offer.

The room is packed by the time I start and it's a great gig.

Afterwards I chat to some of the audience out in the chilly beer garden. One guy asks me, 'So you play a lot in Germany?'

I say I do, and he tells me, 'I was in prison in Germany for fifteen and a half months.'

'Really? Where in Germany?'

'Bavaria.'

'Ah. They'll put you in prison there if you cross the street in the wrong place. What did you do?'

'Me and my mate were sharing a room with this bloke in Berlin one night. He seemed alright, but when we woke up the next morning he'd stolen my passport and my car keys—and my car. We knew his address in Munich, so we hitched down there, did it in a day, but he wasn't home, so we broke in to his place. We couldn't find the passport but we found an enormous wine cellar so proceeded to offload as much of the wine as we could. We got a wheelbarrow and made a few trips out to the edge of the property and dropped the bottles over the wall into the neighbouring park. The problem was, when we went into the park to take away the wine, we decided to try some of it first. We drank quite a lot. That's where the police found us, unconscious in the park surrounded by loads of expensive wine bottles. They showed us the photos of the ruts we left in the garden from pushing the barrow over it. We explained about the passport, but the guy didn't show up to court so they just banged us up. When he finally turned up and admitted to stealing it the police came to my cell and said, 'You're free to go.' After fifteen and a half months. No apology, no compensation, nothing.'

Clive and a few of his friends walk me to the end of the road, where they intend to take a left and head towards a pub with late opening hours, and I sensibly decide to take a right and head to the hotel. Clive asks if he should come with me to make sure I find the place. 'It's literally straight up this road isn't it?' I say, hoisting my bag over my shoulder. 'What could possibly go wrong?'

Even as I say it I realise my foolhardiness, but in fact I'm back in the Wise Old Owl ten minutes later, and apart from the fact that the key doesn't work for the first few attempts and I have mysteriously got white paint all over my jacket, everything is fine.

## 12th January LONDON

I'm awake at 8:30 because I accidentally set the alarm an hour early—must figure out how to work my new alarm clock—but that means I'm able to get downstairs by 9:30, in time for the last breakfast, where I can't resist pocketing a few of the mini Marmite sachets. I know it's technically theft but no giveaway trails of wheelbarrow ruts were left on anyone's lawn and somewhere along the way during the coming six week tour through Europe with the UK Subs I'll be glad I did it.

I take a mid-morning train back to London, where I have a quick turnaround at home before heading off to guest at Tom Robinson's annual Castaway Club gig. Tom was an inspiration to me when I supported him on my first solo tour at the beginning of the nineties and since then I've always jumped at the chance to play his fan club gigs. Lately I've usually been on tour myself when they take place, but this year was auspicious—not only do I have the day free but he's chosen a venue in West London, just a short bus ride and walk from where I live. On the downside, he's doing it with an eight piece band which I'm supposed to be part of, and due to his commitments presenting his radio show on the BBC the only chance for rehearsal was yesterday, when I was in Maidstone. Consequently I'll be playing on some songs I haven't played on for a long time. When he sent me the setlist through I had to explain that I'd never heard two of the songs before; but then he sent me links on YouTube showing me playing them on stage with him five years ago in Belgium.

I arrive at the Tabernacle in a state of mild confusion as it's been completely renovated since the last time I was here. Where there used to be a dilapidated stage and seating there is now a posh bar and restaurant crowded with people, many of them waiting for the show this evening. I wander around lost for a while until someone finally takes pity on me.

'TV—it's *up the stairs...*'

Happily there's time before doors open to try out the two songs of mine we'll be playing—and very fine they sound too with the whole band backing me up—but unfortunately no time to practice Tom's songs. Backstage I see a setlist for the first time and notice that one of the songs I'd been diligently practicing at home has moved into the section of the set before I come on, and another song, which I hadn't been expecting to play and can't remember, has moved into the part of the set where I am on stage. So Tom shows me how that one goes and I have a surreptitious practice.

Looks like at least five hundred people in the room when the band start. I get called up after a while and my songs go down brilliantly, then I settle myself at the back of the stage and play along with the rest of Tom's set, enjoying not being the front man for a change.

All the musicians and their partners hang around the venue after the audience has gone to have a meal together, then Gaye and I walk up to Notting Hill to take the night bus home. It's only on the bus that I remember that the new clip-on tuner I lent Tom during the set is still clipped on. To his guitar. Maybe I will ask for it back at the next Castaway Club I play at, probably five years down the road. Meantime I'm happy to know that my shiny blue tuner is in the possession of one of the nicest, most generous and supportive men in the music scene.

## 18th January WIGAN

The first red alerts for snow in the UK for two years, and coincidentally also my first gigs of the year in the North, precisely in the same area and at the same time as the heaviest snow is forecast. It's already snowing in London by early morning and there's a decent covering by the time I leave home at midday. Luckily, after a number of falling-over-in-the-snow incidents last year, I have a pair of snow grips to slip over my shoes and I make good headway down to the tube station, slowed only by the roller suitcase I have to drag behind me. At Euston the concourse is very crowded due to a number of train cancellations and soon after I arrive I see the 'delayed' sign flash up next to my train, so I ease my way past the hundreds of people gazing hopefully up at the Departures board towards a quieter area near the platforms where I can get a coffee. I've just bought it when my train is announced. It's leaving from the platform right next to where I'm standing, and I turn around to see a tidal wave of bodies surging towards me. Keen not to get caught up in the flood, I make a dash for the platform too—not easy as I am rolling a suitcase and carrying a guitar and a coffee, which in theory requires three hands.

Never have I been more happy that I pre-booked a seat; people are standing in the aisles and carriage ends, and it's only the fact that I was one of the first on that means I found space for my guitar and suitcase—the luggage racks are bulging. All around me people are opening up their phones and tablets and are all trying to connect to the internet at once, with the result that they are all staring at arrows and wheels and spinning beach balls. Soon we are off, only ten minutes late, and by the times we have reached the outskirts of London we have reached our average cruising speed of three miles per hour.

Much, much later I reach Wigan. I can't be bothered to put the studded shoe straps back on for the walk to the hotel, but a few skids along the way remind me how effective they are. The hotel has been renovated since the last time I was here and is warm and comfortable, so I can't complain about the thirty five quid advance price I paid for it. At that price there's no breakfast of course—good because I won't have to wake up for it—but when I notice a giant supermarket in the distance from my third floor window I decide to don the studs and go out to buy some for when I do get up tomorrow. A pot of emergency instant porridge would do the job nicely.

These studs are great on snow but seriously jar the knees when you're on solid ground. I have the feeling I might be leaving a trail of holes in Tesco's floor, but don't look down so as not to draw attention to myself. It's only the *clippety clop* noise that gives me away. A few shoppers look round in the mistaken belief there is a horse loose in the aisles.

Soundcheck is underway at the Boulevard, where support band Kanada Kommando are running through some songs accompanied by much feedback. That's not too surprising as they are playing quite loud, but I am surprised when the feedback continues for my soundcheck as well. There's even feedback when I'm not playing anything. We eventually track the problem down to a faulty microphone, and then everything is fine.

The gig is also fine, a decent turnout despite the bad weather, and one of the band even gives me a lift back to the hotel at the end of the evening so I don't have to find out how good I am on the ice after a few beers.

## 19th January DERBY

There's no snow falling and not much on the ground when I leave the hotel. I don't even have to wear the knee-breakers. The rail companies seem to be having more problems with the weather than I do though. I get to Wigan station to find that my train to Crewe is delayed, then I have an eighty minute wait in Crewe for my connecting train to Derby, which is cancelled. I'm advised to take a train to Stoke, where I should be able to get a Derby train. Should. Never a reassuring word when spoken by someone in a rail information office. This is all uncomfortably similar to a day at the end of last year when I went to play the Rebellion Christmas Festival in Birmingham. I got to Euston to find all trains to Birmingham had been cancelled, and was advised that I should take the next train to Bletchley, where I *should* be able to get a connecting train. There was one eventually, but in the meantime I had to wait nearly two hours in the freezing cold at Bletchley station—a fate if not worse than, then very similar to, death.

It's what they don't tell you that hurts. All trains to Derby from Stoke have been cancelled, something they obviously already knew in Crewe but didn't like to break to me. At the misinformation desk a man tells me that I will need to take a replacement bus service to Uttoxeter—wherever that is—and I should be able to get a train from there. *Should.* I ask him where the bus leaves from and he gets on the walkie talkie and after a long exchange establishes that the bus is outside but currently there is no driver. 'He's gone AWOL somewhere.'

There are two buses parked outside. With the help of another member of staff I find out which one is bound for Uttoxeter and get on it to wait for the driver. When he arrives and we finally set off I notice that the roads are remarkably clear of snow, so why no trains are running is a bit of a mystery. Nervous about ending up stranded in Uttoxeter I text Dave, tonight's promoter, and he contacts National Rail enquiries and lets me know that there is a train from Uttoxeter to Derby leaving in an hour. I finally get to Derby six hours after leaving the hotel in Wigan—a journey of a little over eighty miles.

Dave has got me a reasonably-priced room in a good hotel, but all I have time to do there before heading off to the venue for soundcheck is unpack my merch into a smaller bag and turn the room thermostat up to full.

The venue is a new one for me in Derby, a room above a bar called The Hairy Dog. I walk right past it three times because the pub's name is covered up by the awning erected outside to create a smoking area. The place is all kitted out with the P.A. and lights from a larger venue in town that closed down recently so it's surprisingly over-equipped for a room of its size and even has a decent stage. The two opening bands have pulled out because of the bad weather but that still leaves another three acts to go on before me, so after a quick soundcheck I settle in for the long wait. The audience trickle gradually in, most of them huddling at the back of the room with their coats on. I tell the lighting guy that I want lots of reds on stage when I play to give the impression that the place is warm. I'm surprised to see my friends Jon and Sophie turn up. They recently moved over from Florida and now live just outside London. In Florida they had to drive for a few days to get to a gig, so they're not going to let a bit of snow worry them and made it here in two hours, a third of the time it took me from just up the road.

As it gets near to my stage time there is a bit of an atmosphere starting to build in the room despite the chilly temperature, and people are gradually coming forward a bit. During my first song they come forward even more because the club's D.I. box on the stage carrying the signal from my guitar to the P.A. stops working and I have to carry on acoustically until the sound man plugs in a new one. After that the ice is broken, almost literally, and it's a good gig.

## 30th January ROTTERDAM

Six weeks on tour in Europe with the UK Subs…after more than thirty-five years playing music it's the longest tour I've ever done. I say goodbye to Gaye and head out into the unknown.

The unknown starts at Folkestone Central, possibly the most dangerous railway station in Britain. The ramp from the platforms down to the ticket hall is covered with polished floorboards so slippery that your feet skid out from under you as you walk. I have to take little tippy-toe steps down the one-in-three gradient and my heavy roller suitcase keeps accelerating and bumping into the back of my knees. That would be a great start to the tour: run over by my own suitcase.

After this I'll be travelling in the van with the band. Driver Andy could have picked me up from home earlier before he went to load in the equipment and fetch the other members, but that would have involved a long journey via Brighton and I would have had to get up at four in the morning. If I wanted to get up at four in the morning I would get a proper job.

They're running late, so I order a coffee from the refreshments stand in the deserted ticket hall. 'Stand' is the appropriate word as there are no seats. The only place to sit is in the photo booth, but I feel pretty stupid in there so after a while I go outside and sit on my suitcase in the weak winter sun instead.

Some time later I look up from my book at the sound of a horn and see the van pulling up in front of me. The cast: my old mate Alvin, bassist; Jet, guitarist; Jamie, drummer; the inimitable Charlie Harper, band leader and singer for more than thirty years; and his wife Yuko who unofficially tour manages as well as doing the band merch. Andy, who is driving the band for the first time, comes bounding out of the van to take my suitcase and one thing is immediately clear: he's the only one of us not wearing black. In fact he is wearing two shades of purple and looks as if he's going on holiday.

Perhaps it's his lack of punk clothing and general air of normality that gets us through customs without being searched—'First time ever!' says Charlie as we are waved through—and we find ourselves at the front of the queue for a Eurotunnel train that leaves only thirty minutes later than the one we were originally booked on.

A Polish tourist coach parks beside us in the adjacent lane, and Yuko points out the the three signs on the side of the driver's door—no smoking, no ice cream, no chips. 'I've got to take a photo of that,' she laughs, then gets out of the van and holds up her mobile phone to it. The driver, who is smoking a cigarette nearby steps forward and puts his hand in front of the lens.

'No photos,' he says.

As we're running half an hour late we elect to go straight to the club when we arrive in Rotterdam rather than checking in to the hotel. Yuko and I set up the merch while the band get their equipment on stage and have a soundcheck. After they've finished I have a quick soundcheck myself then go back to the merch area and watch the audience trickle in. Some of them notice me as they go past and exchange a few words. I don't play very often in Holland, and it's interesting to notice the difference in attitude between the audience here and in other countries. Many of them can't grasp the concept that I will be playing solo rather than with a band, and a few seem disappointed.

After that negative feedback I'm feeling a bit nervous when I go on stage. It's not an ideal start to the tour as my guitar strap breaks during the first song, which leads to a short pause while the sound man gets on stage and fixes it with gaffa tape. The audience remains quite reserved so I'm not sure how well the set is being received. Afterwards the singer from the support band tells me, 'A lot of the young punks out there are complaining, but *I* loved it.'

Later, someone else says, 'It takes a lot of nerve to get up on stage in front of all those punks and play solo!'

It is a kind of compliment, but also only a small linguistic step away from, *'You've got a nerve, getting up on stage in front of all those punks and playing solo...'*

On the other hand, one by one people pass by me at the merch stand as the Subs play and tell me that they really enjoyed the set, and quite a few of them also want to buy CDs.

Even though the gig was supposed to finish by eleven, it's two in the morning before we're packed and out of there. We drive through the featureless suburbs to our hotel then unload our suitcases from the back of the van and haul them across the car park to the hotel entrance. The clear skies have led to a chilly night, and there's an icy wind blowing as we wait for someone to let us in. Eventually a cleaner turns up at the door and tells us we are lucky we caught her, there's usually no one around at this time of night. That surprises us as Yuko phoned earlier to make sure it would be okay to turn up late. There was supposed to be a 24 hour check-in service but the bleary-eyed woman at Reception doesn't look like she was expecting to be disturbed and seems to be having trouble finding our reservations. While we wait Jet takes one of the free lollipops from the bowl on the desk and sucks away on it. Punk rock!

It is with a sense of inevitability that the we receive the news from the receptionist that there are no rooms booked for us. After a number of phone calls we establish that the promoters have given us the wrong address and we are booked into a hotel belonging to the same chain but six miles away. We trail back across the car park and load all the suitcases back into the van. 'Looking on the bright side,' says Jet, 'because we are going to another hotel we can have another lollipop.'

The hotel is in darkness, but to our relief lights flicker on in the reception area as the van pulls in. With a huge sense of relief we ascertain that they have the rooms for us, but filling in the lengthy registration form at this time of night feels punishingly unnecessary. Why do they need to know where I was born? We ask what time breakfast is and are told, six—as if we are going to wake up in three hours for it—and when we clarify *last* breakfast we are told nine. So no breakfast. I grab a banana from the bowl on the desk. I don't think I will want a lollipop breakfast.

Jet and I have rooms on a different floor to the rest, so we squeeze in the lift together with the three guitars and two suitcases. As I'm in room 58 I'm initially confused to find that there is no fifth floor, but then Jet points out the notice saying that rooms 31 to 60 are on the first floor. He presses the button marked *1* and we wait for a while but nothing happens. We look around for a slot to put in the key card to activate the lift, but there isn't one. 'You know what,' says Jet, 'I think in Holland 1 means the second floor.'

I'm not quite sure I follow the logic of this, but I'm prepared to give it a go. I press the *2* button, and it lights up red just like the *1* button but the lift still doesn't move. We've been in it for a couple of minutes now. 'Let's just take the stairs,' I say.

The stairs are right opposite the lift, and in ten seconds we're on the first floor, and in our rooms.

The rooms are fine and, importantly, warm. Even though smoking has been banned in Dutch hotels since 2008, my room has a strong smell of that room deodorant they use to cover up the smell of smoke and next to the 'no smoking' sign there is an ashtray. Jet and I go back down the stairs to join Alvin in his room to share the bottle of red wine from the drinks rider which we've saved for now. We established the tradition of the ironically un-punk 'UK Subs Wine Club' on our tour together a year ago as it's nice to have a drink and a chat in a relaxing environment when all the stress of the day is over. Quite often last year that bottle of wine would stretch to two, but tonight we're all tired after the long day and soon wander back to our own rooms. Jet and I are halfway up the stairs when I say, 'I still can't understand why that lift didn't work. Let's give it another try.' Jet looks longingly at the door to the first floor just a few steps away, but humours me and we walk back down to the lift, where I press the *1* button, the doors close and seconds later we are up where we almost were already.

So there it was, a mix of ups and downs—not just the lift but the whole first day of the tour. Generally everything went well, but there was certainly a sting in the tail when we ended up at the wrong hotel. The usual, really, and if it all went right something wouldn't be right. Who knows what challenges the next six weeks have in store for us.

Lollipop punks Charlie Harper and
Jet Storm (Rotterdam)

# 31st January BREMEN

I still don't fancy a lollipop breakfast, but I grab an apple from the bowl on the reception desk to join the banana. If things carry on like this I'm going to have a healthy diet on this tour. Breakfast happens at a motorway service station ninety minutes later and is a non-emergency cheese and salad roll.

In the dressing room at the venue there is a plate of ham and salad rolls, and a plate of cheese and salad rolls exactly the same as the one I bought on the motorway. I don't really want another one yet but I wrap one up and put it in my bag as an emergency sandwich for later because although there is enough food for everyone right now, it is *the law* that the carnivores will always eat the vegetarian food first before moving on to the meat.

There's a nasty moment in the backstage toilet when I can't get the door unlocked and almost miss my soundcheck, then it's on to the long wait while the venue fills up. A couple of weeks ago this gig was moved to a larger club after the original one sold out, and by the time I get on stage there are a lot of people in. The first song goes down a storm. Unfortunately, during the second one there is a sudden howl of feedback that swallows up the sound of my guitar. The noise seems to encompass every frequency known to man, and is at such ear-splitting volume that I am unable to carry on. I stop playing and the feedback stops too. I start playing again and the feedback starts again too. I stop. It stops.

The voice of the sound man comes through the monitor box in front of me. 'I think it is your guitar cable. Do you have a spare?'

I don't think it is my cable and I don't have a spare but I explain to the audience that it seems like my cable is broken and for a joke tell them that I'm annoyed about that because it was very expensive. Jet shouts from the side of the stage that he has a spare on his amp so I grab that and plug it in instead of mine. The audience cheers and I launch back into the song but straight away the feedback starts up again. I stop. It stops.

'Ah...,' comes the voice of the sound man through my monitor. 'It seems like the problem is our D.I. box. I need two minutes to replace it.'

This is the same thing that went wrong a couple of weeks ago in Derby. I go up to the microphone and explain to the audience that we need a short break because it's the club's equipment that is the problem. I also mention that I'm happy about that because it means there's nothing wrong with my cable, and everyone laughs. So it's with us all in a good mood that I continue two minutes later and the rest of the performance goes off without any further problems.

After the show, Charlie says to me, 'I'm sorry I wasn't around to help out when you were having that trouble. I could hear something was going on but I was locked in the backstage toilet.'

I live in a khazi?

## 1st February HAMBURG

They're not ready for us to soundcheck in the Fabrik club in Hamburg so Alvin and Jamie suggest we take a walk to a nearby music shop as they need a few things. It's a good opportunity to replace my broken strap so I tag along. When we get there we find the music shop is now a dance studio offering Flamenco lessons. Back at the club we are given directions to where the shop has moved and set off for another try. The only guitar straps they stock have the same plastic locking mechanism as the one that just broke but I get one anyway. Alvin seems keen to leave and when we get outside he says scornfully, 'Call themselves a guitar centre—there wasn't a single bass guitar in there!'

'That's because it's a shop for proper musicians,' I explain.

Back at the venue the sound technicians still aren't ready so I go backstage and set about trying to fit the new strap. I soon realise that the fitting is different so I'm going to have to remove the lock section from the old one and reuse it. I borrow Jet's toolkit and try to prise off the old fitting but can't get it to budge so I have no choice except to carry on with the gaffa tape repair and wait until I get home to fit the new strap. The gaffa is probably the strongest part anyway.

The gig is stunning, more than six hundred people in, singing along and giving lots of applause. After the technical problems during the first song on the first day and the second song on the second day I am fully expecting something disastrous to happen during the third song today — but nothing does, and it's only during the encore as I stamp around onstage that I hear a sudden alarmingly loud bang through the monitors. I recognise it as the sound of a loose connection in the D.I. Box—a sure sign that the guitar will cut out any minute—but I avoid stamping my foot for the rest of the song and get away with it.

It's busy back at the merch stand, people wanting to chat and have photos and buy stuff, and I spend the next three hours there until the club closes. Back at the hotel we decide to convene wine club in the bar. We go up to our rooms to drop off our bags and guitars and Alvin and I are first back down to Reception, only to discover that the bar closed an hour and a half ago. We wait for Andy and Jet in the lobby to tell them the bad news. Andy arrives and heads straight over to the reception desk. 'There seems to be some sort of problem with this,' he says, waving his key card. 'It won't let me into my room.'

The guy behind the counter glances at the card. 'That's not for this hotel, sir.'

Jet arrives, and it turns out he has brought a bottle of wine from the dressing room, and Andy has a few bottles of beer, so we reconvene wine club—well, wine and beer club—for my room. While I'm waiting for the rest I write a little notice saying 'fuck off' and put it outside the door where the key card goes, then as each person knocks to be let in I throw open the door and say angrily, '*Can't you read...?*'

## 2nd February GÜTERSLOH

The front door of the venue is locked when we arrive at 4:30 as requested in the itinerary so we trudge around the complex of buildings hoping to find a way in. Everything's shut. Eventually I call up the promoter and it turns out he's upstairs somewhere. Three flights of stairs actually, as we soon find out. The downstairs venue where bands usually play has been double-booked for some kind of party night so we're in a smallish room on the top floor that looks like it might usually be a youth club. The promoter tells me that we could have still played the other room but the show would have had to finish at ten. Sounds good to me after four days on the road, but a Saturday night punk rock show finishing at ten isn't really on.

The good news is that there is a lift to bring the equipment up in. The bad news is that the only place to put the merchandising table is across the narrow corridor in front of the lift doors, and Yuko and I can't set up yet because the support band will be bringing their gear in soon. Dinner will also be arriving in the lift later, and after the support band have played they will be taking their gear out in it. Worst merch spot of the tour so far.

Half the band go back down the stairs to load the equipment out of the van into the lift while I stay upstairs with Charlie to take it out and over to the stage. When that's done I go down the stairs myself to get some extra CDs and T-shirts from the spare boxes in the back of the van, but I meet Andy coming back up and he tells me he has already driven the van off and parked it somewhere.

Yuko also needs to refill her merch supplies so the three of us walk over to the van, which is in a car park five minutes down the road. It's a good job we go back because it turns out that it's parked in an area reserved for taxis and the drivers aren't happy about it. One of them who is sitting at the wheel of his taxi just a few bays away *drives* over and winds his window down to tell us to move, then reverses back to his parking bay.

The lift requires a mysterious and currently-unavailable key to work it so we have to carry the merch boxes up the stairs to the venue, where the crew still aren't ready for soundcheck and nothing much is happening. In fact nothing much happens for the next four hours and the promised dinner doesn't arrive until just before the club opens, which means it's too late for me to eat it. The meal for the meat eaters is a Thai chicken dish that has so much chilli in it that they can't eat it either. They could eat the accompanying rice to make it a bit milder, but that comes in a big steamer and hasn't been cooked yet. And there are no spoons.

Eventually we have a soundcheck, I'm able to set up my merch, the doors are opened only slightly later than planned and people come streaming in. Some friends of mine from Kassel arrive and come over to the merch to tell me that the evening has now sold out. They were only allowed in after they explained at the ticket desk that they'd driven an hour and a half to get here.

So it's a packed crowd and a good gig. The bar sales must be doing well too because while the Subs play I go behind the merch and am leaning on the lift doors when they suddenly open behind me and I fall into a trolley loaded with beer crates—which then have to be carried out and hoisted over the table and taken to the bar.

It's very busy at the merch throughout the gig, and a lot of people want to talk to me, which is great but also tiring. At one point I tell Yuko that I'm going to take a little break and I slip away to the deserted dressing room across the corridor. Peace at last. You can hardly even hear the band from here. I'm just pouring myself a small glass of wine when someone who works at the club marches into the room, stands next to me, farts, says, 'oh, sorry,' lights a cigarette and blows smoke in my face, then starts telling me in detail about his recent holiday in Thailand until I can take no more and have to go back out.

Afterwards it's a long and complicated process packing away everything and sending it back down in the lift. We're just on the final leg of getting all the smaller stuff—the personal bags and the guitars—out of the dressing room when someone asks for a photo of us all together, which means we have to stop what we're doing and gather round the sofa. Everyone is busy with their individual tasks so this takes some time. We're finally all in position and posed and the photo is about to be taken, but just as the shutter closes one of the women cleaning out the dressing room places a large bag of rubbish on the table right in front of us. She hears the click of the shutter, looks round and realises what she's done. 'Oh sorry!' she says, but before the photographer can get another shot everyone has scattered again. The cleaning woman looks over the photographer's shoulder to check the screen on the camera. 'Oh well—nice photo. With bag.'

No one feels like volunteering their room for wine club tonight, so we have it in the hotel restaurant. Later we raise the stakes by turning it into cognac club. Probably not a good idea: we still have thirty gigs ahead of us.

Thirty.

## 3rd February DORTMUND

We're in a four star 'superior' hotel in Dortmund—something I could happily get used to—and even better, we have four hours to relax in it before soundcheck. Not much else to do—you can't go sightseeing in Dortmund, there's nothing to see.

We see a bit more of it than we intend to though when the Sat Nav directs us down a narrow dead end road. Andy checks the address on his itinerary. 'Wilhelmstrasse. This is where the club is supposed to be.'

'This isn't the club,' I point out helpfully. 'This is a railway embankment.'

The weather is dull and grey, and it starts to sleet as we load the gear into the Kaktus Farm, tonight's club located in Dortmund's *other* Wilhelmstrasse. Years ago this was a regular club on the circuit and bands like the Kinks played here. I've played here a few times myself and one of the best things about it is the authentic sixties-era bowling alley in the dressing room downstairs. The promoter sets it up so we don't have to pay, but when the balls don't arrive he walks down the lane and goes into a door on the side, then we see his legs going past the pins, which kind of spoils the magic. While the Subs are on stage later I go back down to the dressing room and walk down the bowling lane myself to have a look at the mechanism. While I'm nosing around back there the ball-lifting mechanism noisily starts up all by itself and cranks away even though there are no balls to return.

I beat a hasty retreat and go back upstairs to my merch table. At the end of the evening one guy who has spent a long time inspecting all the items finally turns to me and asks, 'What have you got for nothing?'

I say, 'Nothing.'

Back at the hotel I volunteer my room for wine club again. There is no key card slot outside the door so I leave a 'fuck off' sign on the carpet in front of the door, then do the 'can't you read?' routine again to everyone as they arrive. Even to Yuko, who I just sent a text message reading: *Bring corkscrew. Urgent.*

Ones own skittle alley…

…not magic after all
(Dortmund)

## 4th February HANNOVER

I was wrong to think there's nothing to see in Dortmund. A poster in the hotel lobby is advertising 'the oldest pumpernickel bakery in the world.'

We left the equipment in the venue last night, so go to pick it up now. We joke in the back of the van about driving back to the wrong Wilhelmstrasse again and are quite surprised when Andy actually does, only realising his mistake at the last moment. We load the van in a heavy sleet shower which stops as soon as we have finished. As we drive off I notice an Italian restaurant opposite the venue called World Of Pizza, happily abbreviated on the sign in the window to WOP.

We have a few hours free in the Hannover hotel and as the room has old-fashioned radiators rather than the air conditioning type of heating we've had over the last few days I decide to wash out a few things in the sink and hang them out to dry. Punk rock!

In the club a guy somehow gets in before the doors open and collars me to tell me that we have a mutual friend, someone called Christine. There are an awful lot of Christines in the world and I have no idea who he means. He tells me she comes from Rostock, but I've never played in Rostock. 'I'll show you,' he says, and starts looking through his phone contacts, finally holding out a photo to me. 'There! Now do you know her?'

It's just a photo of her eyes.

Despite it being a Monday night the venue is full and we're all very happy with how it goes. Back at the hotel we decide to have wine club in Jet's room as he wants to smoke a cigar—he's developed a taste for them since Alvin introduced him to them a few years ago. It's the UK Subs cigar and wine club. Punk rock!

## 5th February FRANKFURT

We'd been hoping to have a couple of hours in the hotel before going to soundcheck at tonight's gig in Frankfurt but instead we get stuck in traffic on the autobahn and have less than an hour. It's a basic hotel and not a very nice place to hang around anyway, which is a shame as we'll be here for the day off tomorrow too. Usually the first thing I do when I get into a hotel room is switch up the heating, but that would tricky here as there is no thermostat and no radiators. Good job I did my washing yesterday.

The Au club fills quickly and my set goes down really well. At the merch table afterwards one girl comes up and asks, 'Do you have any badges?'

I say I'm sorry but I don't, and she looks annoyed. 'I wanted a badge!'

I gesture at the expansive spread of CDs in front of us. 'I just have music.'

'Music is too expensive,' she says. 'I only have three euros. I could buy three UK Subs badges for that.'

'Or you could get my EP,' I point out. 'That's only three euros. You could have *four* songs for the same price as three badges.'

She shakes her head. 'I'm going to have to think about it,' she says, and walks off.

I have just spent five minutes of my life that I will never get back trying to persuade someone to spend three euros on my music.

Shortly afterwards another guy comes up to me and says, 'I hope you won't take this the wrong way, it's meant as a compliment...'

Here it comes, I think: *you have a lot of nerve, standing up there on stage on your own...*

What he actually says is: 'I liked it when you played 'Gary Gilmore's Eyes' and all those great Adverts songs, but the brand new song you played was the best of them all. Hearing that made my evening.'

Hearing that made my evening.

## 6th February FRANKFURT

I sleep until 11:30 and feel considerably better for it. I'd planned to go and have a walk around the city today but we're out in the suburbs, the weather is miserable, and when I ask the woman at the reception desk how to get into the centre she looks at me as if I am a trouble maker. Apparently there is a bus that goes to the nearest S-Bahn station and I could get a train from there, but the bus only goes once an hour.

In the end I make a plan with Jet to just go and get some coffee locally instead. The woman at the reception desk looks suspiciously at me when I return to ask for directions. Clearly a trouble maker. 'Go left and there are some shops about 600 metres away on the right,' she says grudgingly. 'You'll be able to get coffee there.'

Jet and I trudge up the road in a sleet shower, past allotments and over motorway bridges, and are considering giving up and turning back when we finally see a small complex of shops ahead of us. As we get closer we see that it's a place selling pet food and a Lidl.

But some considerable way further on we find a café, and it's run by a French woman who cooks me an excellent vegetable *galette*. In just a few hours we will all be meeting up for a meal in an Italian restaurant so it looks like I'll be spending most of my day off replacing the weight I've lost over the past week.

## 7th February BERLIN

One of the biggest gigs on the tour today. Unfortunately Charlie and Andy have both gone down with heavy colds, and we have a six hour drive to Berlin ahead of us. We hit the occasional snowstorm on the way but luckily there's not much lying on the roads and we arrive on time. The venue is close to the hotel and Andy is relieved to hear that we can leave the van there overnight so for today his driving is done. He goes back to the hotel to sleep and try to recover. He doesn't look well.

The SO 36 is a large venue and by showtime there are eight hundred and fifty people in. The evening is a big success and I'm very busy on the merch table afterwards. My mates Paul North and his brother Carl have flown over from England for the gig and pass by occasionally looking approvingly as I work away, selling CDs and T-shirts and signing stuff for people. Paul drives quite a few bands around on tour but is better known as a merchandising guy and over the years he and Carl have bullied me into getting my own merch sales organised.

Eventually things die down and people start to leave, but for me the evening isn't over. I've been asked to play the after-show party at the Wild At Heart, just ten minutes walk away, and as it's one of my favourite clubs in Europe I agreed to do it—though right now, if the truth be told, I'm dog tired and would actually rather go back to the hotel.

But I soon liven up when I get on to my second stage of the evening. The sound guy Uli tells me with a grin that he has the same settings on the mixing desk from the last time I was here and the sound is excellent right from the start. I play a completely different set from earlier in the evening and people are still shouting out song titles when I leave the stage, but I'm done.

## 8th February DRESDEN

I'm waiting for the lift to arrive to take me down to Reception. The doors open and Andy is inside. I ask him how he's feeling and he says, 'Absolutely terrible, to be honest. This morning I discovered a new dimension of throwing up.'

As we go down in the lift together the phrases *noro virus* and *tour canceled* run through my head. I try and keep a few paces away as we walk to the venue, where we meet our tour agent Simone, who goes off to an *Apotheke* to get some anti-nausea medicine for Andy while the rest of us load the van.

Luckily it's only a short drive to Dresden and we get some time in the hotel before soundcheck so Charlie and Andy can relax and try and shake off their colds. It's a two radiator room so I wash a few more clothes and hang them out to dry. Hopefully I'll get the chance to do the rest tomorrow in Prague but who knows what the radiator rating will be there.

I've played the *Chemiefabrik* lots of times and know the two promoters Andy and Mario well. They're thrilled to finally get their dream combination of me and the Subs to the club. The only problem is, it soon becomes apparent that the club is too small. It's usually a very late gig here, but people are queuing up outside in the snow before the doors even open. The room already seems full when I play, but when the Subs go on it's so packed I can't even get in there to see how they are going down.

When I get back to the hotel my room is like a sauna, but the clothes are dry so I fold them up and pack them carefully away. Punk rock!

## 9th February PRAGUE

So that's Germany done for now and it's off to the Czech Republic, where the hotel receptionist asks me to put my name on the form next to where it says 'signature of alien.' The room is spacious but I soon find out you have to turn the mixer tap left instead of right to get cold water, the light switch has to be pressed upwards instead of downwards to turn on the lights, and the knob on the radiator has to be turned to the picture of a snowflake to get it to heat up. What you should do in case of a fire is clearly printed on the back of the door: *Carry out the people from life threatening rooms*!

Should the life threatening room happen to be your own, things could be more tricky: *If you do not have any way which enables you living the object, put a wet tissue into the holes around the door. By flourishing in the window or by another way try to draw attention to yourself.*

My room has a tiny high window that looks out over the roof, so flourishing in it probably wouldn't have much effect. The important thing is, there is hot water and two radiators—the right ingredients to get the rest of my clothes washed. I'm just about to tip the bag of dirty washing into the sink when I realise the problem: no plug. I try using the cap of my shaving gel to block the hole but that doesn't work, and neither does the shower cap. I go downstairs but the receptionist says she doesn't have any plugs. When I ask if there are any stores open that might be able to sell me one she tells me they will be shut because it's Saturday. She marks three crosses on my city map where there are shopping centres that will be open but says she doesn't think there is much chance they will sell them, and as they are all located on the other side of the city I decide not to bother. There is only an hour to go before soundcheck and I don't really want to spend the time on a wild goose chase for a sink plug.

Also, I need to change my guitar strings before the gig. I go to get a new set from my bag and notice a roll of masking tape next to them. Normally I use it to stick price tags on the CDs and T-shirts, but it occurs to me that I could use it to stick the shower cap down across the plug hole. I try it out and it works brilliantly. Until I put the water in, then it floats off.

At five we all head off to the van, through a small cobbled square packed with people and food stalls, mainly selling meat. 'Don't look, Tim,' says Charlie at one point. I look to see what I'm not supposed to look at, and am confronted with a whole gutted pig hanging from its back trotters. This is the carnival period in the Czech Republic: *Masopust*, which means 'goodbye to meat' and is the pre-Lent equivalent to *Mardi Gras*. Many people are wearing fancy dress or traditional Czech costume. There is a lot of drinking and revelry going on.

'People having fun,' says Jamie, gazing around.

I say, 'Yeah, I hate that.'

As we leave the square we pass two policeman who look sternly at me. Then one of them bursts into laughter, points, and loudly reads out the sticker on my guitar—*Musik ist scheisse!*—to his colleague who cracks up too. I grin back at them.

At least, I think they were policemen. I suppose they could have been in fancy dress.

The van is parked near the John Lennon wall, which fans have covered with artwork and graffiti in tribute to him. I'm not quite sure what his connection with Prague was, and not all the graffiti seems Lennon related. 'FRED' example.

At the venue we unload the van, the band carry their equipment to the stage, Yuko and I go to set up the merchandising, and Andy collapses across a bench in the dressing room with a coat over him. I'm getting very concerned about his health—the flu or whatever it is doesn't seem to be getting any better. We have a lot of driving ahead of us and although tomorrow is a day off there will be a straight run of seven shows after that before the next one.

The merchandising area is an unused bar downstairs just outside the room we play in. It's a nice wide stainless steel surface with plenty of room behind it to put all the cardboard boxes, though Yuko is concerned about the T-shirts falling into the filthy blocked-up sink with cigarette butts floating in it behind us. I'm thinking about what we could do to stop that happening when I notice the rubber sink plug on the draining board...

Should I?

'Just take it,' says Yuko. 'They never use this bar down here.'

Looking at the state of the sink they clearly don't, except as an ashtray, so I whip the plug into my bag. I am a plug thief and Yuko is my accomplice. She watches as I continue to feel around in my bag for my pen to sign CDs with later.

'Here, I've got a spare pen,' she says.

'Thanks but I really want to find this one. It's my *favourite* pen,' I say. These little things matter during a long night on the merch. Finally I feel what seems to be the pen, but pull out a small plastic teaspoon.

'That is quite sad,' says Yuko.

The air-conditioning is so strong that my books start curling up as if they are on an aeroplane. It gives *The Emergency Sandwich* an authentic sandwich look though.

I'm on stage early and there aren't many people in as I start the first song, but the room soon gets comfortably full and the set goes down well. Afterwards one guy tells me that he has a cabin in the mountains and when the end of the world comes he will be self-sufficient up there. He grows his own potatoes. He has no mains electricity, just one battery which he uses to power his CD player, which is what he listens to his TV Smith records on.

One girl has come from Austria for the show, and has bought her elderly father, a fan of mine, with her. In a few days she will come to the Vienna show with her mother, who is also a fan. They come separately because one of them always has to stay home to look after the dog. He's probably a fan too.

Back at the hotel we convene a quick wine club. I drop my bags quickly off and arrive at Alvin's room to find that his door is still open and he hasn't yet taken all his things in from the corridor. I'm slightly disappointed that he has't even had time to make a 'fuck off' sign. Soon afterwards Jet arrives and we shut the door and open a bottle from the backstage rider and finally relax.

Jet looks around the room. 'Alvin, where is your bass?'

'OH FUCK!'

It's still there in the corridor.

'That just shows you how tired we are all getting,' he says, and shortly afterwards I get a reminder of exactly what he means. When I get back to my room I unpack my shoulder bag, open my guitar case, fold back the cover on the bed, then reach for the bag again to get out my iPad. It's not there. The bag had been sitting around in the unlocked dressing room all night so I suspect someone seized a moment when no one else was in there to look through it. In a bad mood I clean my teeth—first with the hot water, then with the cold—then sit down on the edge of the bed to figure out what to do. My whole life on tour is in that thing. While I'm thinking it over I notice that the bed has an uncomfortable hard patch. I pull back the cover and find my iPad under it. I'd unpacked it and seconds later forgotten and pulled the cover over it.

I'm definitely over-tired, but tomorrow is a day off and I can sleep as long as I want. I set the alarm for midday.

This one will run and run
(Prague)

## 10th February PRAGUE

I wake up at 8:30 and can't get back to sleep.

Interestingly, the shower tap, unlike the one on the sink, has the hot and cold water on the conventional sides, which I find out the hard way. Suitably refreshed, I go down to breakfast, where unexpectedly they are playing Leonard Cohen over the sound system—good, but not generally my first choice to start the day.

Andy arrives, eats half a sausage and says he is going to spend the day in bed. He looks like shit.

Back in my room I remember about the plug I stole from the venue, but when I try it out in the sink I find that it is too big for the hole. Down in the lobby the same girl is behind the desk as yesterday and when I ask her if there are any laundrettes nearby she tells me they aren't common in the Czech Republic and the nearest one is a fifteen minute tram ride away. I explain that I can't do my washing without a sink plug and she says, 'Now the maids are here maybe they can find you one.' She goes to one of the rooms that is being cleaned and comes back with the news that they don't have one now but if they find one they will take it up to my room. She doesn't sound very hopeful.

I didn't really want to spend my day off sleeping and washing clothes anyway, so I head off for a walk around the city, always impressive no matter how many times you've seen it. At one point I walk past a laundrette, closed. I find myself on a wide street, with a large department store opposite and realise this is one of the crosses the receptionist marked on my map yesterday. I head inside. First I try the second floor which has the Travel Accessories section. There are a lot of suitcases and even a promising-looking display with discreet travel wallets and electrical adapters—but no sink plugs.

Up on the fourth floor I soon find out that 'Small Domestic Appliances' are located up an elevator leading from the middle of the children's section; you have to backtrack from the juice bar. Anyway, it's up the elevator, which makes it floor five really. Why don't they just come out and say it?

They don't have any sink plugs.

I'm a bit underdressed for the weather, which is hovering around zero, so I walk back to the hotel for a warm up. When I get to my room I find the maids have left a plug by the sink. And it nearly fits.

All I have to do is get a small piece of bubble wrap from my suitcase, put it around the plug and then screw it gently into the hole. As the bubbles pop and the plastic compresses I achieve the perfect watertight fit and my jeans and T-shirt are soon freshly washed and hanging over the radiators. I would like to have washed more of my clothes but it was only a small sink and I'm not fucking going through that again.

Yuko calls to see if I want to go for a walk. She's never seen Prague city centre before and I know it quite well so it's nice to show her around. Charlie still has a fever and can't join us. I'm really worried about how long it will be before I also succumb to this illness that's going around—the only hope I have to cling on to is that I had an awful six week flu at the end of last year so hopefully I've developed some immunity.

Back at the hotel Yuko goes in to see how Charlie is, and I walk on to scout around the area to see where we could go to eat tonight, hopefully a place with a vegetarian option for me. I know that Alvin, who lives in France, likes good French food so I check the menu outside *Le Petit Prince*. Today's special is an *hors d'oeuvre* of snails with herb butter, followed by the main course of 'fallow deer with a rosemary crust and veal reduction.' The next restaurant I come across offers Czech Cuisine. Their special is 'baked rabbit leg on white wine with potatoes and carrots.' Maybe I won't suggest we go to either of those.

The plan was that we would all meet at seven-thirty, but Jamie doesn't feel like going for a meal, Charlie is ill, Andy is ill—and when Yuko knocks on Alvin's door he says he is going down with it too.

So it's just Yuko, Jet and me. We go to eat in the Italian/Czech fusion restaurant around the corner, where the food is quite good but the background music includes 'The Final Countdown' and 'Y.M.C.A.' Jet tells me that after breakfast he went back to bed and slept until 4:30 in the afternoon, then went for a short walk before going back to sleep. He was going to text me while he was out because down an alley near the hotel he spotted a sign saying 'Laundry' with a giant bra and boxer shorts hanging from it. He went to investigate and peered through the window. There were ten old men in there drinking beer. It was a pub called 'Laundry.'

## 11th February OSTRAVA

I sleep well and would like to continue doing so, but as we will be heading further into Eastern Europe today vegetarian food will become harder to find so breakfast is a priority. Yesterday I had some quite good scrambled eggs on toast at the buffet so I go to stock up on that again. The toaster is the type where you lay the bread on a moving metal chain rack that passes slowly between two grills, then tips the toasted bread onto a chute at the back of the machine where it slides back to you. I put two pieces of bread on and go to get some coffee, then come back to find someone has swiped my toast. I put another two pieces on the rack, then go to get some scrambled eggs on my plate while I'm waiting, but there aren't any left. Oh well, just toast then. When I go back to the grill, my toast has been taken again. Unbelievable. Actually, it really is unbelievable as I'd been keeping an eye on it this time and I'd swear no one went past. I check round the back of the grill and find that the chute is set in the wrong position. My four bits of toast got tipped straight down the back of the cupboard, I can see them down there along with many others piled up in the dust.

I have a croissant.

At 11:20 I get a phone call from Reception to say that check out is at eleven, not midday as we'd all thought. Downstairs everyone is waiting around, dejected and ill. Jamie is now going down with the cold too. The van should have a 'condemned' sign on it and someone walking in front ringing a bell to warn people we are coming.

It's a four hour drive to Ostrava, where last year we had the worst hotel of the tour and at the gig the support band trashed the dressing room. This year we have a different hotel and a different support band. We have an hour in the hotel before soundcheck. The rooms are basic but okay: two radiators, and the bathroom has a sink and a bath, both with plugs. Would have been an ideal place to do the washing.

Alarmingly the hotel information leaflet says that check out tomorrow is at ten, but we ask the receptionist on the way out and she assures us that the venue made a special arrangement for us to check out at twelve. We all give a little cheer.

The venue is a ten minute drive away, unfortunately on the third floor but at least there's a small lift. The first load of gear is sent up and loaded out into the corridor but there's a small problem when one side of the club doors won't open, making it impossible to get the bigger boxes into the venue. Eventually one man, who is already so drunk that he falls off his stall when he offers to help, manages to prise open the bolt with his penknife.

I set up the merch with Yuko and after a while realise it's getting near time for the club to open but the band still haven't soundchecked. I go to the backstage and find them all in there, stretched out on the benches, sleeping or just trying to keep warm. Alvin says they are too ill to soundcheck. I go back out to the venue hoping I can do mine but by then the support band are setting up their gear and soon the audience start coming in and then it's too late.

All the same, within a couple of minutes of me going on stage the sound man manages to get a good sound, and the audience enjoy my set. There are more than a hundred people in, not bad for a Monday night in Ostrava, and quite a few of them have seen me before and are shouting out requests.

The Subs come on after me and put on a great show—you would never know how ill they are. I watch them from the back of the club, and quite a few of the audience find me there and want to chat in broken English or have photos taken. One couple achieve what I think is a new record: nine photos of me in various combinations with one or both of them, plus the few photos at the beginning when the camera didn't work properly. Towards the end of the set I find myself surrounded by a cluster of teenage girls who seem quite starstruck. One of them tells me I have 'sexy thighs.'

Back at the hotel the receptionist now on duty is unaware of the twelve o'clock checkout and tells us that it is not possible. When we tell her that there's been a special arrangement she gets all sulky, shakes her head and turns her back on us. We troop off to bed not knowing whether we will be turned out of our rooms early in the morning or not.

## 12th February BRNO

At least they didn't knock on my door at ten—they did on Alvin's.

I skipped breakfast because it finished at 9:30 and it's usually slim pickings for vegetarians in the Czech Republic anyway. Jet got down for it in time, and tells me it was the worst breakfast he has ever had in his life. We drive to a large shopping centre and eat there. There's even decent coffee.

It's just a one hour drive to Brno, the roads clear but heavy snow falling. The hotel is on the outskirts of town and even has its own car park. It's a slippery business unloading all the bags from the back of the van, and when we eventually have them all in the lobby we find that the receptionist doesn't have any record of our booking. A phone call to the promoter elicits the information that he changed the hotel to one nearer the club, unfortunately without telling us. We carry the bags back through the snow to the van and pack them back in. Ten minutes later we see the hotel but Andy overshoots and has to turn back, at first attempting to drive the wrong way down a one-way slip road then doing a rather alarming U-turn. Finally we're at the new hotel and unload all the bags, only to be told by the receptionist that he has no record of our booking. He phones the promoter and after a lengthy discussion they seem to clear up the problem, but when he starts giving out the keys we find out that we've been allocated twin rooms instead of the single rooms stated on the contract. Then there's another phone call and eventually it's agreed we'll get single rooms. The time we'd hoped to have in the hotel before soundcheck has now evaporated to half an hour, and I'm last in the queue to fill out the forms required before we get given keys. Just as I'm about to get checked in Alvin arrives back at Reception to say that he's been given a room that hasn't been cleaned. I wait while the guy behind the desk allocates him a new room, and am just about to finally get checked in myself when first Andy then Jet arrive to say they have also been given rooms that haven't been cleaned. When they have their new keys the reception guy ignores me and turns to another person who has just arrived. I call him a bad name.

Two hours has now gone by since we arrived at the first hotel, and when I finally get to my room I have just three minutes before I have to be back down in the lobby to go to soundcheck.

At the club the promoter is very apologetic. Maybe he had other things on his mind: not only is he organising the gig, he's also playing in the opening band called 'Boy.' The Subs decide not to soundcheck and before I can see about getting one myself Boy are loading their gear onto the stage. I can't even get near the sound man because the band members are queuing up to give him their detailed technical requirements. By the time they've finished the club is open.

Boy arrive on stage after a lengthy intro tape of pompous operatic music. They all wear elaborate stage outfits and launch into a full-on set of fast twin-guitar rock with smoke machines, programmed lights and backing tapes. The singer stands on the monitors and with a maniacal grin waves his arms around and exhorts the audience to join in. Fifty minutes later with one final howl of feedback and pulse of lights they leave the stage to rapturous applause from their local fans. I'm supposed to go on and play my acoustic set pretty much straight away. I think I'll leave it ten minutes.

After I've played I see two Dutch guys I know in the audience. One of them was at the first gig of the tour—which seems like years ago—and asks if it's the same gaffa tape holding my strap together. I tell him it is and he says, great: he put thirty photos of it being fixed on his Facebook site and will report on its progress after tonight.

By the way.

Q: What kind of cake do roadies eat?

A: Gaffa cake.

We agree to have a quick wine club in Alvin's room and I'm pleased to see he has scrawled 'fuck off' in biro beneath his Do Not Disturb sign. Although I'm not sure if it's meant for us or for the hotel staff tomorrow morning.

## 13th February BRATISLAVA

What do we like about Bratislava? We like the fact that last year it was the best hotel of the tour and we're there again this year. Admittedly there are no radiators, but when I've washed out a few clothes and hung them around the room I switch the air conditioning to full fan and full heat so by the morning everything should be dry.

I notice that during the couple of hours I'm in my room the snow doesn't stop falling outside and when we go out to the van the pavement surface is like an ice rink. Glad I have my strap-on shoe grips.

I don't usually eat before a show but I make an exception today as the vegetarian meal is a tofu, vegetable and rice dish—a pleasant change from the statutory bread and cheese that has been the staple of my diet since we got into Eastern Europe. I eat it quickly as I still have to soundcheck, and leave just as the whole trout dishes arrive for the rest of the band.

The venue is on the ground floor but it's still a difficult load out at the end of the night because we have to get the equipment through a narrow bar area where drunken audience members show an extraordinary reluctance to get out of the way and let us through. Outside we carry the gear through deep snow to the van. At least the club has provided a couple of people to help us, which speeds up the process a little, particularly as we are one man down because Andy is too ill to help. While we are loading the van I overhear one of the local crew say he's going to try and get Andy some medicine to help him with the nausea. That's worrying: he's clearly not well but he hadn't told us he was still feeling sick.

Back at the hotel plans to hold wine club in the bar are abandoned because it's shut. We have a bottle of local wine from the venue with us, but Alvin tried it earlier and wasn't impressed. 'I'm not drinking that shit!' he declares, and heads to his room

Yuko and Jet and I, the only three people still healthy out of our party, have shit wine club in my room. 'Winners' club,' says Yuko. 'Cheers!'

Jet looks around the room at all my stage T-shirts hanging up to dry. 'Oh, I never realised—I thought you only had one of them.'

Then the talk returns to a familiar subject: we have more than three weeks of touring ahead of us, the hardest part and the longest drives still to come. None of us feel safe with a sick driver. His concentration has been noticeably worsening over the last week since he went down with this cold: earlier today he drove through a red light and we were seconds away from being sideswiped by cars coming in from another street. We are literally putting our lives in his hands.

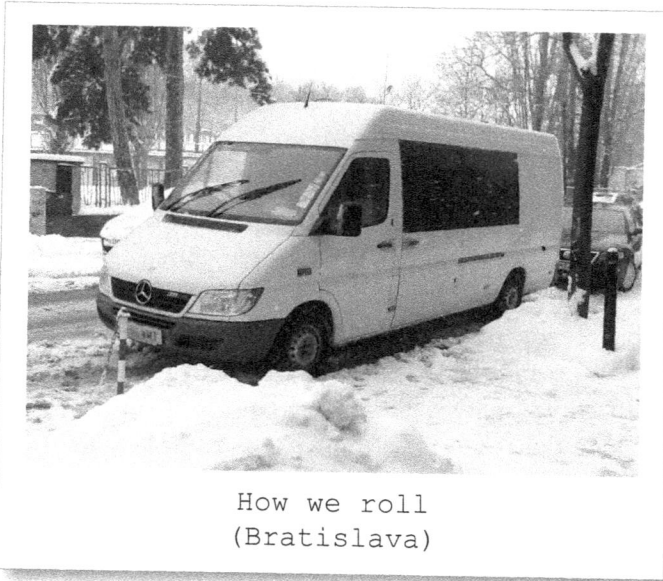

How we roll
(Bratislava)

# 14th February VIENNA

I come down to breakfast to find just Yuko and Andy there. Andy looks terrible and I decide to confront him with the situation. I explain about the long drives and hard work ahead of us and say we're worried that if his health doesn't improve we could find ourselves in a dangerous situation. 'What can we do about this?' I ask.

'I dunno,' he says. 'Maybe I should go to a doctor?'

Maybe he should. But he doesn't.

The Chelsea club *is* punk rock. It was the first club I ever played in Vienna and although not many people came that night, club owner Othmar kept on asking me back and gradually the audiences increased until every show I do here now is comfortably full. In the meantime the people who work here have become my friends. We get a nice welcome from Othmar and promoter David when we arrive. We unload the van, then Andy goes back to the hotel to sleep.

Tonight is sold out and the Subs and I both have great gigs—for me the best of the tour so far. But there is only one thing on our minds: What Are We Going To Do About Andy?

Wine club decision is that he has to go home.

## 15th February LJUBLJANA

The morning consists of a number of meetings in various rooms to discuss how we can continue. We call up Paul North who's now back in England after coming to see us at the Berlin gig. None of us had any idea back then that nine days later we would be asking him to come on tour with us. As luck would have it he is available for all except the last three days of the tour so in theory he could fly to Milan tomorrow and take over. We'll have to figure out what to do about the last three days when the time comes.

We drive back to the Chelsea to load the gear into the van, and Yuko and Alvin break the news to Andy that we are going to send him home. We had been worried about what his reaction would be but he accepts the news with a sense of resignation—I think he realises things can't go on the way they are. Yuko gets on the internet to book all the necessary flights, and meanwhile I chat with Othmar and David, who tell me that last night was the best night they've had here all year. They also tell me they've been speaking with my tour agent in Berlin and have already booked in a gig with me and the Valentines to play the 'Best Of The Adverts' show later in the year. This surprises me slightly as I wasn't sure until now if the tour was definitely happening or not.

By the time the flights have been booked we're late setting off for Ljubljana and there's a somewhat sour atmosphere in the van as Andy digests the information that for him the tour is over. The journey takes five hours and there's no time to check in to the hotel when we get there—instead it's straight to the club, where we load out and Yuko and I set up the merch. The band get their equipment ready on the stage, but when they hear that a local support band will be on first they decide not to bother with a soundcheck until just before they play.

I get collared for an interview while the band and Andy go out to a restaurant. The journalist is called Gregor and starts talking about punk and how I came to start playing solo, but after a few questions the support band begin their soundcheck and it's too loud to continue. We move into the short corridor just inside the front door. There's just enough room there for Gregor and his photographer and me to squeeze in.

Gregor switches the microphone back on and starts to ask about my books.

'Not many people know you are a writer too,' he says. 'What are your books about?'

'They're tour diaries,' I explain.

'What do you write about in them?'

'Well, just funny little things that happen on tour.' I say. 'Like having to do an interview in a corridor in a club in Ljubljana.'

His eyes light up. 'So I'll be in the next book?'

'You could well be. But you'll still have to buy a copy.'

'If you put me in I'll buy ten copies,' he says.

Done.

Shortly afterwards the club opens and I go back to the dressing room to find the stage times pinned up on the wall. It seems that I'm supposed to play before the local support band and I'm due to start in a few minutes. I walk on stage to lukewarm applause from about thirty people, and there are only twice that many in when I finish forty-five minutes later. Worst gig of the tour.

The Subs get back from the restaurant, but when they realise there's still another band to play they decide to go and check in to the hotel, which is only five minutes walk away. I go to the merch stand at the back of the club. No one is buying anything, but one guy comes up to me and say, 'TV Smith! I saw you here last year! You're still good!'

An hour later the Subs are due on stage. Alvin tells the promoter that the support band have to come off stage *now*, the evening is already running late and we have a long drive to Milan ahead of us tomorrow. The promoter duly pulls the band off stage, but then we realise that no one knows where Charlie is. Back at the merch table I see him come through the front door and amble past. He looks over towards Yuko and shrugs his shoulders. 'I got lost!'

I get the feeling Alvin isn't really into doing this soundcheck. His vocal check for the monitors is: 'One, two! Cheese sandwich! Body hair! Bollocks!'

During the gig I get the feeling Charlie isn't really into promoting the brand new UK Subs CD with limited edition booklet: 'What can I say? It's very bad. It's got lots of albums on it. It's like a little Harry Potter book...'

Back at the hotel we all agree we're not having wine club tonight. Jet tells me that he has to get on the computer and book some flights. He has just heard that his cat Fatso is ill and may be dying and so he plans to fly back to London from Bologna on our upcoming day off then back to Munich for the next gig. 'That may sound sad,' he says, 'but to me Fatso is family and I don't care how much it costs.'

I get into my room. I see myself in the mirror as I go by. I look tired.

## 16th February MILAN

A long drive to Milan, out of Winter and into Spring. Almost as soon as we cross the border the snow starts to melt away and at the first rest stop we make we're able to soak up some sunshine. I put my scarf back in my bag.

During the journey I ask Jet what happened about the flights and he says he was up for hours booking them and they were really expensive. Then his girlfriend called this morning to tell him that Fatso has recovered. 'He tricked me!'

Seven hours after setting off from Ljubljana we pull into the hotel car park in Milan. Through the entrance doors I can see Paul North in the lobby ready to meet us. There is an awkward moment when we introduce him to Andy.

It's going to be a late gig tonight, so we decide to leave it an hour before we go to the venue. My hotel room is fine but a bit shabby, with peeling veneer on the cupboards. Sink plug but no radiators. The first thing I do is tighten the screws on the bathroom door handle with a five cent coin. That's all it needed to stop it rattling around every time you open it. To complete the faded seen-better-days ambience there is a Corby 5000 trouser press on the wall, a design classic that you don't see many of nowadays. I'm so excited I almost press my trousers.

The plan was that Andy would carry on being our driver for tonight and Paul would start tomorrow. Unfortunately just as we leave the hotel there is an unpleasant argument between Andy and the band. The exchange gets increasingly bad-tempered and ends up with him throwing the van keys on the floor, grabbing his bag and storming back into the hotel.

So Paul unexpectedly has to step up to the driver's seat a day early, and the difference is clear. Immediately we get the impression that someone is taking care us. We pull up to the venue and Paul rolls down the window and says to the guy waiting for us, 'Ten strong lads to help in with the gear, please,' then leads us to the dressing room and goes to supervise the load in.

For the first time on the tour, instead of carrying stuff we go inside and have dinner.

The venue is a big cold place with the vibe of a squat. Nothing much seems to be happening, and three bands are scheduled to play before me. Paul spots me checking the timings in the itinerary and says, 'Why are you bothering looking in the Book Of Lies?'

I finally start my set just before midnight. There's a chest-high metal barrier a few feet in front of the stage keeping the crowd away, so it's hard to get a sense of how they're reacting. It all seems to be going quite well but the applause dies away quickly after each song. I'm not too worried about it as I've noticed in the past that Italian audiences can be quite reserved. One exception is the guy at the side of the stage going nuts the whole time and shouting 'I love you!' after every song. When I come off stage he grabs me in a bear hug and says, 'TV, you are the grandmother of punk!'

Back at the hotel the 'fuck off' sign is on my door and we gather to celebrate a new start to the tour. Tomorrow we'll be halfway through.


## 17th February BOLOGNA

This morning there is only hot water available from the tap so my teeth get particularly clean.

We've just reached the outskirts of Bologna when we get a message that the promoter has changed the hotel for tonight so we stop and re-set the Sat Nav. Usually a change of hotel means a downgrade, but this one actually seems a bit better than the one we were promised. When we ask about the rates we find that the promoter got a very cheap deal for tonight, but tomorrow—when we stay here on our day off and have to pay for the rooms ourselves—the price doubles.

The venue is shockingly small, so the Subs decide to leave most of their gear in the van and use the local support band's stuff. It also has a terrible merch spot: a small table in the freezing cold entrance corridor. There is no coffee, no heating, and no loo roll in the toilets. I wander off to get these three items in a nearby cafe and cause a bit of a stir when I use the toilet there and accidentally pull the string for the emergency alarm instead of the flush.

Back at the venue there are more people hanging around outside than could possibly fit in the room, among them Mars Valentine, who plays guitar for me when I go on one of my occasional band tours with The Valentines. He also runs a good club in Bologna called the Covo—why we're not playing there I don't know. He gives me a copy of the club calendar for this year. Each month has a photo of people who have played there. I am Mr. September.

This place we are playing, the Freak Out, does seem to attract a few big names. I read on their poster that a few days ago they had a gig from Mike Watt, who plays bass in Iggy Pop's band. Alvin used to play in Iggy's band too, which means that in the space of a week this tiny club with no backstage or toilet paper has hosted two Iggy bassists.

As the support band play I notice another thing missing from the facilities—lights. There are none whatsoever on the stage. Typically, when I start my set I almost immediately break a string—for the first time on this tour—and it takes ages fumbling around in the dark to get a new one on. The gig is good after that though, with the audience up close and obviously enjoying it. However, afterwards all I sell on the merch is one bottle opener.

The gig runs late and the Subs don't get on until nearly midnight. It's Alvin's birthday tomorrow and he's resigned to the fact that he'll be spending the start of it on stage. It doesn't turn out that way though: when he plugs in to the bass gear all that comes out of the speaker is a distorted farting noise, so he actually spends the start of his birthday running out to the van in the freezing cold with Paul to carry in his own speaker cabinet.

## 18th February BOLOGNA

A decent sleep, then I take the bus into Bologna to spend the day off wandering around. It's one of my favourite cities. In the evening we all meet up with Mars and his girlfriend Angela at a restaurant they have recommended to celebrate Alvin's birthday. All of us except Jet, who has gone home to Fatso, and Jamie, who hasn't replied to our text messages.

'Where is Jamie?' asks Angela.

'He's a drummer,' says Mars.

After an excellent meal of home-cooked local specialities we retire to a nearby bar for wine club. While we're there someone comes in trying to sell some gimmicky novelty cigarette lighters. He gives a big sob story about how he has to do this to get enough money to feed his family and Alvin takes pity on him and spends five euros on one of the guitar-shaped lighters as a present for Jet. It's only when he gets back to our table and show it to us that he finds out it doesn't light. He chases after the guy and demands he exchange it for one that works, and gets told that will cost him another two euros.

## 19th February MUNICH

We have a long journey ahead of us to Munich so make an early start and all goes smoothly until near the end of the Brenner Pass over the Alps, when suddenly the traffic grinds to a stop. Apparently there's been an accident ahead of us, and it seems to have affected both carriageways because there are very few vehicles coming in the other direction either. We crawl along for over an hour, waiting for the accident to come into view and fully expecting bodies, blood and wreckage. Eventually we see a juggernaut lorry that has broken through the concrete central reservation and jackknifed. The driver's cab has come to rest precariously balanced on top of the concrete wall and the bed of the lorry has turned over beside it, spilling its load of boxes over both carriageways. Miraculously no other cars have been involved and no one seems to have been hurt. An army of policemen are gathering up the boxes and loading them on to trolleys. As we get nearer we see what the boxes actually are. Wine! Enough to fuel the UK Subs wine club for years! Stop the van!

We park right outside the Feierwerk club in Munich and unload the gear in a snowstorm. It's great to be back in a large club where there is plenty of space to hang up the T-shirts and display the CDs. I've already run out of the gaffa tape and masking tape I bought with me from home and am making quite a bad job of attaching price stickers with parcel tape, which is all I have left. Paul sees me struggling and comes over. He glances disapprovingly at the price tags I've attached crookedly to the shirts, rips them off and screws them up, then removes the parcel tape from my hands and lobs it into a cardboard box. 'Leave this to me.'

Next time I pass by he's made nice new big easy-to-read stickers and rearranged the way the shirts are displayed so they look good.

As always at the Feierwerk my gig is well-received and afterwards I hang around the merch area and chat with people. One slightly scary-looking tattooed guy tells me that he is a big fan of mine and also of my friends Garden Gang. He says he is happy he could be here because he has only been out of prison for three days. He remembers seeing me and Garden Gang playing together shortly before he first got locked up seventeen years ago.

'Seventeen years! What were you in for?' I ask, and he tells me he broke someone's neck. I say, '*What?*' and he thinks I haven't understood his German. He reaches out his hands and puts them around my neck then gives a tiny twist to demonstrate.

Later my friend PamP from Garden Gang tells me that everyone thought the guy was dead as no one had seen him for years. The story is that he was actually working in an immigrant hostel seventeen years ago when some neo-Nazis broke in and started punching a pregnant Turkish woman. Was he justified in killing one of them? It's a moral dilemma I can't answer, but I can still feel my neck going *criiiik...* as he put his hands around it.

Outside, the van is stuck in the snow and the band have to push it to get it out of the car park. I would loved to have helped but I seemed to be terribly busy doing something terribly important somewhere else. In the warm.

## 20th February STUTTGART

In the van on the way to Stuttgart, Yuko tells me that she just heard the news that back in England Andy now has pneumonia. I feel bad for him, but can't help thinking about what would have happened if we had kept him on…we'd certainly have had to cancel some dates, maybe the rest of the tour. And he could have died. We all could have. One of the basics ground rules about choosing a driver for a six week tour is that he shouldn't have pneumonia.

Anyway, having Paul on the tour has turned out to be the best thing that could have happened. Driving a band around is not always straightforward though—as we soon find out when we get to Stuttgart. The hotel is right in the city centre and there is nowhere to park near it. Paul pulls up at the curb and I go and ask in Reception if there is anywhere to park. We're in luck. Not only is it a really nice hotel but it has a secure gated parking area behind it. Charlie hops out to start the check-in process while I get back in and direct Paul around the block to the entrance to the parking, where someone waves us in to the reserved bay for the hotel. Paul gets out of the van with a smile of relief and a double thumbs up—a good hotel and a parking spot! We go to the back of the van and start unloading the bags, then see Charlie coming out of the hotel waving his hands at us. They can't find the booking. We put the suitcases back in the van and troop disconsolately into the reception area, where the nice lady behind the desk phones up the promoter, who gives her the address of the hotel we have been moved to. Alvin asks to speak to him but the promoter hangs up. I try and ring him up using my German phone and find he has switched his phone off. The lady looks at the hotel address she has written down and says, 'Don't tell him I said so, but *I* wouldn't put anyone in there…'

As we pull out of the parking lot, Paul glances back and says, 'This is what you could have won.'

There is no parking space outside the new hotel, and it's on a main road with heavy traffic and trams going past. Alvin and I get out of the van and go up to the shabby first floor reception area, where a sullen young man finds our booking and tells us that parking isn't allowed anywhere nearby. All we can do is try to find a space on one of the side streets. While we are having this conversation, the only thing I can think about is the fact that this guy looks uncannily like my website manager Klaus.

Back down the steps to unload all the suitcases from the back of the van again, then Paul goes off to try and park somewhere. Upstairs I find Yuko in fits of laughter. I ask her what's up. She points at the guests' comments book lying on the reception counter, open at the most recent page where something has been written in Japanese. She translates it for me: '*I never want to come back to this shit hotel ever again.*'

When I'm finally in my room I email Klaus to tell him he has a *doppelgänger*, and ask him if he has family in the Stuttgart area. He writes straight back to say that it really is him, he changed his career path to have more time for beer, etc. *Great acting, right? You really believed I didn't know you!*

I write that I'm going to Reception to have a word, and just as I send the mail there is a knock on the door and I find the other Klaus outside. 'Mr Smith says you must go to the club now,' he says. The promoter is also called Smith. This is all getting very confusing. Not only that but what right has he got to tell us when to go to the club, considering he moved us to a shit hotel and hung up the phone on us earlier?

Actually, I'm surprised the promoter is acting like this: he has put on a few gigs for me in Stuttgart over the years, usually without any problems. He doesn't even recognise me when we get to the club, even as we wrestle a box of drum parts down the stairs, one of us on either side. When I come back with the last load of merch boxes I hear him asking where I am and Alvin points over towards me. The light dawns. He comes over and says hello and apologises effusively for the problems. It's hard to stay angry with him, but there is no escaping the fact that the hotel problem cost us an hour of desperately-needed relaxation time and a lot of frayed nerves.

After all that though, it's a cracker of a gig—sold out, and we leave promising the promoter that we will come back, and him promising us that he won't mess up the hotels next time. And now the stress is over, the hotel doesn't seem as bad as it did at first. The night receptionist lets us use the breakfast room for wine club, and even gets us glasses. Generally we have to use the plastic cups from the rooms.


## 21st February LINDAU

It's not too far to Lindau and we pull up to the hotel mid-afternoon. I won't actually be staying here tonight as my friends René and Mariann will be taking me back to their place in Switzerland after the gig and driving me to the next gig in Lucerne tomorrow. I'll be off the tour for eighteen hours!

Meanwhile I don't have anywhere to hang around before soundcheck, so I jump back in the van with Paul, who's driving down to the venue. The crew are all ready for us at the club and hoping that they can start a soundcheck. We explain that the band aren't going to be coming for a couple of hours, but there will still be plenty of time for everything. 'They set up very quickly,' says Paul. 'As long as there aren't any support bands cluttering up the stage with their gear we'll be fine.'

'That won't be a problem,' says the promoter. 'We just have one guy playing on his own so he won't have any equipment.'

'That's me.' I say.

The crew help us unload the van, show us the two dressing rooms upstairs, introduce us to the cook who is preparing an evening meal for us, and then I have a soundcheck, which goes very well. There's even time to sort through all my merch, which has been gradually falling into disarray over the last few weeks. Once everything is put into its correct boxes I feel much more relaxed and start looking forward to the gig.

The band arrive complaining about the hotel, which falls somewhat below the standard agreed in the contract. 'My room was cold, so I got the woman to give me a new one,' Alvin tells me. 'The radiator was full on in that one but it still hadn't heated up, so I went and fetched the woman. She walked in and said, "this isn't cold!" I said, it might not be to *you...*'

Also there's no breakfast included. Looks like I have chosen a good night not to stay in the hotel.

Shortly before I go on stage I am introduced to two girls in their early twenties, twins, both of them blind. They are incredibly well-informed about my music and ask me lots of intelligent questions about my songs and how I write. The conversation switches smoothly between them as one of them lets a sentence hang and the other one takes over. In some ways it's like talking to a single person. Despite their handicap they beam out positivity and happiness, and although they seem very excited to talk to me I feel I have gained much more from being able to talk to them, and I leave for the stage in a very good mood, two angels on my side.

The gig is up in the top ten of the tour so far, and afterwards the twins tell me how much they liked the new songs. Another guy starts to tell me how much he enjoyed it, but then runs out of words to express himself, even though I suggest he says it in German rather than struggling with his English. He backs off and lets me carry on selling CDs and T-shirts to the people who are gathering around the merch table, but a few minutes later he returns, clearly keen to have another go. He slips around the side of the table where he can get within whispering distance and says, 'TV, I don't want to molest you...'

I say, 'Good.'

Then he says exactly what he said last time again and I thank him again and then he goes away again.

I leave the Subs to pack away, apologising that I won't be there for wine club tonight, then it's just an hour's drive to Winterthur, where René and Mariann and me have a wine club all of our own.

## 22d February LUCERNE

A leisurely late breakfast and a pleasant day at René and Mariann's apartment. I even get my washing done. In a proper machine.

We get stuck in traffic for an hour on the way to Lucerne but I'm still in time to check in to the hotel and drop off my suitcase while René parks the car. From the hotel it's a short walk in sub-zero temperatures across a railway bridge to tonight's club, the Schüür. Wish I hadn't left my snow grip shoes in the van yesterday.

The Book Of Lies stated that I would be on stage at 9:30, but the timings are pushed back and it's two hours later when I actually start. It's a high stage and a big club and I feel a bit remote from the audience, but afterwards everyone tells me how much they enjoyed it and how good the sound and lights were. Jamie shows me a photo he took during the gig that makes it look as if I am ascending into heaven.

After that it's time to say goodbye to René and Mariann who have to drive back to Winterthur. It's a strange feeling seeing them go because usually when I play in Switzerland I go back with them. Then it's wine club in the backstage room where we can make as much noise as we want, then back to the posh hotel, where we can't.

## 23rd February LYON

Time to leave Switzerland and head off for our first gigs in France. Just before the border we stop at a large rest station that seems more like a shopping centre. There are plenty of shops here so I have a quick look for a sink plug and gaffa tape but they don't have either of them. Charlie, who is getting his appetite back now he's finally getting over his cold, goes off in search of hot food, and Paul and Alvin and I sit at the coffee bar. I ask Paul if he actually threw away my parcel tape when he was fooling around the other night but he says he didn't. 'The good news is that I picked up two really good rolls of gaffa over the last few days though.'

'Picked up? Your mean you stole them?'

'To be fair, I was given the first one. The other one I—er—I just didn't know who to return it to.' Changing the subject quickly, he adds, 'I tell you what I have got though: a lovely roll of white gaffa. That's great stuff, strong as you like, you can stick things up, write prices on it, so much better than the ordinary stuff...'

I turn to Alvin. 'Alvin, have you got any gaffa anecdotes?'

We hit France and unfortunately also hit traffic, which means we have to crawl along for hours among lanes of cars packed with winter sports gear. It's the first day of the school holidays. There is deep snow as far as the eye can see on the fields and hills on either side of the road. The chance of being able to check in and relax in the hotel for a couple of hours before the gig is starting to look increasingly unlikely.

In the end the journey to Lyon that should have taken less than five hours takes eight. We follow the Sat Nav directions to the hotel and Paul negotiates the one-way system to get as near as we can. There's nowhere to park so he pulls the van over on a narrow side street and suggests we get the suitcases out and go the rest of the way on foot. He'll wait in the van—we're already late for soundcheck so there will only be time to pick up keys and drop the bags in the rooms anyway. Bearing in mind some of our previous check-in disasters I suggest we leave the bags for now and make sure we're actually booked in first. By then Charlie is already beetling up the road and round the corner towards where we think the hotel must be. Given his notoriously bad sense of direction, Alvin and Jet and I rush after him. There's an icy wind blowing sleet in our faces. Charlie is already at the end of the road as we turn the corner, way up past where the hotel should be. We reach the number of the street given in the Book Of Lies and find that it is a police station. Charlie is out of sight. We hurry back to the van and I explain to Paul that we've lost Charlie and we're going to try the other end of the street as there's obviously a mistake with the number. I go back round the corner, where Alvin is getting directions from a local person who says the hotel we're looking for is way down the other end of the street by the tower block. Miraculously Charlie arrives back at the same time as us and we hurry back into the comparative warmth of the van. We explain to Paul that we have to go left and all the way down to the tower block, but there's no left turn allowed so we have to turn right instead and drive up the road past the police station then all the way around the block so we can approach the street from the other end. The first time we try it we come in one block too early and find ourselves still some way up the road from the tower block and have to go all the way up the one way street past the police station again, then round the block again, leaving it a little longer before we turn in this time to make sure we have really reached the end of the one way street. We get beyond the tower block but then there is no right turn allowed to get us back to it so we have go left instead. We then hit a right to get us running parallel to where we want to be but in the wrong direction, and snake our way back through a maze of one way streets until finally we find ourselves at the tower block, where there is no sign of a hotel.

'Maybe it's one of those workers' apartments type of hotel, there are individual key codes down here for each room' says Paul doubtfully, looking at the Book Of Lies. 'Someone should go and ask if it's in this building somewhere.'

Alvin steps out and goes up to the entrance of the building where he gets into conversation with an elderly lady. Suddenly he comes running back to the van. 'She's going to take us there! That's her car!'

A Peugot nips past us at speed, but we are blocked in by a stream of cars close behind it. We are finally able to nose out and see the Peugot in the distance, up by the police station. Soon there are only a couple of cars between us and we are speeding up the road we drove in on from the motorway. 'Apparently it's miles away!' says Alvin.

'Why on earth did they give us this address?' says Paul, glancing at the Sat Nav.

Five minutes and a good few kilometres later the lady is indicating for us to pull in. We're now in a street with the same name as the one we went to before, but this one is in a suburb called Bron, not Lyon itself. She's not exactly sure where the hotel is but this is the right street.

We thank the lady, who now heads back, and drive slowly on up the street keeping our eyes peeled on either side. To our surprise, at the far end we find our hotel. We're really late now so unload the suitcases as fast as we can and hurry into the lobby, where the girl behind the counter says she has no record of our bookings.

We drop the bags and show her the reference numbers in the Book Of Lies but she shrugs and says she can't help. We persuade her to phone up the promoter to try and clear up what's going on and a very long conversation in French ensues which ends up with her apologising a lot and telling us she does have rooms for us after all. A frustratingly lengthy check-in process follows and I'm the last to get my keys. I open the door to find a very small room which is almost all bed. There's a double bed, but they've also squeezed in a single bed next to it so the two beds stretch from wall to wall. There's a ledge to put the suitcase on by the window on the far side of the room but I can't get to it without climbing over the beds. It's also freezing in there. The radiator is already turned up full but is stone cold, and the warm air heating system above the door doesn't work at all. I know we're in a hurry to get to the venue but I can't come back to a room like this later. It's going to be minus six outside tonight.

I dash back down to the lobby, where the rest of the band are waiting for me. I explain my problem to the receptionist and she goes to a wall panel and fiddles with a few controls. 'That should be okay now,' she says.

I hurry back to my room and wait a couple of minutes, but the radiator still isn't heating up and the ventilator still won't work. Back down to the lobby. The band aren't there any more and I see that they are all sitting in the van. I have to join a queue of people trying to check in before I can get to the lone receptionist and tell her that the heat still isn't working and I need to change my room. I have to leave right now, I explain, and I can't waste any more time trying to get the heating working. She says there are no other rooms free. She goes back to the control panel on the walls and fiddles around with it again. 'That's got to work now,' she says. 'I'll go up to the room and check it for you in ten minutes if you like.'

Excuse me for looking unconvinced. I run out to the van and apologise to everyone for holding them up. 'My room was boiling,' says Alvin. 'I couldn't switch the heater down.'

So finally we're off to the club, opening time fast approaching and the decision already made between us that we'll abandon soundcheck tonight. There won't be time for it, and there's a local support band so their gear will already be set up on the stage by now. The Subs consider the possibility of borrowing their equipment—then we wouldn't even have to unload the van.

It probably shouldn't come as a surprise that the club isn't as easy to find as we hoped it would be, but all the same we groan in despair and Paul holds his head in his hands as we pull up at the address given in the Book Of Lies and find ourselves in an industrial estate. Suddenly we spot a couple of punks ahead of us. 'They've got to know!' shouts Paul and roars up towards them. 'Warm Audio!' he calls out of the window, and they point in the direction we've just come from.

The street is too narrow to turn the van around in, so we drive on until we can get to a turning place, then back past the punks to where they seemed to be pointing, but there is still no sign of the club. We drive on for a while, over a railway crossing, everyone in the van keeping their eyes open for anything among the deserted industrial units that could possibly be a club. Eventually we reluctantly admit that we must have missed it again. The street is too narrow to turn the van around in so we drive on until we can get to a turning place, then drive back and reach the railway crossing just as the barriers come down. When the train has passed we drive on and see the two punks disappearing into an alleyway on the right. 'It must be there!'

It is. For a club called Warm Audio, it's bloody cold. Jamie eyes up the support band's kit on the stage and realises it's so different from his that there's no way he can use it so we have to unload the van after all. There's a freezing wind and snow in the air, but people from the club help us and soon we have everything inside and can wind down in the backstage room, where a large spread of bread and local cheeses has been laid out for us. No one seems to be worried about the fact we are so late. One of the people running the club is also in the support band: they're on tour at the moment and got stuck in traffic today too so he knows what it's like.

Not long afterwards the place is completely sold out. I push my way through the crowd to get to the toilets at the far side of the room and join the queue of women in the corridor. A guy gestures me past them and shows me the row of six urinals round the other side of the wall. There's no distinction between the men's and women's toilets but the women are queuing for the one cubicle. In broken English the guy tells me he's happy to meet me and is only here tonight to see my show, he's not so interested in the

Subs. I take my position at the nearest urinal. The guy gestures at the furthest urinal and says, 'Zat's for ze shy ones. An' ah am shy.'

He heads towards it, then turns back and stands at the urinal next to me.

'But ah take zis one because ah want to talk to you while ah pee.'

He unzips and there is a long pause. He looks down dejectedly.

'An' now ah can't.'

The Subs and I both have fantastic gigs. After a day like that, the evening went better than we ever expected. Apparently it went better than the club expected as well. They ran out of beer.

Back in my room the heating isn't working. I find a little clockwork heater in the bathroom. I wind the heat setting up to full, then turn the timer all the way up to the maximum two minutes and it starts ticking away. But it doesn't heat up.

## 24th February MONTPELLIER

I can't help noticing as I make my way towards Reception past the open doors of the rooms that are being cleaned that they all have just the regular one bed in them. I got the arse room.

There is one common aim today, and that's to get into the hotel in Montpellier in time for a short break after the drive so we can arrive at the venue fit for the night ahead. We're staying in a hotel belonging to the same chain as yesterday, and as we arrive at the outskirts of the city we see a sign for it just off a large roundabout. The hotel comes into sight. It looks a step up from the one we were in last night, and has the word *superior* after the name.

'My Sat Nav says there's another half a mile but we'd better duck in and have a look,' says Paul. He drives the van into the spacious car park and Yuko and Alvin go in to see if they have our bookings. They return shortly afterwards with the news that they don't, and that our hotel is in fact further down the road.

'It looked really nice though!' says Yuko. 'Price of the rooms was twice as much as yesterday!'

As Paul pulls out of the car park he says, 'This is what you could have won.'

He follows the Sat Nav directions and drives back up to the big roundabout, then off a slip road to the motorway, branching back into the industrial estate on another slip road. We turn a corner and see the hotel ahead of us. It looks very similar to the last one and is also a *superior*. As we get closer we see that it actually is the same hotel, we've just approached it from the other direction.

'I don't believe it,' says Paul, and drives back up to the roundabout, avoids the slip road and takes the adjacent road we were on when we first saw the hotel. This time we carry straight on and take a right into some industrial warehouses and soon find the correct hotel, a smaller version of the one up the road.

The woman at the reception desk is very friendly and helpful, checks us in with minimum fuss, hands out the keys and explains that there is someone at the desk 24 hours a day in case there are any problems.

The problems don't take long. Before I've even left for my room Alvin is back at the desk because his room is cold and the heater doesn't work. I go to my room and open the door to a wonderful blast of heat, the fan running at full power. But the room hasn't been cleaned. I go straight back to the lobby where the receptionist is about to take Alvin to his room to show how to work the heating. When she's back I explain about my room, so she looks for a different one. 'Please make it a nice warm room,' I beg, and explain about yesterday. She says, no problem, and hands me a new key. At least the room only has one bed in it and is reasonably warm, but after I've taken my jacket off and been in there a few minutes I realise that reasonably warm isn't warm enough. Nothing I do to the control pad makes any difference so in the end I head back to the receptionist, who follows me back to my room and struggles with the controls herself for a while. After a while the fan switches on and warm air comes streaming out.

'Great! How did you do that?'

'You 'ave to press *enter* each time you change one of zese controls.'

'But I tried that and it still didn't work...'

She shrugs her shoulders. '*Je suis magicienne.*'

The magician of the central heating.

After all that there's not a lot of time left before we have to leave for the gig. The venue is called 'The Secret Place.' The Subs played it about five years ago and say that it is aptly named because it is very difficult to find. Since then the whole area has been developed into a vast industrial estate and there are no recognisable landmarks. Luckily we have the Sat Nav.

Paul programmes in the address and we set off out of the hotel car park and through the industrial estate. We come to a T-junction where we should turn left, but the one-way system only allows us to turn right. The right turn takes us past a circus on the other side of the road.

'Look at that—camels!' shouts Jamie.

We drive on for a bit until Paul can find a place to turn around, then back past the circus, where we all have another look at the camels, and on past a fast food restaurant called 'Quick.'

'I went to a *Quick* in the service station yesterday and ordered the *Giant Burger*,' says Jamie. 'It took ages for them to serve it, and it was really small.'

The Sat Nav leads us to another big roundabout with a Harley Davison shop next to it. 'This is where the club is supposed to be,' says Paul—but it clearly isn't so we go around the roundabout again and take the slip road just before the shop in the hope of finding something in the area behind it.

'Is this ringing any bells, anyone who's played here before?' asks Paul from the front. No response.

There's a surprising amount of traffic for a Sunday evening and it's all bunching behind us as we drive slowly along looking out for the club. It's a narrow street and there's no room for anyone to overtake us. 'This is ridiculous, says Paul despairingly. 'Someone had better ring up the promoter and get directions.'

Alvin rings and gets the information that we should go to the roundabout with the Quick restaurant next to it, drive on to the next roundabout, follow the sign to *Setes*, then take a right at the first lights.

'Does anyone remember how to get to the Quick restaurant?' asks Paul.

'I think we have to go back to the circus,' says Jamie.

'We never left the circus,' I mutter.

We drive back to the circus, pass it, turn around at the roundabout and head back past the circus again towards the Quick restaurant. We're bored with the camels now, and anyway they are quite hard to make out as it has got dark since we left the hotel. A huge illuminated sign flickers into life on the front of a shop selling air conditioning systems on the other side of the road: Keep Cool!

We find the Quick restaurant next to the roundabout and start to follow our directions but shortly afterwards we spot *another* Quick restaurant, also next to a roundabout. This one actually seems more likely to be the one the promoter meant as it's much nearer the address of the club, and as we approach it we see the sign for *Setes*. We take the exit road and turn right at the first set of lights, and find ourselves in a bus station.

'Hang on folks, let's stay calm,' says Paul, as he wrestles the van around. 'There's a lot of metal around here and I don't want to be hitting any of it.'

We drive on down the road a bit in case the promoter meant the second set of lights, and on the way come across another Quick restaurant. I don't think we're in

Kansas any more Toto. We take the next right but end up in a smart residential area, clearly not the place for a punk rock club, so Paul turns the van around again and heads back towards the bus station. 'How do they get any post?!' he exclaims in exasperation.

The phone rings. It's the promoter wondering where we are. Alvin asks him to come and meet us by the Harley Davison place so he can lead us to the club from there, and he says he'll be there in two minutes—he'll be in a small red car.

Unfortunately we're quite a lot further than two minutes away. 'By the time we get there he'll be gone,' fumes Paul as he negotiates the van through a queue of traffic and out onto another roundabout. We reach the Harley Davison shop a few minutes later, and just as we pull off the roundabout into the slip road next to it we realise there is a small red car on the slip road facing in the other direction, a few cars queuing behind it, the driver looking around anxiously. He spots us at the same moment we spot him, but one of the cars behind him sounds their horn and he has to pull out into the roundabout, narrowly avoiding getting winged by one of the cars speeding round it, while we are already heading down the slip road back into the industrial estate. There are cars on our tail and no space to turn around so we go on to the next roundabout and double back, passing the promoter's car which is now speeding the other way.

I turn to Alvin. 'I'm thinking of becoming addicted to drugs.'

The promoter must have turned at the same roundabout we did because soon we notice him a few cars behind us, unable to overtake because the road is too narrow. I suggest it might be funny if we drove direct to the venue now with him following us, but nobody laughs.

We pull over to the side of the road and eventually there are enough breaks in the oncoming traffic for the cars behind us to get past, and then at last the promoter's car is in front of us. He leads us back onto the roundabout, then on to the roundabout with the Quick restaurant next to it, where he ignores the exit we took marked *Setes* and instead takes the next one, also marked *Setes*. A couple of kilometres down the road we turn right at the lights and then left into an alley with an illuminated sign saying 'Secret Place' at the end of it.

From the front seat Charlie says, 'Ah yes, I recognise it now.'

The merch area is in the beer garden, where the temperature is a few degrees below zero. There's just one little heater up on the wall so I tell Yuko I'm not going to do any merch tonight—if I come off stage sweating and out into this I could be the next candidate for pneumonia. Yuko says she's going to put out the Subs merch anyway so she'll cover for me. Inside there's quite a nice little club, a low concrete stage, not quite level. Back out through the beer garden I find the backstage, which is a small caravan. When I try and shut the door the handle breaks off in my hand. Inside the caravan a heater blasts away ineffectually. Soon the food arrives, a huge bowl of chips with a whole chicken for the meat eaters and a potato bake for me. Potato bake and chips. I would have had some of the potato salad as well but there was ham in it.

We hang around in the caravan while the support band plays, and Charlie attempts to keep the door shut by sticking it up with gaffa tape. Gaffa may be strong enough to hold together a guitar strap for twenty five days but it can't keep a caravan door shut.

By the way, what sort of...oh, never mind.

Alvin tells me about some of the other ridiculous circumstances the Subs have found themselves in on tour. At one gig they arrived to find the venue was a barn in a field full of six foot high weeds. Alvin walked out of the barn in despair and Charlie told him encouragingly, 'It'll be alright once they get the horse out.'

I take the stage with quite low expectations, but quickly realise that the audience are really enjoying what I'm doing, and we have a brilliant gig. Despite not having a soundcheck the Subs play brilliantly too, and it's one of the best nights of the tour so far.

Afterwards a youngish guy comes up to me and says, 'I have never felt anything like that before. You made me totally happy and totally sad at the same time. Incredible.'

That's why I do this.

## 25th February MONTPELLIER

At last another day off. Untroubled by an alarm clock I sleep most of the morning, then go in search of breakfast. I'd like to have had it in the historic Montpellier city centre but we're so far out in the suburbs that getting there would involve a taking a number of buses and I'm not confident I'd find my way back. Instead I wander around the industrial estate and find a patisserie in a faceless modern unit, crammed with customers from the surrounding businesses. They sell me a good croissant for next to nothing but I'm directed over to a machine for the coffee, which is quite bad. I get a much better one back at the hotel, then spend the rest of the day catching up on my emails, glad of some time on my own, finally getting to bed at two in the morning.

## 26th February DONOSTIA

We make an eleven o'clock start for the long journey south to the Basque Country. By late afternoon we're in Donostia and looking for our hotel. The correct street number wouldn't come up on the Sat Nav so Paul has programmed in the nearest it would accept—59 instead of 61—and it takes us straight to a building that looks like it could be a hotel but is in fact a military training academy. Number 61 turns out to be a couple of kilometres away up out in the countryside along a twisty steep road not much wider than our van.

The hotel is a large building on top of a hill that looks like it is aimed at a clientele of summer hikers. The rooms are basic and cold. Alvin enquires about the heating and is told that it comes on between seven and eleven—exactly the period when we won't be there.

Miraculously there's a parking space right outside the venue and it's an easy flat load in. We stand at the bar with a good strong coffee. I'm chatting with Alvin when I notice a woman coming out of the toilets beside us and realise I don't know the Basque for *Gents* and *Ladies*, one of the first things you should learn in any language to save embarrassment. I check what's written on the door: *Noka*. I turn back to Alvin. 'So, *Ladies* is *Nokas*. How am I going to remember that?'

The upstairs dressing room is a literally a toilet and we dump our bags in the shower area next to it. There's a very fat photographer bustling around setting up his equipment in the technicians' room across the corridor which looks out over the club towards the stage. The photographer's name is up on the posters too, bigger than mine. He comes out of the room, sweating profusely, and says something to me and Jet accompanied by a lot of arm waving and macho gestures. He repeats the same words a few times, but we don't know what he means. Then he points at one of his armpits and wafts his hand in front of it, and I realise he is saying, 'I stink!'

He does too. After he's gone back into the other room, Jet turns to me with a bemused expression and shakes his head. 'He wasn't ashamed about it at all. He was actually proud that he smells.'

The singer from the support band says what an honour it is for him to be sharing a stage with the UK Subs and TV Smith and begs us to watch his show, so we follow him down the stairs. A couple of songs into the gig, he asks someone from the audience to bring him a beer. When it eventually arrives he immediately pours it over his head—tediously *rock'n'roll* and a waste of good beer.

I turn to Jamie, who is standing next to me. 'Later in the set he pours shots over his head.'

Jamie chuckles. 'Yeah, and right at the end a sambucca. Then he sets fire to it.'

If he makes much more of a mess up there I might light the match myself.

Paul is busily mopping the stage with towels as I get up there with my guitar, which gives me an ideal opportunity to say, 'You missed a bit.'

The place is pretty full for a Tuesday night, but it's an audience that's not familiar with me or the concept of anyone playing solo acoustic punk. They take a bit of convincing, but after the first few songs they start to gather closer to the stage and I hear people clapping along a bit. By the time I finish I'm getting warm applause so I leave the stage feeling I've made a good first impression.

As usual I watch The Subs from the merch area but after a while I have to go upstairs and fetch another T-shirt and a jacket from the toilet dressing room because the club has turned the air-conditioning on. The vent is right above the merch table and blasting icy cold air across me and Yuko. The T-shirts are flapping.

The day has one final surprise in store for us when we finish loading the gear into the back of the van at the end of the evening: Paul unlocks the front passenger door and the key breaks off in the lock. Now we have just one spare key between all of us, and if anything happens to that we'll be in big trouble.

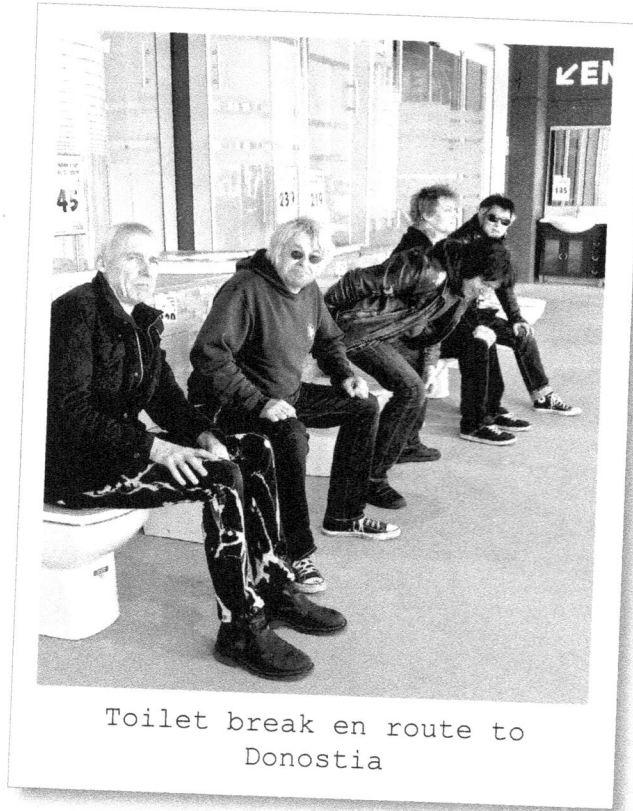

Toilet break en route to
Donostia

## 27th February LOGROÑO

I dreamed that I opened my bag and all that was inside it, neatly lined up in a row, was a roll of black gaffa, a roll of parcel tape, a roll of masking tape, and a mini roll of Sellotape. I think my subconscious is telling me that my life needs order..

It's a sparkling clear sunny day but a lot of snow is lying on the fields around us as we drive over the mountains. After a couple of hours we pass a sign for a large DIY superstore and turn off the motorway to look for it in the hope that they will have a key-cutting service. We drive around an industrial estate for a while and finally spot the place ahead of us. Charlie says he's just going in to find a toilet and when we catch him up we find him in the entrance sitting on one of the display models, grinning. The rest of us line up on the toilets next to him and Yuko takes our photo. I've heard of a toilet stop but this is ridiculous. Paul returns with the news that they don't cut keys here, and the photo session breaks up when a uniformed security guard with a furious expression marches round the corner towards us.

A couple of hours later we reach Logroño, where tonight's gig will take place, and as we drive in through the suburbs we spot a Mercedes garage, exactly what we need. One of the mechanics comes out and tries to get the broken piece of key out of the lock with tweezers. He doesn't have any success but reckons they will be able to cut a new key so at least we'll have a spare. The process is not as easy as you might think, requiring a lot of form filling and registering of chassis numbers and double-checking with the van hire company in England. When they finally cut the key it then has to be calibrated electronically with the engine so that it can start the ignition as well as open the doors. We're at the garage for nearly two hours, which leaves us with less than an hour at the hotel before we have to get back in the van and go to the venue.

The club is called the Biribay Jazz Club, perhaps not the most fitting name for a punk rock gig, and it's a bit smaller than the usual places the Subs play, but it's ideal for a solo gig so I feel at home as soon as I walk in. Also, the kids running the place are very friendly and helpful. When we see that one of the bottles of wine in the backstage is a semi sweet Italian rosé Lambrusco, we ask them to change it for a decent local *vino tinto* and they hurry to give us the best Rioja they have. We are right next to the town of Rioja, after all.

Soon afterwards I treat Paul to this joke:

Q: What wine does the Lone Ranger drink?

A: Vino Tonto.

He doesn't seem all that impressed by my sharp wit as he bustles about preparing the stage. I notice him trying to move two large boxes out of the way from the front of the stage until the sound man points out that they're actually subwoofers and are part of the PA system. Usually they would be set below the other speakers at the sides. Paul comes over to me exasperated. 'I don't believe it: the subs are right in front of the stage!'

I say, 'I think you'll find that the Subs are in the dressing room.'

He gives me a withering look and I say, 'I'm getting my stand-up comedy routine ready for when all this music bollox falls through. Which won't be long the way things are going.'

It's soon time for me to play, and I feel right in my element on a low stage and with the people right in front of me. Clearly most of them have never heard of me before and don't know what to expect but I can tell that they're into it right from the first song and it's a very enjoyable show.

## 28th February MADRID

I'm not all that surprised to find, as I wind my way down the corridors towards Reception glancing in at the open doors of the rooms being cleaned, that I got the arse room again. Wi fi didn't reach it, there was no bath, and it was smaller than the rest.

We set off for Madrid, over the snow-covered high plains, and arrive in time to spend thirty minutes in the hotel before Charlie and I have to go off for a radio interview with national Spanish channel Radio 3. The guy doing the interview really knows his stuff, and between the chat plays lots of records from both me and the Subs. On the way back to the club in the luxurious car booked by the radio station we lounge in the back seat and I say to Charlie, 'This is nice. Maybe you and me could tour like this in future and send the rest of them in the van.'

The plan was that the band would soundcheck while we were at the radio station, but we arrive at the club to find that there's been a power failure so nothing has happened. The tiny dressing room smells of damp so they are all hanging around in the club, which smells of bleach. With only half an hour to go before the doors open and still no electricity except the emergency lighting, the band finally decide to go off to eat. A few minutes after they leave, the power comes on, and I get a soundcheck.

The club is sold out with 220 people, and most of them are already in when I take the stage. It's a good gig.

Back in the smelly dressing room the Subs prepare to start their set but their intro tape keeps cutting out.

'What's going on?' says Jamie

'Spain,' says Alvin.

And the final results on the merch tonight: two CDs sold! One stolen!

## 1st March VALENCIA

Quite happy with last night's room, it was the same as everybody else's.

Not sure how happy Jamie was with his as he's not in it. In fact we don't know where he is when we gather at the van at 11:45 to start the four hour journey to Valencia. His phone broke yesterday so he can't be reached, and Yuko has to ring someone in England who knows someone in Madrid who he might be staying with and eventually she gets a message to him and half an hour later he arrives at the hotel in a taxi, apologising profusely. He's so contrite that you have to forgive him, but it has cost us two hours.

Paul hammers it down the motorway and we only make one brief stop and manage to arrive in the Valencia region soon after five and still in good time. Unfortunately he's put the wrong address in the Sat Nav and it's only at the last minute that we realise we are heading for the club instead of the hotel. We are not risking going to the venue without picking up the hotel keys first, so we re-set the Sat Nav and drive another six kilometres to the address we've been given for the Ronda hotel. The Ronda turns out to be three hotels in a row, one of them a three star, the next a two star, and finally the Ronda Hostal, which doesn't have any. The address we've been given is for the two star so we try to check in there first, but the woman behind the desk says she doesn't have a record of our reservation. We move on to the three star, where they tell us we are in the two star. Help me Ronda!

'I bet we're in the hostel,' I say to Yuko. Look what you could have won.

She goes to ask at the hostel, but while she's gone the woman in the two star finds our booking. There's literally just time to drop the bags in the rooms and then we leave for the venue.

Although this is officially the Valencia gig, a closer inspection of the Book Of Lies reveals that the Rock City club is actually on an industrial estate in a neighbouring town. We're the first punk gig they've ever put on there. Tomorrow there will be an extreme metal festival. It's big and smart and expensive to get in, and there's a six foot high stage—not ideal for a solo gig. There are also not many people in by the time I start at 9:30, and for one of the few times on the tour so far I feel dissatisfied with how it went. Maybe the scattering of people down there liked it, but they were too far away for me to tell. There are more people in by the time the Subs play and they go down well, but I find myself sinking into a bit of a depression. Is it all worth it?

## 2nd March ZARAGOZA

There's no bath plug so I have a shower, and when I open the window to let the steam out afterwards I notice that the gap between the double glazing is one-third full of water. If I could just get a fish in there somehow it would make a nice novelty aquarium feature. Would have to be a flatfish.

Outside, the weather is gloriously warm and sunny. It's the first time on the tour that I haven't had to wear a jacket. I enjoy this brief taste of Spring a great deal while I'm loading the suitcases in the back of the van, but then we have to get in the van ourselves and drive to Zaragoza. Soon we are back in Winter, heading up into the hills, the snow sparkling in the sunlight.

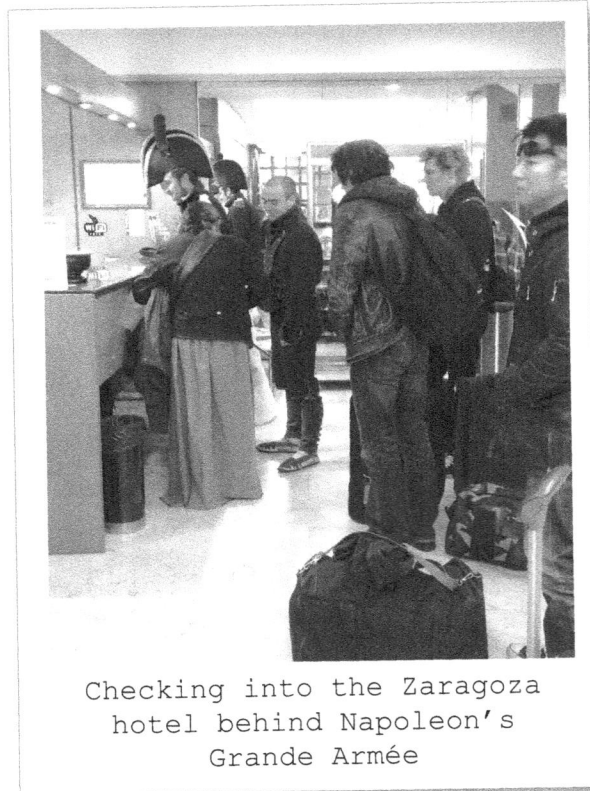

Checking into the Zaragoza
hotel behind Napoleon's
Grande Armée

By the time we get to Zaragoza it's late afternoon and the warm weather is back. There's a delay checking in to the hotel because Napoleon's *Grande Armée* are in the queue ahead of us. It's the anniversary of a famous battle in the Peninsula Wars, where the Spanish held back the French at the bridge over the river here, and some of the people involved in the re-enactment are checking into our hotel in full costume. The hotel is situated on one side of the bridge and the club on the other. The central location is wonderful for me, not so good for Paul as the place is full of tourists and there's nowhere to park so he has to drive to the venue and sit in the van for two hours to make sure it won't get towed away.

I'm in a beautiful corner room looking out over a small square and a church. Bath and sink both have a plug so I do the washing. Then there's still time to go across the road to the main square where the Spanish troops are gathering, trumpets blowing and drums banging. I have a quick look in the cathedral, where mass is just finishing and people are shuffling towards the altar to receive the sacrament. A solo voice sings a lament that reverberates around the building. I'd like to spend more time here but I've got a punk rock gig to go to.

Beautiful view from the room
by day...

But by night...they gather...

While the Subs are setting up for soundcheck I do an interview on video for two guys who do some kind of internet music site. I find it hard to concentrate because there's a magnificent view of the cathedral through the window behind them, and on the street right outside the club the French army are marching past. The guy doing the interview starts with a few questions about the Adverts and what made me want to play solo, then asks me about the tour diary books. He's already got volume one and really enjoyed it, and says he will get volumes two and three from me later. I tell him that he and the cameraman will probably be in a future volume. Might get another couple of sales.

Dinner tonight is a buy-out, which basically means the club gives us ten euros each so we can go and get our own food. In my case that means pocketing the money and making an emergency sandwich from the supply of snacks laid out for us on the bar. For the first time for a few days there is a selection of vegetarian items apart from the usual processed white bread and cheese—there's hummus and olive paste and dark rye bread with seeds in it. I make up a sandwich and put it in my bag in the dressing room. A moment later Yuko comes rushing in: 'Tim, don't eat it! There are anchovies in the olive paste!'

She's saved me from a fate worse than fish.

After soundcheck most of the band go back to the hotel to rest, while I sit around with Jamie in the dressing room using the free wi fi and catching up on emails. As the club opening time approaches Paul comes into the dressing room and says, 'Have a look at this, they've switched the indoor fountain on!'

We go out into the club to have a look and there's a lengthy discussion about whether it's a fountain or a water feature. There's a lot of water coming downwards but very little going upwards. In my opinion that makes it a water feature.

Paul groans in exasperation. 'Look, you're in a club with a fountain *inside* it—or a water feature, whatever you want to call it—and there's that big church thing out of the window. You can hardly complain!'

'Big church thing?' I say. 'It's the *Basilica de Pilar*, reputedly the first cathedral in the world to be dedicated to Mary and founded in the first century. It's not a 'big church thing'.'

I can see he's impressed and he'll never know I only know that because I've just looked it up on Wikipedia in the dressing room.

The club opens and the local support band start their set. I watch a couple of songs then go back to the window to have another look at that big church thing. The French are lining up their canons on the bridge and there are people bustling around everywhere. It's all action at the zebra crossing just below the window, where a policeman in a *hi vis* jacket is waving a hunched pedestrian across the road, using a lighted baton to stop the traffic. I do a double take when I realise it's Charlie on the way back from the hotel.

Good gig. Wine club in my luxury room. The view from the window into the cobbled square is a bit spoilt by the eight wheelie bins of rubbish parked in the middle of it.

## 3rd March BADALONA

The sink plug isn't actually attached so in theory I could just walk off with it, but with just one week to go this will probably be the last clothes wash of the tour.

It's twenty degrees centigrade at the rest station halfway across the scrub desert plain on the way to Badalona. While the others go and eat in the restaurant I have my emergency hummus and salad sandwich at the picnic area out in the sun.

I'm tired by the time we reach the hotel and in theory there is time to nap for an hour or so before going off to the gig, but we're right on the seafront and it's a shame to waste the opportunity for a walk along the beach. I drop my bag in my room and head straight back downstairs, where I see Jamie's bag all on its own in the middle of the lobby. I put it behind the reception desk and when I get back from the walk it's still there so I take it up to my room, which is right opposite his, and put a note under his door. Two minutes before we leave for the venue I hear his voice in the corridor, 'Oh *fuck*!'

The view from the venue isn't quite as good as yesterday, it's a graffiti-covered warehouse on an industrial estate. The band do their soundcheck then Paul takes most of them back to the hotel. When he returns, Yuko and I are still setting up the merch. 'Here he comes,' I say to her. 'Look busy,'

He strides over and when he's within earshot I say to Yuko, 'I don't know why we're even bothering to set up. Bloody North is taking all our business.' It is actually true that while our merch has slowed to almost nothing the last few days, his second hand punk singles have been flying out.

'Bloody North.'

'Yeah, bloody North. Let's get Andy back.'

'You know what?' says Paul. '*I—don't—care*. It's a twelve hour drive tomorrow. Barcelona's got a perfectly good airport. I can be on the next flight to Manchester. You can sort yourselves out.'

'Typical bloody North!' I say. Then I think about the two days in the van we've got coming up before the next gig in Rennes. 'Actually, I've had enough. I'm off the tour too.'

'Are you coming to the airport with me Tim?'

'Yes I am mate.'

Quite a good gig. Then a brief and somewhat subdued wine club in the hotel lobby, the thought of the nine o'clock start and the long drive tomorrow hanging over everyone's heads.


## 4th March CHALAIS

We drive. Over the border and into France. Hours later we have a rest stop and I have the following conversation with the woman behind the food counter:

*'Il y a un sandwich végétarien?'*

*'Non.'*

*'Peut-être un quiche sans jambon?'*

*'Non.'*

*'Quelque chose d'autre végétarien?'*

*'Non.'*

When we get back on the road we get pulled over by the *gendarmerie* who weigh the van on a portable weighbridge attached to a laptop, which tells us we are overweight. Alvin promises them that we will be unloading some gear at his place in Chalais in a couple of hours, and we are allowed to carry on after paying a ninety euro fine. In fact we have no intention of unloading anything at Chalais but they will never know that.

In Chalais we buy some food from the supermarket then drive on to Alvin's house where he prepares sleeping places for everyone. Then we drink our own weight in wine from his fine collection and get to bed at around three. So much for the planned early night.

## 5th March RENNES

Jet doesn't look like he's really enjoying the forty-five minute drive down twisty country lanes until we hit the motorway, and we have to pull over for a couple of minutes so he can get a breath of air, but apart from that there are no real casualties from wine club *chez Alvin*.

It's a long day in the van though, and we don't reach Rennes until five-thirty. We pull up to the budget hotel on the outskirts of town and unload the bags, but then find out from the Receptionist that we don't have a booking. Fools! Will we never learn? While we're hanging around in the lobby waiting to find out from the promoter where we are supposed to go I log on to the free wi fi and find an email saying that advance sales for my solo gig in York coming up next week are so poor that the promoter is thinking of pulling it. I write back to say that he should hold his nerve.

The hotel we've actually been booked into is slightly better than the other one, but by the time we get to it we don't have any time to spend in it.

Once again we are so late at the venue that there is no time to soundcheck before doors open, but once again the place is quickly packed out and I have a great gig.

I'm not sure how enthusiastic Alvin is about the pre-gig soundcheck the band has to do with the audience already in and bunching around the stage. His vocal monitor check goes, 'One, two! Cheese sandwich! Washing line!'

The club is so full that I can't get out of the upstairs dressing room to watch because people are standing in front of the door. I can hear what's going on at wall-shaking volume though. Even the talk between the songs is clearly audible. Charlie plugs the new album: 'It's got like a little Beatrix Potter book with it. It's full of ditties for young people.'

After another song I hear him say to someone in the audience, 'You've been after my beer all night. Can you just go to the bar and buy your own—because *I can't!*'

Over the drum microphone Jamie says: 'And he doesn't want to catch your herpes.'

After the gig there's not a lot of action at the merch table, but someone offers me a gig for the coming summer: an open air festival by the sea, organised by a shop which sells varieties of beer from all around the world, *La Mer Bière*. The beer sea! If it happens I'll be paid well and will get to stay in my own private apartment with a swimming pool. I can even stay on for a few days for free and have a little holiday. Pinch me, I must be over-tired.

Back at the hotel lobby, Yuko, Paul and me are the only takers for wine club. 'Winners club!' says Yuko. When we go back to our rooms there is still the chance of eight hours sleep—more than we managed on the day off yesterday.

## 6th March VERNOUILLET

One good way to get a band out of the lobby and into the van is to test the hotel fire alarm system. Twice.

When we're on the road Jamie tells us that he got a message from Andy this morning: he's feeling much better and wants to thank us—sending him home was exactly the right thing to do.

We make good time to the suburbs of Paris and should be able to have ninety minutes in the hotel, but we get there to find that not enough rooms have been booked and it takes more than an hour to reach the promoter and sort it out. After that I just have time to change my strings before we have to leave.

The Book Of Lies claims that the gig is in Vernouillet in Germany. Of course we know that Vernouillet is actually in France, but it's only when we arrive at the venue that we find out we're playing the first day of a five day festival and that two bands will be on before us. The venue is an indoor basketball court and has had a P.A. installed and a stage built. Things seem to be moving fairly slowly. Neither the Subs or I get a soundcheck before the doors open, and when the first band play the room only has about one hundred people in so looks fairly sparse.

The leaflet for the festival says that my set promises 'lots of surprises', and it's certainly a surprise for me when my scheduled time to play arrives and I have to stand around on stage for ten minutes while the technical team try to get the P.A. working. All that is coming through the monitors in front of me is what the DJ is playing, very loudly. I speak a few words into the microphone but can hardly hear my voice over the music, and the guitar isn't coming through at all. I retreat to the side of the stage, where Jet is standing with a cheeky expression. He deadpans, 'Tim, I think it is your guitar cable.'

Eventually the crew reckon they have the problem fixed and I tentatively start a song but there is a lot of feedback and the voice and guitar take it in turns to cut out completely. There is clearly something seriously wrong so I jump down from the stage and play acoustically. The crowd love it so I stay down there. After the third song Paul arrives next to me and says to me, 'They think they've got it sorted now, you can get back on the stage.'

I get back on the stage and start playing but immediately there's a screech of feedback and the guitar cuts out leaving me singing *acapella*. I unplug and jump back down among the crowd again. 'From now on that is not a stage any more,' I tell them. 'That is a table to put my beer on.'

I play for another half hour and it goes down a storm, best audience reaction of the tour.

## 7th March DUISBURG

What I think is my alarm going off is actually the warning beeps from a heavy vehicle reversing in the building site outside my window. Then the earth boring machine starts up. I am a noise magnet. I could put the earplugs in and go back to sleep for another hour but I just had a dream that my guitar was broken and it's such a relief to realise it isn't true that now I prefer to stay awake.

Today we're back in Germany for one gig in Duisburg, which is just up the road from where my mate Vom lives, and he's going to come over and join me on drums for a spontaneous TVOM! show.

It's a gruelling drive and it soon becomes clear we're not going to make it on time to check into the hotel before the gig, which is rather worrying considering the problems we've had on the tour so far. When we get to the venue, the promoter has picked up the keys for us so at least we know that in theory we have rooms. Waiting at the club for us is Alex, who drove us on the tour a year ago—he will be taking over tomorrow when Paul goes off for the dates he is booked for with a band called the Hi Fi Spitfires.

The club is packed with people soon after opening and there are so many familiar faces it's quite overwhelming—they all want to chat with me but I'm so tired now that I can hardly string a sentence together, and I keep on accidentally answering in French or Spanish instead of German.

My concentration soon picks up once I get on stage, and Vom and me lock in and have a fantastic gig. It's so tight that it's hard to believe the last time we played together was a year ago on this same tour.

The van is packed and it's time for Paul's last session behind the wheel. Just before we leave for the hotel the promoter comes running out with two foil-wrapped packages, the vegetarian meals for Paul and me that we didn't have time to eat earlier. Everyone else ate before the gig. With Alex now on board there is no spare space in the van so I have to balance the foil cartons on my lap.

We're halfway to the hotel when Jet suddenly shouts out, 'Paul!'

Paul turns his head, 'What Jet?'

'PAUL!'

'WHAT?!!'

'No—Paul, POLE!!'

There's a waist-high pole in the middle of the carriageway splitting it into two lanes, but it's unlit and almost impossible to make out—Jet was the only one of us who noticed it. Paul swerves around it just at the last second. Would be a shame to blot your copybook on the last drive. Two minutes later we are stopped in a random police check and Paul is breathalysed. He is clear of course and we are allowed to drive on. 'Unexpectedly tough last session that,' he says as he switches off the engine for the last time and hands the key to Alex.

Something else unexpected has happened, I realise as I stand up. The foil food cartons that have been sat on my lap during the drive have been leaking, and my jeans and the bottom part of my jacket are completely soaked in oil. Alvin grabs his bag from under my seat only to find that it too is sopping wet. We attempt to clean up the mess but we only have one tissue between us, and soon our hands are all slick with oil as well. Paul tries to help and is soon oiled up too. We're so annoyed about it that we dump the meals straight in the bin without even looking to see what they were. This is what you could have won.

So, after a brief wine club in the lobby I wash my jeans and bottom half of my jacket in the sink in my room. There is no sink plug but I manage to get most of the oil off under hot running water using the honey-scented liquid soap. The radiator isn't working but I drape my wet clothes across it anyway in the hope it will come on in the morning.

## 8th March DRACHTEN

I wake up swelteringly hot at eight, two hours before I needed to. The radiator did indeed come on, and how—my clothes have cooked nicely. The only thing is, my trousers now look extremely rumpled. There's never a Corby 5000 in the room when you need one.

We leave Paul in the hotel lobby surrounded by his bags, waiting for the Hi Fi Spitfires to come and pick him up. Alex takes the wheel and we head towards Holland and the final two dates of the tour.

What's going on? We're at the hotel early enough to spend a couple of hours in it, they have our keys ready for us, and check out tomorrow isn't until midday. They even do breakfast until eleven so I might catch that. Admittedly the place is a bit shabby. The room is small but with an enormous radiator—better than the other way around in my opinion—and has more mosquitoes in it than you might expect from a Dutch hotel in the middle of winter but it's such a relief to be able to relax for a while in my own space that I don't care.

Yes, we're on a roll. The club is just a couple of minutes down the road, it's an easy load in, and snacks are laid out in the spacious upstairs dressing room. There's a comfortable area for me and Yuko to do the merch and soundcheck goes fine. After that, the band eat in the club's dining room. I ask the cook if he can put my vegetarian dish aside for later and he says, no problem—though he will be more drunk later. I say, so will I.

As usual in Holland, it's a thoughtful listening crowd for my set who then turn into a completely bonkers punk stage-invading crowd for the Subs. While they play I go into the kitchen to get my meal. I don't know if the cook is more drunk than earlier or not: he's not there. And neither is the meal. As I come out of the kitchen I notice him moshing at the front of the stage to the Subs, fists punching in the air, throwing himself all over the place with a wild expression on his face. I go upstairs to the dressing room and have an emergency peanut butter sandwich.

Wine club is convened in my room back at the hotel. I'm still scribbling the 'fuck off' sign when Alvin arrives. Jet and Yuko soon turn up too so it's quite cosy. We're all so tired we can hardly speak. After a while Jet goes off to his room to smoke a cigarette and never returns. 'We'll have to expel him from wine club,' says Alvin. But he and Yuko soon call it a night too. Yuko takes the 'fuck off' sign to slip under Jet's door. I hope she gets the right room.

How does a toothbrush work?

## 9th March EINDHOVEN

Jet arrives in the lobby with a bewildered expression, holding the 'fuck off' sign. 'I smoked a cigarette and sat down for a minute. Next thing I knew it was eight o'clock and I was still sitting there with all my clothes on.'

There's an icy wind blowing and the skies are a leaden grey, sleety drizzle in the air. Snow forecast for the trip home tomorrow. All we have to do is hold it together for one more gig and we're done.

Only a couple of hours to Eindhoven, and according to the Book Of Lies there will be a good hotel when we get there. The Gods of Touring are smiling on us at last. We stop off at a petrol station to fill up the van on the way and I go in to get a coffee. Keen to get rid of some of the small coins clanking around in my pocket, I count out the one euro seventy cents required, but when I press the button on the machine it delivers the coffee before I even put any money in. I don't know whether to be pleased or annoyed.

The hotel room has a bathtub and a sink, both with plugs, and a large radiator—perfect for doing the washing, but it's the last day of the tour. I don't know whether to be pleased or annoyed.

Breakfast was a long time ago and the motorway stop offered nothing vegetarian, so I decide to go out and find something now. The first shop I find sells fetish gear. The second is a café, but it's closed. The next looks promising—through the window I can see a group of men sitting around a table drinking coffee—but when I get to the door it turns out to be a funeral parlour. I strike out in another direction and soon find a supermarket, where I get a healthy-looking spinach, walnut, courgette and goats cheese salad and take it back to the hotel, where on closer inspection it turns out to be a microwave meal that should be cooked for a few minutes and eaten hot. No matter how long I stare at the safety deposit box it will never become a microwave oven. In the end I eat the meal uncooked, and it's very nice.

Good job I did find something to eat because there's nothing at all at the venue. The sound man isn't there yet either and when he does turn up he's very slow setting up. When I soundcheck there is a familiar loud clonking noise and it's not my guitar cable.

I go up to him and we have this conversation:

'Have you got another D.I. Box? This one is making all that noise.'

'Yeah, I've got another one. It's in that big box by the side of the stage.'

Pause.

'Erm, could we swap them over?'

'It'll be fine.'

'Well, it won't be fine—this one's broken.'

'It's not broken.'

'It *is* broken, every time I move it, it makes that horrible noise.'

'Don't worry. It'll be fine.'

'I'd really rather we swapped it over.'

He shrugs his shoulders. 'Ooookay.'

We go to the stage and he gets out the new D.I. Box and hands it to me and I unplug the old one and plug in the new one and the problem is solved.

So with a noise-free guitar, the strap still held together with the same emergency gaffa repair made six weeks ago on the first date of the tour in this same country, I take the stage for the last show. Fifty minutes later I leave it again, exhausted, happy. Job done.

I go for a ten minute break in the upstairs dressing room but I've only been there a few minutes when two girls come charging up the stairs shouting, 'Free beer!'

They see me sitting there dripping with sweat and get a bit sheepish. 'Sorry. Jamie said it was okay,' says one of them as she raids the fridge. They sit down and chat with me for a while, then one of them says to the other, 'I need to fix your tits.' She goes to Alvin's toolbox and takes out the gaffa tape and rips off two thin strips and puts them in a cross over one of her friend's boobs, then does the same to the other one. 'I am a bit childish,' she says, then gets her friend to put crosses on hers. I think about telling them my hilarious gaffa tape joke, but they hurry back down to watch the Subs before I get the chance. Probably best.

As soon as I get my breath back I go to watch the band too, making a quick visit to the Gents on the way. The bloke at the next urinal looks over ands says, 'Wow! I never thought in my life that I would piss next to TV Smith. And now I did.'

Every now and then one yearns for a backstage toilet.

I go and watch the Subs from behind the merch table, which is right by the side of the stage. The band are in fine form for the last night of the tour and there is a large good-humoured crowd singing along and waving their arms in the air.

I lean over to Yuko and nod towards the audience. She takes out her earplugs.

'People having fun,' I say.

She nods in agreement and puts her earplugs back in. After a moment I lean in again and she takes her earplugs out again.

'I hate that.'

## 15th March LEEDS

Back in the UK, the Subs tour over, on the train for a gig in Leeds. I change at the main station on to the branch line to Burley Park, and from there only have to roll my merch suitcase ten minutes over the unevenly paved backstreets to the Brudenell, a former working mens' club now serving as a well-kitted out medium sized venue. There's no sign of headliners Ruts DC when I arrive, so I go ahead and do my soundcheck. Soon second support Louise Distras turns up, then, just as the promoters were starting to get worried, the Ruts arrive. They left London in their van quite some time before me but got stuck in traffic on the motorway.

Playing guitar for the Ruts these days is Leigh Heggarty, which is a bit strange for me as I'm used to him playing duo sets with me. When we soundcheck together I usually joke around that I have to have a better sound and lights than him as he's just my sidekick—now I have to deferentially get my stuff off stage so he can set up.

After the Ruts finish Louise goes to the stage to get ready for her soundcheck, and is chatting with me and Leigh when he suddenly sneezes and blood starts to pour from his nose. He grabs a tissue but it fails to staunch the flow and soon the stage around him is splattered. Louise looks on aghast. 'I want to help but I don't know what to do!'

Leigh kneels on the stage pinching the bridge of his nose with a bloodied tissue. 'Ibee awright ib I judd thday dike diss for den middets.'

His caring band members leave him stranded on stage while they go and check in to the hotel, which means that ten minutes later when the bleeding stops Leigh and I have a good chance to catch up while we're setting up the merch and waiting for the club to open. When my stage times arrives the place is nicely full. I notice as I plug my guitar in that Leigh's pedal board is stuffed with tissue paper in case his nose explodes again. You can get away with it in soundcheck but it could be awkward during a gig.

All goes off without a problem, there are a couple of hundred people in and everyone has a great night. It's the first time I've played the Brudenell and it's already become one of my favourites clubs in Britain, I hope to come back. Afterwards my mate TJ drives me back to stay the night at his place in Clifford, a few miles outside Leeds, and as he's a real ale fan and has a good selection of craft beers we have Beer Club.

## 16th March YORK

The excitement never stops. Last time I stayed at TJ's place we went on a trip to a nearby village to buy new vacuum cleaner bags. This time he promises an even more thrilling day out, though the secret is rather spoiled when I notice the note he has left upstairs for his wife Lisa: *Gone to Wetherby with Teev to buy shaver.*

That's not all though, we also get a new battery for his alarm clock. While we're in the shop I take the opportunity to scour the shelves of the Travel section for a sink plug, but they don't have one.

TJ and Lisa drop me off at tonight's venue in York and go off to get something to eat while I soundcheck. Because advance ticket sales have been poor, promoter Chris and I move some tables and chairs in front of the stage to try and make the room cosier. After soundcheck I set up my iPad on one of the tables with a view of the stage in the background and try to record a promotional video for the tour in Argentina that I'll be embarking on in a couple of weeks. Mariano, the promoter over there, has told me more or less what he wants me to say, and I've written out the names of the clubs and towns I'll be playing on a sheet of paper, but I'm not even sure how to pronounce some of them. I manage to stumble through the filming without too many mistakes, but afterwards I find that I've just taken a still photo. I put the iPad on the correct setting and try again but when I check it back I look ridiculously serious so decide to go for a third take. I don't know what the people getting the club ready for opening think about me sitting on my own repeatedly saying 'Hi, I'm TV Smith…' but it has to be done. During the third take Chris, who is still moving the furniture about, falls over a chair with a huge crash and everyone in the club bursts into laughter, including me, so I have to stop the video. Take four goes perfectly, but all the way through it I'm still holding back the laugh about Chris falling over so the people in Argentina might wonder why TV Smith looks in such a good mood.

Louise Distras is supporting again tonight, and to try and boost numbers Chris has booked a last minute local support, who are pretty good musically, if a wee bit pretentious. While I'm backstage I hear their singer announce, 'The next piece is called…'

I turn to Louise. 'Will you be playing any pieces tonight, or just the usual songs?'

As expected, not many people turn up but there are enough to fill the tables and chairs in front of the stage and create a good atmosphere, the sound and lights are excellent, and I enjoy playing a more intimate concert. Then it's back to TJ's for Beer Club.

## 23rd March LONDON

Down to South London for a gig in New Cross. This time Leigh Heggarty is back playing with me. We have a great gig, no nosebleeds, and afterwards I get a great place to stay: I go home.

## 29th March BIDEFORD

Devon: a place where a gig was hard to find when I grew up here. If any bands came at all it would usually mean an hour or two's drive to the nearest city, Exeter or Plymouth. But now I've got an invitation to play a club called the Palladium in Bideford, Gaye's home town before we moved to London. She still has quite a few friends there but ironically I'm playing the same weekend that she goes to Norway for a Black Metal festival, so she can't come.

To my surprise, there's a good crowd in the club, lots of the people there are in bands themselves, and I find myself having an excellent gig. I would have killed for a club like this when I lived around here. I remember when I couldn't wait to get away from the Southwest; now I can't wait to come back.

## 3rd April LONDON

I stayed on in Devon for a few days to visit my parents, who still live there in a small town on the edge of Dartmoor. I drove them to nearby Exeter for a shopping trip yesterday and had quite a successful shop myself: got a thick winter jacket in the sales so I'll be all ready for the Subs tour next year and, more importantly, in a camping shop I finally found a travel sink plug.

I arrive back home in London mid-afternoon to find an email from a producer on a radio station I've never heard of called Absolute Radio. He explains that they are currently running a phone-in competition to win an all-expenses-paid trip to the USA to watch an American wrestling match between two fighters called The Undertaker and CM Punk. The contestants have to answer some questions live on air, and yesterday the station got an undertaker in to ask them. Today they want a punk. Could I come and do it?

Not particularly interested, I write an email saying that I've just arrived in London and can't get to their Soho studio in time. I assume that will be the last I hear of it, but the producer emails straight back to say, well, could you do it tomorrow? I say yes. I always do.

## 4th April LONDON

A young guy on an internship takes me upstairs and tells me a little about the station, which is broadcast nationwide and is aimed at a demographic of twenty-four to forty-four year olds. *They'll never have heard of me!* Then he hands me a sheet of paper with the questions I have to ask and takes me over to the studio. As the surprise guest I'm supposed to wait outside until it's time for the competition, but presenter Geoff Lloyd spots me through the window and comes out while a record is playing to shake my hand. 'I had no idea it was going to be you,' he beams. 'I saw you play in Manchester once—it was one of the best gigs I've ever been to…'

The first caller is on the line and I read out the questions, most of them related to punk or wrestling. One of them is: 'Which designer do you associate most with punk: Vivienne Westwood or Jeff Banks?'

I don't mention that the jacket I bought a couple of days ago in Exeter is a Jeff Banks one. There's no time to explain that I could never afford a Vivienne Westwood one and anyway I don't think it would keep me warm in the back of a minibus with a broken heater driving through Poland in February. This is radio so everything goes along at a fair lick and ten minutes later the competition is over. As the next record plays I get a lot of compliments about how well I read the questions. The co-presenter, who sits the opposite side of the desk to Geoff and is working her way up the ranks from Traffic, says brightly, 'You should go for the job on Mastermind!'

I have other plans.

Tomorrow I will be fifty-seven years old.

## 9th April LONDON— 10th April BUENOS AIRES

Long haul flights in Economy never get any better. It's only the anticipation of my first visit to Argentina that gets me through the seemingly endless hours of cramps, fidgeting and aching muscles. At least there's no one in the seat next to me which means I can distract myself by inventing ever-more improbable ways to get into something approaching a horizontal position in a space as long as my leg. Sleep is impossible and I look forward to the meals and drinks service like a prisoner waiting for his rations to be doled out—though they would probably be slightly more tasty—and there is plenty of time to ponder questions such as: why do they give me a portion of butter with the vegetarian meal but no bread roll? Do they expect me to butter the cup?

The plane lands at eight in the morning and I'm soon through Immigration and have picked up my guitar and suitcase and joined the massive queue to go through customs, very much hoping I won't get asked why I have seventy CDs in my bag. It's quite a lot for a tourist, particularly when they're all mine. As I wait in the queue I try and think of what I can tell the Customs people if I get stopped: *I REALLY like listening to my own music....my wife put them in while I wasn't looking...I'm on strong medication and mistook them for socks...* But nothing really sounds like it would convince. And actually the queue is moving so slowly that I'm beginning to wonder if I'll ever get as far as Customs. There are now twenty lines of people shuffling forward, filling the hall as far back as the baggage collection area, and in marked contrast to the way the English wait, the entire crowd gradually breaks out into a slow handclap accompanied by jeering whistles. An hour later when I finally get to the X-ray machine the humiliated Customs official can't hurry me through fast enough. He doesn't even seem to be interested in the form I dedicatedly filled out on the plane, somehow forgetting to mention the CDs. I wave it towards him: 'Er, did you want this?' He grudgingly takes it from me without even glancing at it.

Outside in the Arrivals hall my promoter Mariano is waiting for me. I've known Mariano ever since he first came and visited me and Gaye in London in the mid-nineties, and we've discussed the idea of me playing in Argentina many times. Now it's finally happening: four dates supporting Duncan Reid from the Boys. Duncan arrived yesterday and is rehearsing with a local band, I'll be playing solo as usual.

It takes an hour to drive into Buenos Aires, the traffic as dense as every other city I've ever visited in South America. You just have to accept the fact that when you get into a car here you won't be getting out again for a long time. Enjoy the ride. Mariano checks me into the hotel he's booked, the Pop Hotel—there wasn't a Punk Hotel?—and we arrange to meet in the coffee bar next door with Duncan and and his wife Liz as soon as I've settled in. It's a basic but pleasant boutique hotel and I have a corner room looking out onto the street. There's an internet connection if I stand by the door or in the shower.

Down in the coffee bar Duncan and Liz are looking considerably fresher than I am as they are over the worst of the jet lag. We drive to Mariano's home to pick up Duncan's keyboard player Alex—the only member of the band he uses in England to come with him—and then on for a bit of sightseeing, which kicks off at a cemetery in the north of the city called La Recoleta, most famous for being Eva Peron's final resting place. Even though I'm tired from the long flight I enjoy wandering around the aisles of ornate tombs, particularly as the weather is warm and sunny—a great relief after this year's long harsh English winter.

Unfortunately the good weather is not destined to last. We leave the cemetery and take an outside table at a nearby restaurant but soon the wind comes up, the skies cloud over and there is a chill in the air. The food is good though, and it seems that the warnings I've had from everyone back home about not finding any vegetarian food in Argentina are going to prove inaccurate. There is an expansive selection of wine and soft drinks too. I point out an item on the Energy Drinks menu to Duncan and say, 'That ought to wake me up: *Vodka with Speed.*'

We drive on to La Boca, the harbour area, past the presidential palace. 'That's the balcony where Peron made the famous speech,' says Mariano, pointing. 'And—oops—that's the motorcyclist I nearly ran over.'

The normally tourist-filled area of La Boca is fairly deserted this late in the season and with the weather worsening most of the stalls selling tourist tat are closing up for the day. We wander around the pretty cobbled streets past brightly coloured corrugated iron-fronted houses and the vendors watch us hungrily. One stall holder calls out, 'Great trousers!' I look back and see he is giving me the first finger and little finger devil's horns salute. 'Yay! METAAAL!' he shouts.

'Thank you,' I say. 'But they're punk really, not metal.'

He looks confused. 'Oh...punk.' He hesitates, then gives the salute again, not quite as confidently as before. 'Puuunk!'

In the evening we drive to a rehearsal room where Duncan is to have a final run-through with his local pick-up band. I tag along because I'm going to come on stage with them at the end of the gigs so we can play 'One Chord Wonders' together. The band have already learned the song and after a couple of times around I can finally go back to the hotel and get some sleep. It's past midnight and I have now been awake for forty-five hours.


## 11th April TANDIL

I wake up to the disappointing sound of the wind howling and rain slapping against the window. On the plus side, there is a triumphant first outing for my travel sink plug from Exeter. In the coffee bar next door I have an excellent breakfast of fresh fruits, yoghurt and granola, then meet up in the hotel lobby with Mariano. We have a long drive to Tandil for our first gig tonight and we're going to be using three cars to get us and all the equipment there. One of the drivers is called Julian and I find him outside smoking what appears to be some kind of pipe. I noticed quite a few people smoking these yesterday and am embarrassed to find out that he is in fact drinking *yerba maté*, the local equivalent to tea or coffee. It's the crushed leaves and stems of a rainforest shrub that are placed in a small gourd like a pipe bowl. Hot water is poured over them from a thermos and you sip it from a metal tube that siphons off the tea from the bottom of the bowl. Julian offers me a sip and is quite surprised to find I like it. It tastes a bit like green tea and has a mildly stimulating effect. 'I need this to keep me awake for the drive,' he says.

And it's quite a drive. It takes the inevitable hour to get through the traffic and out of Buenos Aires, then the straight road stretches ahead as far as the eye can see, mirage puddles shimmering on the horizon. The approach to overtake the numerous lumbering lorries on the two track highway starts half a mile before reaching them. White herons crouch alertly on the banks of the swampy ditches on either side of the road. Beyond there are endless flat grasslands dotted with scattered herds of cattle and horses, and here and there tree-lined dirt paths lead off to ranches with names like *La Rosalita* and *Santa Fé*.

We pull into the town of Tandil in the late afternoon and drive straight to our hotel, where the promoters and various members of the support band have gathered outside to greet us. A few fans are also there and ask us to sign their posters and get photos with us. It's a great welcome, tempered only by the fact that by the time the meet-and-greet is done I only have twenty minutes left in the room, which turns out to be disappointingly shabby. There is a squeaky bed and an unusual smell, and in the bathroom there is no sink plug—*I don't care*—and they have found out the hard way that you can't fix a broken porcelain towel rail with Sellotape.

It's a ten minute walk to the club, where we go upstairs to find a low smallish stage and basic sound system and lights. Quite a few people are hanging around the place, clearly keen to watch soundcheck, and some wander over to say how much they love English punk rock and how much they are looking forward to the gig. 'Tandil is only a small place and we really appreciate you coming.'

The myth of there being no vegetarian food in Argentina is once again exploded when we all go back to a bar opposite the hotel and I'm served a delicious pumpkin and cheese tartlet. I'll have plenty of time to digest it—my stage time is one in the morning. The bar also serves a variety of locally brewed craft beers.

Back at the club they can't do enough to look after me, and I'm swamped with members of the audience wanting photos and autographs. When the first support band play I retreat to an area behind the bar that serves as a backstage. It's actually the closed-off balcony to the large club downstairs, where a local band is playing some melancholy songs with a strange beat. It sounds to me as if the cymbal crashes and musical accents are occurring in completely random places but Duncan's guitarist Tomas points out that this is Argentinian folk music set to a 6/8 beat. It makes an interesting combination with the music blasting out of the upstairs club where the band are playing Ramones covers in strict 4/4.

One o'clock comes around, I finally get on stage and play to a satisfyingly enthusiastic reaction. Duncan follows, the excitement level in the audience ramps up even more, and then for the grand finale I get back on stage for One Chord Wonders.

Afterwards people are all over me to tell me how much they enjoyed it. I'd been a bit worried that they wouldn't understand the concept of a solo punk show here, so I'm particularly happy when one guy says, 'You started off solo and then after a few songs I thought I could hear a whole band!' Almost everyone who talks to me, no matter how little English they speak, holds their hand over their heart in the international gesture to say they were moved. It's been worth coming already and a great way to remind myself that the way people react to music demonstrates how similar we all are, no matter where we come from.

There are some cultural differences though. When we eventually leave the place at four in the morning there is a long queue of people outside waiting to get *in*.

## 12th April ROSARIO

I'm a fool. I thought 'we meet downstairs at 9:30' meant 'we leave at 9:30' but in fact it's Argentinian for 'we leave at 11:00'. I've just thrown away a potential extra ninety minutes of much-needed sleep.

The newspapers report freak floods in some areas yesterday, but today the sun is out and it seems like the storm front has passed. There's a chilly wind but we don't notice that once we get in the car, our home for the day. On the nine hour journey over pot-holed roads to Rosario we don't see a single town. What we do see is grassland plains, scattered clumps of trees, cattle—future meat—ditches, hawks and herons, wild dogs, more bloody plains, the road evaporating ahead into shimmering puddles, lumbering lorries, grain silos, dirt paths to ranches with names like *Santa La La*, crooked lines of telegraph poles, plains, more plains. The evening drags the colour out of the sky and leaves a fingernail sliver of moon hanging in the blackness.

We walk into the lobby of our hotel to find our promoter Guille in the lobby to welcome us. He tells us he is also in the support band tonight and will be coming to the rest of the dates on the tour even though his band isn't playing them—he doesn't want to miss the party.

We take an hour in the hotel to recover from the drive. I'm in room 306, the same number I had in Buenos Aires so I don't need to write it down again. The room is large and clean and has everything you need except a sink plug. I laugh at the lack of a sink plug, ha ha!

I'm glad we don't agree to the suggestion of the fifteen minute walk to the club because it's actually a fifteen minute taxi ride. Three people squeeze in the back seat and I sit in the front with the guitar case squashed in front of me like a novelty air bag. The club has a disturbingly high stage and on the wall is a giant luridly coloured Warhol-style screenprint of someone who looks very much like Arthur Askey. Surely not—it would be hard to think of a more unlikely folk hero for the Argentinians. Guille steers me away from the local *Quilmes* beer in the backstage fridge—'hangover beer,' he warns—and brings me a few safer bottles instead.

When we heard that we would be playing an hour earlier than last night Duncan and I were both happy. But my stage time of midnight turns out to be Argentinian for 1:30. By then there are quite a few hundred people in the club and the atmosphere is electric. Once again the audience reaction is stunningly good, and after the gig I get kissed and hugged by just about everyone who is there. It's a hard life being loved, but to be honest I wouldn't trade it for being back working in the Vaseline factory.

## 13th April BUENOS AIRES

The drive back to Buenos Aires seems like nothing compared to yesterday's marathon: it's less than four hours and on a proper road so we don't get shaken to pieces along the way. We have to shift the luggage around between the three cars though because Julian reckons the pot holes yesterday damaged his suspension and he's not sure if he's going to make it back.

We check into the Pop Hotel again—slightly confusing because my new room is laid out in a mirror image of the last one so that everything is on a different side

Tonight's club is called the Roxy Live. After soundcheck I hang around in the backstage area upstairs and Tomas shows me how to play the folk tune we heard the other night in Tandil. The style is called the *chacarera*, he tells me, and borrows my guitar to show me the rhythm and chords. Then he hands the guitar back to me to have a go. There's one chord in it I don't recognise so I have to look it up on an app on my iPad. It turns out to be a B7 over F#, which is a long way from One Chord Wonders and I can't get my fingers around it.

In contrast to the previous two nights I theoretically have an early stage time of 9:20 tonight, even though there are two support bands playing. 'Yeah, right,' I think, and tuck into the superb vegetarian empanadas Mariano brings over from a local restaurant, safe in the knowledge that we are running on Argentinian time.

To my surprise the first band start right on schedule and after a ten minute changeover the next band start on time too. The singer is called Pil—no relation to John Lydon's band—and is well known in Argentina after a hit single he had with his previous band *Los Violadores* which was subsequently covered by my German friends *Die Toten Hosen*. Pil has told me that he wants to cover my song 'Immortal Rich' and we're due to drop into a studio before I leave Argentina to record it. At various points during his gig tonight he refers to me as 'the immortal TV Smith,' but what with the jet lag and fatigue I'm not sure if I can live up to the description. Not only that, but for the first time since I got here my stage time proves to be accurate and I'm still feeling the empanadas weighing me down when I start my gig. Out front though the reaction is similar to the last couple of nights, and when I go out to the merch table afterwards I'm once again surrounded by people who want to thank me and get souvenir photos. Duncan's set goes down a storm too, but before he's even had time to dry off afterwards the security guys are asking us to leave the dressing room so they can prepare for the club night which will be starting up any moment. We go to find a bar in the area to finish off the evening, but after the long drive yesterday most of us are barely managing to stay awake. A couple of drinks and we're done—the long Buenos Aires nightlife must carry on without us, and judging by the number of people out on the street and queuing to get into the bars and clubs it certainly will.

## 14th April MONTEVIDEO

I have noticed that here in Argentina cars run on swear words and frequent use of the horn. There are three major oaths, Mariano explains as he drives us to the port: 'Your mother's pussy, your *grandmother's* pussy—and then for some reason we also have, your parrot's pussy.'

We're heading to Uruguay, a two hour ferry ride across the estuary of the River Plate, so wide that halfway into the crossing you can't see land on either side. The ferry takes us to a pretty town called Colonia, and there we change to a spacious coach for the drive to Montevideo. From my high viewpoint the landscape in Uruguay seems much softer and more pleasing than in Argentina—the endless harsh flatlands have been replaced by rolling green hills fenced off to create human-scale fields, almost English-looking except for the occasional outcrops of roadside pampas and the clear blue sky and blazing sun overhead. The two and a half hour journey to Montevideo would be an ideal opportunity to catch up on some sleep, but jet lag and my body clock contrive to make that an impossibility. Instead I sit and watch the landscape drift by in a stupor of exhaustion, my brain in neutral.

The promoter is at the bus station to meet us, and has a minibus for our use. What with me, Duncan, his band, Liz, Guille, Mariano and various others who have come on the trip, we manage to completely fill it and Alex has to balance on the guitar cases. We drive to the imaginatively named 'Hotel Uruguay,' where I have a faded colonial-style high-ceilinged room with no windows and a plastic air-filled toilet seat. I only notice about the toilet seat when I sit on it and am surprised by a gentle whistling noise. There is a large letterbox-shaped mirror placed confusingly at knee level and the bed has a plastic undersheet. There are also some people noisily having sex further down the corridor. The phrase *knocking shop* occurs to me. I'm quite keen for the ninety minutes we have here to pass so we can go to the club. In the meantime I hang around using the frustratingly intermittent internet connection and try to catch up with my emails. I'm hungry and thirsty but don't want to risk the tap water and don't have any Uruguay currency to go and buy any food.

I'm in the lobby with Duncan, Liz and Alex at the appointed hour to go to soundcheck, and we're all grumbling about how hungry we are. We're wondering why Mariano isn't here yet when suddenly he and the band arrive, coming up the stairs from outside. 'That was one of the best pizzas I have ever had!' says Mariano, licking his lips.

'Why didn't you tell us?' we gasp.

'Oh sorry!' he says, 'I thought you wanted to sleep. There will be some food at the club.'

We load back into the minibus and are driven to the club, where the promoter leads us out through a back door to a large dressing room, with another smaller room next to it, a window between the two. There's a breeze coming from somewhere. I look up and see the sky above and suddenly realise we are actually in a high-walled yard. There is a table loaded with many varieties of empanadas, none of them vegetarian. I feel myself descending into a hunger and fatigue-induced bad mood. Mariano goes to try to organise some spinach empanadas but it's too late—the hunger switches off, as precisely as if someone has flicked a switch. I grab a beer and go and sit on my own in the room on the other side of the yard which at least has a roof. I stay there peacefully for a while and play some guitar and start to cheer up.

In the club, soundcheck is turning into a lengthy process. Alex comes out to the yard shaking his head, and grabs a banana from the bowl on the table. 'It's one of those soundchecks where I can leave the stage, go to the dressing room, eat a banana, then go back to the stage, and they still won't be ready,' he says.

It's not the greatest sound in the world. The PA speakers are underpowered and one of them is sort of hidden around a corner, but eventually the band soundcheck is done and I get to do mine. Then it's the long wait to show time. It's getting a bit chilly in the yard so I hang around in the club watching the people slowly file in. Quite a few of them notice me and come over to say hello. One guy says, 'I saw you at The Sidecar in Barcelona in 2007 when you played with Suzy & Los Quattro. I lived there then and you used my drum kit.' He points at the stage, 'That's it.'

Uruguay time is quite similar to Argentina time. I was originally told that I would go on stage at 10:00. The next time I heard it being discussed it had mysteriously moved back to 10:30. It's already past that now and I've been in the little room next to the yard—which I've come to think of as my private space—for quite a while, playing some guitar and getting in the mood for the gig. When the support band finally finish I pack the guitar into its case and head for the door but Duncan sees me and tells me that he thinks there is another band before me. I'd been told there was only one, but I glance in to the club and see that there is indeed another band setting up. I say to Duncan, 'I'll go back down to level 3.'

I return to the room and get out the guitar again. Gradually the rest of the people in the courtyard start to notice that I have commandeered the room for myself. At one point I pop out to get a bottle of beer from the ice bucket and as I head back in Duncan's guitarist Juan laughs and exclaims, '*El casa del TV!*' I poke my head back out through the window and make an expansive gesture: '*Mi casa es tu casa!*'

Actually it really does have a homely feel to it. Even the four lengths of heavy timber in the centre of the room propping up the roof have been covered with a length of carpet to disguise their purpose. Admittedly not every home has a shopping trolley dumped in it, but hey. The potential for a photo opportunity quickly starts to become apparent too, and soon the members of our party are taking it in turns to come in. '*Bienvenido a mi casa!*' I say to each of them, and I show them around a bit: '*Esta es mi mesa. Esta es la puerta. Eso es el techo.*' The Spanish lessons are finally paying off. Most of my visitors have their photo taken with me, Mariano snapping away through the window or doorway. Finally we have a group shot outside. This takes quite a while as there are a lot of us and everyone wants a copy on their own camera. After a while I start to feel it's gone on long enough. 'What are all these bloody people doing hanging around my house?' I say to no one in particular. 'I was trying to have a quiet Sunday night in!'

There aren't as many people in the audience as we've been getting in Argentina, perhaps around one hundred, but if anything they are even more enthusiastic. At the end of my set they demand an encore, my first of the tour, and afterwards the owners of the club invite me into their private room where they bring me ice-cold beer and take photos, and their twelve year old daughter translates for them so that they can tell me how much they enjoyed it and what an honour it was to have me play in their place.

Duncan starts his set and after watching for a while I go back out to the yard to cool down and get some peace for a few minutes. Overhead in the night sky the plough constellation is perfectly framed by the four walls. Mariano pokes his head around the door and sees me standing there.

'You're not in your house?'

'I couldn't keep up the rent. They threw me out.'

After the show the plan is to go to a bar called Clash City Rockers, which Duncan visited after his last gig here with The Boys and enjoyed so much that he wrote a song about it called Montevideo. It has become an anthem for the bar, and they are hoping we'll both turn up and play a few songs acoustically. I'm feeling exhausted and seriously consider going back to the hotel and getting some sleep even though it's only two-thirty—*only!*—but we all get in the minibus and after we've dropped our bags off at the hotel and we've realised that Duncan will need to borrow my guitar I find myself swept along and back in the van and on my way to the bar with everyone else. I'm glad I did. There are many more rounds of drinks and photos and compliments and the tiredness soon becomes a minor nuisance that you swat away like a mosquito and before I know it I'm up on the table stamping my way through a few more songs, the whole crowd clapping along. I hand the guitar to Alex, who accompanies Duncan, and we spend an exciting hour or two taking it in turns to sing until Duncan brings the session to a close with the third play today of Montevideo.

It's six in the morning and time to go back to the knocking shop.

How they hold the roof up
in *mi casa* (Montevideo)

Mariano in *mi casa*

Duncan in *mi casa*

Who are all these people outside
*mi casa*?

## 15th April BUENOS AIRES

At ten-thirty we gather blearily at the breakfast table and the first round of goodbyes starts. Duncan is staying on here for a day because this afternoon he will receive a medal from the town in a formal ceremony to thank him for promoting the image of Montevideo in his song. A few of his band members are staying too—for the rest of us it's back in the minibus to the bus station, then the drive back to the port and the ferry to Buenos Aires, where I have an appointment in the studio with Pil. During the ferry ride Guille tells me that he'll be getting the bus straight back to Rosario when we get in to Buenos Aires because he has to work tomorrow. I ask him what he does, and he tells me he's a cardiologist. It's a responsible high pressure job and weekends like this allow him to let off steam so he can do it properly.

The rest of Duncan's band will be taking the bus back to Tandil, so there are more goodbyes when we get off the ferry. Then it's back to the Pop Hotel where this time I'm in yet another strangely familiar yet different room. While Alex and Mariano wait in the café next door I whip a new set of the strings on to the guitar as it had around three sweat-soaked hours of being played yesterday. Then there are just ten minutes to spare before we're due in the studio so we get a taxi down there.

While I record the guitar track, Pil and his guitarist work on a Spanish version of the chorus, then they record a rough version of it which I copy so they can use it for backing vocals later when the song is finished. *Pero un día podemos rascar esa picazón—rico inmortal!* When the album is released people will think I'm fluent in Spanish—and if I can keep up the motivation to continue learning, who knows, perhaps I will be. I've certainly got a yen to come back to Argentina. The people here understand what I'm about and I like the South American temperament and relaxed way they have of doing things, particularly at a time when Europe seems to be getting more conservative, more regulated, more grey. Here they haven't forgotten how to factor enjoying yourself into the equation.

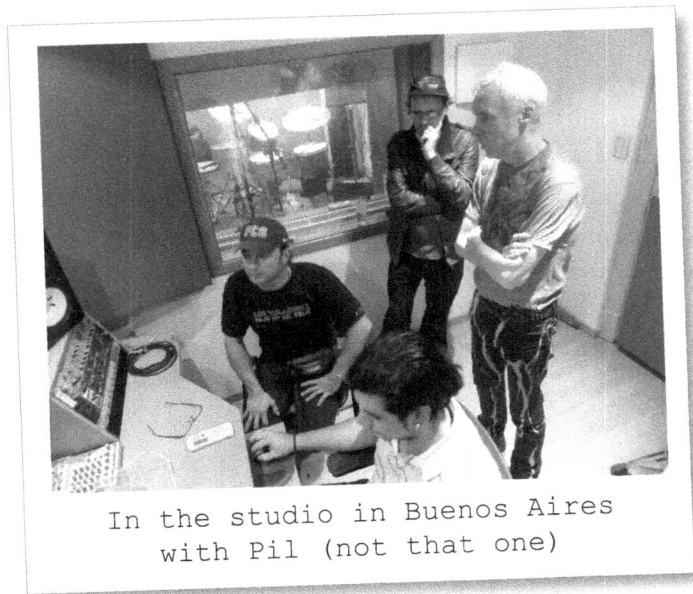

In the studio in Buenos Aires
with Pil (not that one)

## 20th April DUSSELDORF

Thirty-five hours awake, then three days at home, now I'm back on a plane heading for a one-off acoustic festival in Düsseldorf. I'll be playing it as a duo with Vom on cajon, and to make the trip more worthwhile I'm going to stay on a few days and take the opportunity to record him on some of the new songs for my next album. Normally he could do it in one day, but a lot of our friends are coming to the gig and it's certain to turn in to a long night so I'm not sure how much we'll get done tomorrow.

The gig goes down a storm, the highlight being when Vom's fourteen year old son and his musical partner sixteen year old Meg join us on stage to play guitar and sing along on 'Lion And The Lamb.'

Afterwards the two of them stay out in the hall to play their own after-show set acoustically. Probably a good idea that they don't come into the dressing room, as Vom and I get persuaded to do a video interview that we have absolutely no interest in, for a website I've never heard of. We've just come back from ninety minutes on stage and want to wind down and enjoy ourselves so can't take it seriously. The woman who insisted on the interview backs out at the last minute and asks her friend to take over. He clearly has no idea what to ask, and from his first question—'So, TV, tells us who you are and what you do...'—the interview is a non-starter. Somehow ten minutes later I am wearing a poncho made out of a giant sheet of paper from the flip-chart board with 'Kick Me' written on it, and Vom has his trousers down and the interviewer is combing his balls with a hairbrush.

## 21st April DUSSELDORF

Bit of a late start. We get to the rehearsal room where we'll be recording mid-afternoon. The drums and microphones are already set up and ready to go. Vom gets straight in and puts two tracks down fast, but the third is less successful and we decide to go back to his place to get something to eat and refuel. But after we've eaten we feel more tired than ever and decide the best strategy is to get a good night's sleep and start fresh in the morning.

## 22nd April DUSSELDORF

There is some urgency to today's schedule as Vom has to rehearse with the *Toten Hosen* at 3:30. We have a contingency plan for him to come back to the studio after rehearsal or, if the worst comes to the worst, before my flight tomorrow, but in the end he puts down all five songs, plus a scorching new version of the one that didn't work so well yesterday, with an hour to spare before the rehearsal even starts.

## 25th April LONDON

Since I got back from Germany two days ago I've been busy working in my home studio—actually the garden shed—on the new songs. Now I have real drums on, not just the loops and midi drums I'd been using before, everything is sounding great and I have a much clearer idea of the direction I'm heading with the new material. I'd been expecting to break off this afternoon because I'm supposed to go into Soho to play a few songs on Absolute radio—a session offered after I'd done my quizmaster guest appearance a few weeks ago—but in the morning I get a text from the producer to say that Geoff, the presenter, has a lot of meetings today and can't be there—can we re-schedule? That's the last I'll hear of that, I assume, but in fact he gets back to me with an alternative date: tomorrow. Meanwhile, back in the shed.

## 26th April LONDON

The session goes well. They tell me they want to record two songs and also a short chat with Geoff to go out 'as live' on Sunday night. I say I might as well do another song as well since I'm there, it will only take another three minutes and then they can either use it or drop it if they want. With an eye for promo, I present Geoff with a copy of the latest CD and tour diary book. Somehow I doubt if the twenty-four to forty-four year olds will be interested, but at least Geoff mentions them both during the on-air chat and suggests people go to my website to buy them. Afterwards everyone seems happy, and by mid-afternoon I'm back in the shed.

## 27th April LONDON

I get an email from the radio producer to say that because they only had a nine minute slot they had to cut one of the songs. To my surprise it's Gary Gilmore. They thought it would be better for their audience to air the newer ones. The twenty-four to forty-four year olds are going up in my estimation. He also tells me that one of their interns is a huge fan. He was in the control booth during the session and didn't want to interrupt to say hello, so Geoff gave him the book afterwards and he was thrilled. I email back to say, glad it's gone to a good home! It's not exactly the promo opportunity I had been hoping for but secretly I'd expected both the book and the CD to go straight in the bin as soon as I was out of the door.

## 29th April LONDON

I was out visiting friends yesterday when the session was supposed to be broadcast so didn't hear it. Today I check the website and see that it did in fact go out, although the promised two songs got reduced to one. A prominent slot on nationwide Sunday evening radio is clearly a powerful selling tool: 24 hours later sales through my website have been...zero.

## 3rd May STOKE-ON-TRENT

It's less than six months since I played in Stoke, which is notably one of the most economically depressed areas in Britain and has suffered the largest cuts to its council budget in the entire country, slashing services across the area. What I like about it is not just the fact that they have a great little gig in the Glebe, promoted by a couple of music enthusiasts, but that the people who come here are friendly and feisty. They greet me like an old friend as the pub starts to fill and much of the conversation is about the economic situation: if the council is in so much financial trouble, why is the historic council building next door lying empty, and new multi-million pound council offices being built elsewhere? Why hasn't it been publicised that a bill has just gone through the Lords laying the grounds for privatisation of the NHS? Someone tells me, almost apoplectic with anger, that even the prison meals service has been privatised and the contract given to McDonald's—the warders go over there and pick up the breakfasts.

It's also a pub with a great atmosphere and great beers. Along with the great people in the audience that can only lead to one thing: a great gig.

## 4th May GLOSSOP

Mainline train to Manchester, then the branch line to Glossop which chugs leisurely along stopping at every station along the way—Ardwick, Ashburys, Gorton, Fairfield, Guide Bridge, Hyde, Newton, Hattersley, Dinting—the embankments strewn with the usual railside debris: hubcaps, crisp packets, spent asthma inhalers.

My hotel is right across the road from the station, a place called the George. It's a bank holiday weekend so the bar downstairs is full of lunchtime drinkers and it takes a while for the landlady to find the time to get me my key. Upstairs I find myself in a small but perfectly comfortable room with the St George's flag flapping noisily outside in the stiff breeze blowing off the Peak District hills.

There's plenty of time before soundcheck so I go to look around the town. It's almost literally one street, which does give me concerns about how many people will turn up tonight, particularly as I've never played here before. I've soon exhausted the sightseeing possibilities and retreat to the large park I notice on the town map. I have a lively walk around the lake and then settle down on a bench to eat the economy cheese baguette I bought earlier from Greggs. Around me people are walking dogs or playing with their kids, trying to ignore the icy wind. At least the sun is out. The park has a narrow gauge railway, and I sit a while longer to watch the little train draw slowly out of the station past the miniature golf course and head off to the woodland circuit, excited children in the back sitting wide-eyed on their parents laps.

Then I hurry back to the hotel to warm up, passing the park café on the way, where a sign sternly warns: *Attention. Parents who allow their children to climb and mess on the rides do so at their own risk.* I nearly cause a miss-throw incident as I walk by the bowling green and the elderly contestants spot my bleached jeans.

At six I head to the venue, a five minute walk from the hotel, and climb the narrow stairs of the pub to find a small, pleasant room with a good stage and sound system, tables and chairs spread around for the audience, the walls lined with old vinyl and record sleeves. I get a welcome from the sound engineer and the promoter, who I'm surprised to find is a guy called Brian, who used to put on gigs for me at a venue in nearby Hyde.

Soundcheck goes off with no problem and then I wait for the evening to begin, hoping a few people will turn up. The sound guy takes me downstairs to the bar to recommend some of the local cask ales, telling me that it looks like they're putting on one now as the barman is fiddling with one of the pumps. 'What have you got on tonight?' he asks, when the barman finally looks up.

'Er…T—V—Smith, I think it is…'

'No—I mean, what *beer* have you got on tonight?'

Support act Steve O'Donaghue arrives, suffering from a heavy cold, and gamely ignores the good-natured ribbing he gets from Brian and the sound guy, both clearly old mates of his. He supported me once in Hyde, his home town, and I enjoyed his set then. By the time he gets on stage tonight there aren't that many people in, maybe about twenty, but his gently melancholic songs work well in this intimate atmosphere, and he chats affably between them and gets everyone on his side. At one point he explains how he's had a sore throat for three weeks and was told by his doctor that the best way to soothe it would be to massage it using a vibrator on his neck. The next day he went into a branch of Ann Summers to buy one When the girl working there brought out an array of different types of vibrator and started to explain their features he said, 'No, you don't understand—it's for my *throat*.'

Which was somehow worse.

You couldn't say he's arrogant. He finishes off his set with the words, 'That's all from me. If any of you see me on the streets of Hyde, please don't point and laugh.'

When I get on stage the audience are well warmed up, and by the time I finish ninety minutes later they are out of their chairs punching the air. A rewarding gig, although—as not many people turned up and I was on a door deal—not in the financial sense of the word.

At least the hotel was only thirty quid, but I'm a bit concerned now because it's one of those with an entry code rather than a key, and the landlady told me that there is a strictly defined route from the front door through the bar area to the stairs. If I deviate from it—towards the bar for instance—it will set off the alarms. I'm carrying a lot of gear and have had a few beers: what if my guitar swings into the path of the invisible beams? What if I fall over? I've never fallen over in a hotel lobby before but tonight could be the night…

As it turns out the pub is still open and doing good business, even though it's nearly one. In fact it's so noisy that when I get to my room sleep seems unlikely and I do something I rarely do in hotels: I switch on the television. The first channel that comes up is a static screen with the words: *Ideal World. Back at 5 a.m.*

Maybe I should set the alarm.

## 5th May LINCOLN

I'm in Lincoln to play a two day punk and ska festival. My stage time is mid evening and as there are lots of other bands playing there won't be a soundcheck so I have a couple of hours in my hotel before I need to be there. Unfortunately the only affordable hotel I could find was a Premier Inn just outside the town, so I have to get a taxi out there. The driver seems very interested in who I am. 'You look just like Johnny Rotten,' he says. 'It's the eyes. You could make a fortune in London doing an impression of him.'

I have other plans.

I arrive at the venue at around seven, enough time to soak up the atmosphere for a couple of hours before I play. The festival is being held in the back yard of the Jolly Brewer, one of the oldest pubs in Lincoln. The stage backs on to the next door church, the spire towering over the yard, and there is currently a pre-arranged break from music while Evening Service takes place. 'We were here before they were,' the landlady tells me. Typical, the new neighbours move in and start throwing their weight about.

At eight the bands begin again and I'm on soon after nine. I have an enjoyable gig, then set up a merch stand at one of the tables at the back of the yard and watch a great ska band called the Activators. Every now and then people from the audience pass by to chat or buy stuff. The guy who has been introducing the bands during the evening wanders over and says, 'You might not believe this looking at me now, but I used to be a policeman in London in the seventies.' He tells me his claim to fame. 'I was working in Paddington police station, and after the 100 Club bottling incident we had Johnny Rotten and Sid Vicious in the cells overnight. I had to negotiate with my colleagues so

I could be the one to take their breakfast in. I didn't speak to them or anything, just put the tray down. They were like a couple of scared kids.'

This was presumably before the McDonald's prison breakfast days.

The last band finishes and people start to disperse, and I'm left thinking what a pleasant evening this was—no overblown prices or corporate advertising, just a few music lovers putting on a little festival, some good bands and a good turnout from the audience to support it. This sort of thing really gives me hope for the grassroots live music scene.

And as the icing on the cake, the landlady even gives me a lift back to the hotel and saves me a taxi fare.

## 6th May MAIDSTONE

It's a bank holiday Monday and because of the reduced rail service the only route I could book in advance to Maidstone involved five changes of train and a forty-five minute walk between two stations in Newark. Consequently I'm quite surprised when I arrive in Lincoln station and find a one-carriage train just about to leave for the Newark station that I actually want. I make a quick decision, drop my just-started sandwich in my bag and jump on. When I return to the sandwich a few minutes later I rather wish that I hadn't chosen the one with the onion relish, as there's now more of it in my bag than in the sandwich.

Due to my sudden change of schedule I find myself in Newark with nearly two hours   before my connecting train leaves. I buy a coffee and sit it out in the cafe, my eye drawn to the sign on the window opposite: *This is not a waiting room. For reasons of safety please use the area further down the platform.*

Yes, people sitting around. On the chairs. I can see how dangerous that could be.

When I finally get to Maidstone I have a feeling of *deja vu* when I get to the busy hotel where I'm supposed to be staying, only to be informed by one of the overworked women at the bar that they have no reservation for me. Out of all the hundreds of gigs I play every year my hotel reservation has only ever been lost twice before: once in Chicago several years ago, and once here in Maidstone four months ago. Luckily there are still rooms available, but the woman dealing with me doesn't know how to use the computer system to book one and can't find the manager, so I get out my iPad and book it online in front of her. 'Ah yes, Mr Smith,' she says, peering at the screen. 'You're just coming through now...'

The gig is part of the two day Maidstone fringe festival, so once again there is no soundcheck. When I arrive at the Style & Winch the sunny beer garden is packed and there is a hog roast smoking away at the far end of it: a marked contrast to last time I was here in the depths of Winter and it was deserted, everyone huddled inside the pub. I drop into the music room at the back to say hello to Clive, who invited me to play in January, and again today. One band is just finishing in there and there are a couple more still to go. I pass the time chatting with some of the people who came to the gig last time I was here, as well as some who missed it and are looking forward to this evening. I also take the opportunity to scout around for places to set up the merch table, but the place is so busy that I can't see anywhere obvious—every potential table is covered with glasses.

The gig is exciting and the room is encouragingly full. Towards the end I tell the crowd, 'After the last song, I'm going to go and set up a table to sell CDs outside by the dog bowl.' I've never said that before.

There are a few people waiting for my by the dog bowl when I get out there, and they help me set up a folding table and put out the CDs. I hang the T-shirts out on the branches of the potted plant behind me. After a while chatting and selling stuff the evening starts to get a bit chilly so I ask one of the women festival helpers who has been hanging around the stall to look after it while I go and put something warmer on. When I get back she has been replaced by a large extremely drunken man who doesn't know who I am and attempts to sell me my own merchandise.

The evening draws to a close and I have one final beer with Clive before heading off. He can finally relax now the festival is over. He started it a few years ago to try to get something going in Maidstone; this year it has involved 150 bands over seventeen stages and has been a big success. Maybe there is hope for music yet.

## 9th May LONDON

Off to Oxford Street for a gig supporting the UK Subs at the historic 100 Club. After six weeks on tour together at the beginning of the year it's strange to walk in and see them already having a soundcheck—I'm usually there for the start!—and Yuko already setting up the merch—shouldn't I be helping?

But it's great to see them again, even though the evening is pretty hectic so we don't have much of a chance to catch up. The gig is sold out and there's a great atmosphere as we have a lot of mutual friends and fans in London. At the end of the evening they get in the van to head for a Travelodge in Reading on the way to their gig in Bristol tomorrow, and I head for the tube home, ready for my gig tomorrow in Wakefield. There's not even time for Wine Club.

## 10th May WAKEFIELD

The route from Wakefield rail station to the Travelodge I'm staying in involves walking right through the centre of town so I soon get a sense of the place. Almost straight away I pass the venue I'm playing tonight, which is surrounded by clubs called things like 'Tequila' and '80's!'—sure to be dangerous later this evening—and then I'm into the pedestrianised town centre where an impressive cathedral sits marooned opposite a row of downmarket shops. Within the space of a few hundred yards there's Poundland, Simply Pound, Super Pound Store, Pound World Express—and if you're feeling peckish, Pound Bakery.

In my room I briefly ponder over whether to bother taking any merch to the gig with me as it all costs more than one pound, but I pack some anyway and struggle with my bag and guitar back across town. The soundman is ready for me in the venue, which is a pleasant real ale pub with a music room upstairs. Within a few minutes he has got up a great sound and I'm looking forward to the gig, just hoping that a few people will turn up as I don't recall ever having played Wakefield before.

Louise Distras arrives. Once again she's playing support tonight, but she took a bit of arm-twisting to do it as Wakefield is her home town and she reckons people don't like her here. She's not that keen on the town either—in fact one of her songs is about the violence on the streets here at night. 'So, what do you think of Wakefield?' she asks, when she sees me.

'I'll tell you if I manage to get back tonight without getting beaten up,' I say.

'Oh God, I hope you don't…' she says. The fact she took me seriously is slightly worrying.

While we're waiting for the club to open the sound man tells me that he's not in the best of moods today. He owns an analogue studio here with lots of vintage equipment in it, he tells me. 'The trouble is, it's too well soundproofed.'

'How's that?' I ask.

'I was doing some mixing in the control room today, and while I was in there someone broke in to the studio and stole a load of microphones. I didn't hear a thing.'

There's a decent turnout by the time Louise starts and though she's nervous about playing in front of her home crowd her set goes down really well. Admittedly, when she asks if there's anyone in the audience actually from Wakefield no one puts their hand up.

My set goes really well too, and afterwards there's even a bit of action in the Ten Pound Shop.

Soon the audience thin out and I'm just packing away my guitar when a guy comes over and says, maybe I'd come to the bar and let him buy me a drink—him and his mate would love to have a chat about punk. When I get there the guy introduces me to his mate, who immediately gets into a discussion about the state of the country, which continues for a good half hour until he goes off to the loo. When he's gone, his mate says, 'I didn't realise we were going to be talking politics—I thought we'd be discussing obscure Adverts B-sides and stuff. New Day Dawning, what a great song that was!'

Then there's the question of getting to the hotel. All the people who'd earlier been offering to walk back with me have already gone so I grab my guitar and bag and head out into the heaving streets, trying to avoid eye contact with anyone. There are mobs of people outside the strip of clubs on the main street. All the girls have too-short skirts and all the men have too-tight T-shirts. One of the two lads walking in front of me says he's going up to the Rainbow. That's right opposite the Travelodge! I manage to edge around them and speed ahead. There's one policeman, but he's in Subway in the queue to get a sandwich. Things quieten down in the central part of the town by the cathedral and Pound Shops, then I hit another patch of clubbers. One guy is shouting angrily at his girlfriend and she is shouting gamely back: 'I saved your life back there! He had you on the floor!'

I glide past, invisible.

## 17th May LONDON

Across London to the opening of an art show that Gaye and three of her friends are putting on in a new gallery called Red Door. I'm going to play a short set during the course of the evening. If we ever get there: East Ham is twenty seven stops away on the District Line—I've got to gigs in Germany quicker.

Gaye's fellow artist David picks us up from the tube and drives us to the gallery. The owner of the place is called Dolores and introduces everyone to everyone else. As each new person arrives she goes round the room doing all the introductions again. David and I struggle with the P.A. for a while, which steadfastly refuses to work even though we stand over it for a long time fiddling with various bits. We look like two blokes peering in to the open bonnet of a broken down car going, 'It could be the fuel pump...?' Eventually we've tried every combination of knobs and it finally works and sounds great. David suggests I go on at around 9:45 and play a half an hour. 'Dolores will be saying a few words first,' he mentions. I joke that I hope she's not going to introduce everyone in the room to everyone else as there are already quite a few people in and it could take a while.

When the time comes to start I switch on the microphone for Dolores, plug my guitar in and stand behind her while she delivers a speech of Oscar acceptance length, thanking everyone who's been involved in helping get the gallery ready and putting the exhibition together, the people doing the bar, the people who put the snacks out. I raise an eyebrow at David when she thanks her plumber—'I think he's here tonight!'—and then the time comes round to me. 'It's a great honour to have someone so famous in our little gallery,' she says. 'We didn't get much of the obscure British punk thing in the corner of Canada where I come from, but *you* all seem to know him!'

Once I get started I have an enjoyable gig. Afterwards someone wants a word. 'Gary Gilmore,' he says. 'Is it right, he just donated his cataracts?'

'His *cataracts*? I don't think they'd have been much use!'

The guy looks affronted. 'I'm not an eye specialist!' he says.

## 23rd May NOTTINGHAM

It's my first time in Nottingham for a while, and satisfyingly Foremans bar is sold out in advance—although it has to be said that it only holds fifty people. Jason, the owner, has warned me that it's probably the smallest place I've ever played. I've played plenty of small places but when I walk in I have to admit it is up there with the smallest of them. Or should I say down there. Still, there's a tiny low stage in the corner and the sound is good so I'm in my element. The sound man tells me he was in East London last week, staying just around the corner from the Red Door Gallery on the opening night of the exhibition, but when he got in from work he was too tired to go. He's off to work now too and will have to leave another guy in charge of the sound now he's set it up. I congratulate him on managing to miss me twice in one week.

Jason takes me over the road to a café to have a chat with a young girl student who is doing a PHD on punk. He points out that we are in a posh street of shops and restaurants with just Foremans opposite standing out from the ubiquitous high street names, 'Punk Rock' proudly emblazoned above the door. He's been running the place for years, moving in when the street was derelict and now all this has sprung up around him. Tourists come and take photographs of the bar, seeing it as a curiosity.

The three of us chat for a while about punk and music generally. The talk turns to music in the Eighties and I say, as I often do, that the Eighties were the worst period of my life. Afterwards, on the way to check in to the Travelodge I see a club with the sign: *80's Fun Bar. Remember the good times!*

I try and try but I can't.

When I get back to the venue the stand-in sound man is there by the desk.

'So you're the guy I have to shout at if it sounds terrible?' I ask.

'You can if you like,' he replies. 'I'm deaf.'

There's a great atmosphere in the room when I squeeze through the throng onto the little stage. I still can't think of anywhere smaller I've played but I don't want to give Jason the satisfaction so I start the set with the words, 'I've played *bigger* places...'

A while later, when introducing one of the Adverts songs, I say, 'As far as I can remember, I think the Adverts used to play in Nottingham Cricket Club.'

'It was the Boat Club!' someone shouts.

Boats...cricket... I'm always getting those two mixed up. It's caused some embarrassing incidents on the pitch.

All in all a very enjoyable gig. Afterwards I set up a merch table on the stage—it actually takes up the entire stage—and a few people chat with me and buy things. A group of lads come over and one comes forward to shake my hand. 'Rilly enjoyed it, like'

Seeing me struggle with the accent, his mate says, 'He's from the North East.'

'Doorum. I bet you dinna na Doorum.'

'Durham? Of course I do,' I reply, 'I've got mates from up that way.'

'Whereaboots?'

I know I'm falling into a trap but I say it anyway. 'Sunderland.'

He shakes his head. 'I'm gan off yer na.'


## 24th May MANCHESTER

Stormy weather. The tree outside the Travelodge window is shaking around so much it looks in danger of being blown down. Must be careful of that when I leave. Always a bad start to the day, having a tree fall on you.

I'm now pleased that I'm playing the warm-up night for Strummercamp tonight, rather than the festival itself over the weekend, which had originally been the plan. Tonight the live music will take place indoors, in a function room in the Cheadle Rugby Club, rather than in the marquee in a field outside, which is where the the bands will play over the following two days. The way the weather is looking I can't see that marquee staying attached to the ground for long. I'm also happy that I'll be staying with my mate Mick in Manchester rather than camping like most of the audience.

I take the cross country train to Manchester, then the bus over to Mick's place, dodging the hefty showers for the final walk. A lollipop lady stops the traffic outside the school so I can cross the road and we exchange wry comments about the lovely summer as the rain comes pelting down again.

Mick drives us over to the rugby club and during the journey I recall the last time I came here with my friends Jon and Sophie and we got hopelessly lost. 'I've been lost here before!' I say as we drive through the suburban maze of commuter houses, clearly nowhere near the festival, following the directions Mick has printed off the internet.

As it turns out the postcode given on the Strummercamp website leads us to a primary school. The GPS on my phone comes to the rescue and after only another short stretch of motorway and a few more roundabouts and suburban streets we are in familiar territory. 'I've *definitely* been lost here before,' I say reassuringly to Mick, and soon we arrive at the rugby club, where everything is running late anyway and there is plenty of time to spare.

Outside, people are braving the cold to smoke, shivering in the evening chill. I'm jokingly treated as some kind of rock star when people find out I'm staying in a house rather than camping. One couple tell me they're already on their second tent, the first got ripped to shreds in the storm last night. The woman tells me, 'I was clinging to the metal fence with one hand and the tent pole with the other, trying to stop it blowing away.'

Instead of the planned 10-ish start, it's nearly 11:30 before I get on stage. I ask one of the guys up there who's setting up a D.I. box for me if he's the sound engineer, and he says, 'Actually, we don't have a sound engineer. It's all a bit chaotic and we're all just trying to help out.'

I suppose that when you're a festival trying to raise money for charity you have to dispense with some of the non-essentials. Like sound engineers. Rather disconcerted by this information I launch into the first song and as expected the sound is terrible, but the crowd are so completely on my side that I soon stop worrying—if they're happy, I'm happy.

Tomorrow the weather forecast is for sun all day and rising temperatures. I'll be back home and in my shed, but I'm pleased for the people who have braved the elements to come here to this great little festival. After a miserable start, hopefully Strummercamp will become Summercamp.

## 31st May NEWCASTLE

The announcement comes round for the third time, 'Once again ladies and gentlemen we'd like to apologise for the late running of this train. This was due to having to wait at a red light south of Newark Northgate station.'

As far as an excuse goes this makes about as much sense as saying, 'We'd like to apologise for the delay. This was due to us being late.'

I want more detail. *Why* was this red light unexpectedly holding up our otherwise impeccable progress? I wait for more explanation but by the time we finally get to Newcastle none has been offered.

I am now running late due to the fact I am running late so I jump in a cab to get to the venue. The driver asks what kind of guitar I have and tells me he has a guitar too. I have a bit of trouble understanding his rather strange Geordie accent until I realise he is Italian. 'I used to have a clarinet,' he tells me. 'My father made me play it and sent me for lessons. The teacher persuaded me to buy one and recommended one at a special price he could negotiate. Two weeks later my father found the same clarinet on sale for fifty thousand lire cheaper.' He pauses the story while he negotiates a roundabout, then adds meaningfully, 'My father went and *had a talk* with the teacher.'

After that, he tells me, he gave up the clarinet and started playing guitar.

As we near the venue he asks me if I believe in UFOs and aliens. 'No,' I say, and he is clearly disappointed but carries on with what he wants to say anyway.

'It may be that aliens are highly sophisticated, refined beings. I have read that if you make noise they don't like it and they move further away but if you make music it attracts them. Maybe when you make your music tonight they will come nearer.'

Blimey. I'd be quite happy with some humans.

I'm not sure how many of them to expect tonight and the venue could hold quite a few. It's a nice room though, and I feel comfortable as soon as I walk in. It's an ex studio theatre in a half-round with some banked seating on one side. The acoustics are great, but there is a slight problem in soundcheck when a peculiar loud thrumming noise starts coming out of the PA system. 'I've never had that one before,' says the sound engineer. I wonder if it might be the aliens, but it turns out to be more mundane: something on the sound desk out of phase.

The promoter has put out some tables and chairs on the floor space to make the place look less empty in case of a poor turnout, but soon people are coming in and it's comfortably full by the time I start. I play a long set. Great venue, great sound, great audience—great start to the weekend. No aliens.

## 1st June EDINBURGH

It's my third time at the Citrus Club in Edinburgh in the space of a year or so, and hats off to promoter Bryan for persevering with me. It's a good club, and my previous two gigs went down really well but there were woefully few people there for the first and only a slight improvement in numbers on the second. This time he is putting me on supporting the Vibrators and hoping the double-bill will bring in a bigger crowd. The only trouble is, that means me going on at 7:30 as the gig has an early curfew so they can get a second audience in for a club night afterwards.

Just before the doors open at seven I go outside to see if anyone is waiting and find five people out there, all of whom I know personally. I wonder if the double-bill gambit is going to work. I've publicised my start time on the internet and it's on all the posters, but—7:30! No one really believes you're going to start that early on a Saturday night. I leave it as long as I can, and when I walk up to the stage I'm pleasantly surprised to see there are a lot of people in, already more than I had at my previous gigs here, and some of them are pointing to their watches and jokingly reprimanding me. 'It's twenty-to, TV, what's going on? Hurry up!'

Brilliant gig. Scottish audiences can be some of the best in the world. When they turn up.

Afterwards I hang around the merch and talk with a few people. One guy, clearly a free spirit, tells me he is Greek and has just got back from spending some time travelling around America. 'I didn't enjoy it much,' he says. 'Wherever I went I felt *in the way.*'

## 7th June LONDON

Tonight it's the 12 Bar club in central London, originally a sixteenth century forge. It's tiny, totally impractical for gigs as most bands can't fit on the stage, and the audience have a choice of the mini-balcony upstairs where about fifteen people can look down on the top of the musicians' heads or downstairs, where you can only see up as far their heads because the sight lines are blocked by the balcony. It's also one of the best small venues in London with a great intimate atmosphere and a satisfyingly independent booking policy by club manager Barnett. Consequently it's no surprise that Louise Distras is on the bill again this evening. I point out to her when she arrives that it's like we're doing a tour together—it's just that we also play other dates on our own in between.

There's a young band from Brighton going on first. As I finish my soundcheck I see the bass player struggling with a roll of tape, trying to fix the sole back on to one of his shoes.

'Nice Sellotape repair job,' I say.

He says, 'My lucky shoes...'

The gig goes great and afterwards as I'm hanging around by the merch someone comes up to tell me that this morning The Adverts were on Radio 2, the BBC's ultra-conservative middle-of-the-road music channel. 'They didn't play a song,' he hastens to add, 'but you were one of the questions on Ken Bruce's pop quiz, Popmaster! The question was, *Which band recorded Gary Gilmore's Eyes?* The woman who phoned in was given a choice of three answers. She got it wrong.'

Another guy tells me about the occasion he met Screaming Lord Sutch and Terry Hooley, founder of legendary Irish record shop Good Vibrations. 'Terry Hooley took out his glass eye and rolled it across the table. Screaming Lord Sutch nearly shat himself!'

## 8th June SHOREHAM

It's only a short hop to tonight's gig in Shoreham-by-sea, in a real ale pub called the Duke Of Wellington and promoted by my mate Attila The Stockbroker. I bought an advance train ticket for a miserly £6.50, a significant saving on the on-the-day price of nearly thirty quid and give myself well over an hour to get to Victoria station, normally a twenty minute journey, so I have plenty of time to pick it up from the machine in case of queues. The only problem is that my local tube station is out of action this weekend so I'll need to take a bus to Hammersmith, two stops down the line, and pick up the District Line to Victoria from there. After I've waited at the bus stop for more than twenty minutes I realise with growing disbelief that despite all my planning I am in danger of missing my train. Then something else occurs to me: I changed into a different jacket at the last minute because of the sudden summery weather, and left my bank card in the other one. I'm almost certain that I'll need that to get my ticket printed. Still no sign of a bus. I make a dash back for home, suitcase wheels burning rubber on the pavement. Once there I grab my bank card, but a glance at the clock confirms I'm never going to make it back to the bus stop and still get to Victoria in time—even if a bus actually comes—so the only alternative is a minicab. The cab office promises to send one 'right away' but half an hour later it still hasn't arrived and I realise that whatever happens my cheap rail ticket is gone and I'm going to have to fork out full price for a later train as well as having to now pay for a cab. No longer in a hurry and hoping to cut my losses, I phone up to cancel the cab but I'm informed that it's already outside. I look out of the front door and see it across the road, the driver not paying any attention to me but stabbing his finger at the GPS device on the windscreen. He seems quite surprised when I walk up.

'I was just about to cancel you,' I say. 'You're so late I'm going to miss my train,'

'Late? I just got the call from the office a couple of minutes ago, I came straight here...'

I check the time. Twenty minutes before my train goes. Might just still be possible. 'How long do you think it will take you to get to Victoria?'

'I think, about half an hour boss. Traffic. I'll do what I can.'

We shoot off at speed down a narrow road and on the first curve meet an elderly lady driver coming in the other direction. A few feet away from a head-on collision both drivers screech to a halt but there is no room for them to pass. The lady doesn't seem keen to reverse, but finally we have got around her and my driver turns onto the main road, heading in the opposite direction to Victoria.

'You do know where we are going?' I ask.

'Victoria, boss. I'm going to take the M4 to avoid the traffic.'

The M4 is in the other direction from where we are heading. His half an hour estimate now seems vastly over optimistic, because if he wants to get to the M4 like this he will first have to circumnavigate the globe. 'The M4 is that way,' I exclaim, pointing behind us.

'You think so, boss?' He looks at me doubtfully, then looks back at the long line of traffic we are stuck in, leading up to the next traffic lights. 'Well, if you think so...'

He makes a three point turn with scant regard for the oncoming cars and when we are finally heading in the right direction he makes a call on his phone. From the back seat I can hear both sides of the conversation quite clearly.

'GPS frozen boss.'

'Roger. Are you P.O.B?'

'Sorry boss?'

'Are you P.O.B?'

'Eh...'

'Did you *pick up the passenger?*'

'Oh! Yes boss!'

'That's the main thing. When you've dropped him off switch off the GPS then put it on charge and switch it on again.'

We drive in an erratic fashion in the general direction of Victoria, with me occasionally having to point out to the driver that he is about to take the wrong road again. There is one case of bad driving that leads to an argument with another driver that threatens to erupt into a full-on out-of-the-car fisticuffs-in-the-street incident. I groan quietly and check the time once again as they shout through their open windows at each other.

'Why are you driving like a STUPID TEENAGER?'

'FUCK OFF!'

'YOU DON'T KNOW NOTHING!'

I miss the train I was supposed to be on, and the one after that, and catch the one after that with ninety seconds to spare. It's completely full and there is nowhere to sit.

But, ah, the sun is shining on the walk from the station to the the pub, there's a refreshing breeze blowing across Shoreham harbour, and it's hard to stay in a bad mood for long. There's singer/songwriter Wob working behind the bar at the Welly, as the pub is affectionately known, and soon Attila arrives, suffering from a heavy cold but as ebullient as ever, and not long after that dedicated TUTS the Fleagles arrive, shortly followed by Jon and Sophie who were also at the 12 Bar last night. One-time Adverts road manager David, who I haven't seen for years, turns up, lots of Welly regulars come, and soon the room is full of happy friendly faces.

Attila plays first with his band Barnstormer, then it's time for me. Attila introduces me with much heaping on of praise, and as I start it occurs to me that by sharing the same microphone as him I am almost certain to catch his cold. During much of the first song I am doing the mental arithmetic to figure out which gigs might be affected. But then I put the negative thoughts behind me and steam on to a very exciting gig, the little bar packed to the rafters, if it had rafters. All Barnstormer's instruments are still set up around me on the makeshift stage and at one point, as I am stomping around during No Time To Be 21, Attila's bass recorder falls off its stand and the component parts scatter across the stage. At the end of the song, as someone scrambles to gather the pieces together, I turn back to the microphone. 'I can honestly say that is the first time I've ever had a medieval woodwind instrument fall over on stage while I've been playing a 1977 punk song.'

Afterwards as people drift away I stand at the bar with Attila and a couple of his friends, enjoying a glass of the local Hophead ale. Attila, an enthusiastic sea fisherman, is reminiscing about some of the most unusual catches he's made around here. 'Mostly it's flounder and bass,' he says, 'but there was one time in 1986 when I realised I had hooked something really heavy.' This was just a few weeks after then-prime minister Ted Heath's yacht had sunk in the area with two crew members missing. Attila's catch broke loose just as he was about to get it above water, but when he reeled in the line he found 'human hair and skin' caught on the hook.

There was another significant catch some time after that. Once again, it was something heavy. 'I was reeling it in and I could see this big green slimy-looking thing on the end of the line coming towards me. I went carefully to make sure the line didn't break, landed it successfully and found it was an old Subbuteo game playing field.'

The guy with us is the owner of a local tackle shop and has a fishing story too. 'The strangest thing I ever caught,' he tells us, ' was a plastic bag with three dildos in it, weighed down with stones.'

## 9th June PORTSMOUTH

I rouse from my sleeping bag and come into the kitchen just as Attila is going off to walk his cute two year old terrier and get some provisions for breakfast. I ask Attila's wife Robina what happened to Oddball, the other terrier they had last time I stayed, who memorably liked to chew on pebbles and would spend hours dropping them at your feet hoping you would throw them for it. Robina tells me that it's bit of a tragic story, as he escaped out of the gate one day and got run over. Ever since then she's been paranoid about it happening again. For months after he died she kept on finding pebbles he'd hidden around the house. Just then Attila arrives back, gasping heavily from an asthma attack that struck when he came out of the Co-op. He dumps the bag of shopping on the table, then suddenly goes white. 'Oh shit! I FORGOT THE DOG!'

It takes a while for Robina to find him as Attila tied him up in a different place than usual. Happily reunited, the three of them head off back to the Welly to pick up the car and I head off to Southwick station to get a train to Portsmouth.

This weekend is the first anniversary of a Portsmouth punk festival called 'Punk By The Sea,' which got cancelled last year at the last minute in mysterious circumstances. The organisers ran off with all the ticket sales leaving nothing to pay the bands and no money for the local charity who were supposed to profit from the festival. Determined to do something about it, a few of the bands pulled together to put on a show in a barn behind a pub called the Milton Arms so at least the people who had bought tickets had something to see, and it turned into a very special weekend, a great example of DIY punk. This year the plan is to do it again and this time make sure the hospice who were supposed to benefit last year actually see some money.

Of course it's all a bit disorganised and chaotic. As I arrive I get told that yesterday went well, but today various bands haven't turned up, the sound man couldn't make it either so they've had to get a last-minute replacement—and there aren't as many people here today as there were yesterday.

Out in the courtyard leading to the barn I find Mick, who helped get me on the bill at Guilfest last year and later this year is promoting his own festival near Woking, which I'll also be playing at. He plays barrel organ in an Irish band himself and has a few gigs over the coming months. His only problem at the moment is fitting everything in as he's due to go into hospital. A few years ago he had an operation for a brain tumour and the metal plate they put in has to be tightened up. He points at his head, 'I've officially got a screw loose. It's driving my wife mad. Every time I accidentally turn over in the night and lean on it I wake up screaming.'

Mick passes me a handful of flyers for the festival, and I point out that that though there are the logos of lots of bands up at the top of the flyer, some of whom I've never heard of, my name only appears on the long list of bands underneath.

'How come I'm there with the also-rans?' I ask, mock-seriously.

Mick's not sure if I'm really offended or not. 'Printer cocked up, Tim!' he exclaims. 'I just sent them the names and for some reason they did it this way. Anyway—you're at the top of the list. You're number one of the also-rans.'

Someone who has heard our conversation as he squeezes past to go into the venue looks back and says drily, 'Story of your life.'

A band Mick manages called Avondale 45 will be on just before me, but there are still a couple more bands to go. I watch a few numbers from the first of them, a knockabout unrehearsed punk covers band made up of various members of other bands. Local tattooist Bubba gets up on stage to sing one number and as technical problems take over and everything grinds to a halt I wander out to the courtyard to give my ears a rest. Soon afterwards Bubba comes rushing out. 'Where's the sound man? We need the sound man!'

The sound man is getting a burger.

He's outside during the next band too, so I take the opportunity to have a word. As I feared, he doesn't have a D.I. Box with him as he only found out he was needed a few hours ago and hasn't brought one, which means there is going to be no way to get the signal from the guitar into the PA system. 'I've been getting migraines all day. I've taken three Paracetamol,' he says, by way of explanation. When he realises that I'm playing acoustic guitar, not electric as he'd thought, he cheers up a bit. 'Oh, we'll find a way!'

I'm glad he's confident, because now I'm not.

One of the bands who didn't turn up earlier now arrive and set up on stage to play. We're running nearly an hour late. I chat with a few people in the courtyard and one of the girls involved in the conversation asks me my name. Rather embarrassingly, Bubba says, 'You must know his name! He's a star!'

The girl looks at me dubiously. 'Explain to me in five seconds why you're a star.'

I would need longer.

Jon, one of the main organisers, comes round with a tray of cup cakes with the anarchy symbol iced on top. There's a donation box for the hospice we're trying to raise funds for on the tray next to them.

By the time the other bands have got their gear off the stage it's almost time for the last bus and train, and the already-scant audience soon thins out even more. The venue actually does have rafters but it's far from packed to them. I spend some time with the sound man trying to get the guitar working—'I've had four Paracetamol,' he tells me—and to my surprise he manages to rig up a cable from the desk that works and the sound is unexpectedly good. People start to trickle in as I hit the first few chords, and even though I find myself playing to only a handful of people I get a warm response.

Afterwards Jon thanks me sincerely for coming. The takings from yesterday, after all the costs were paid, came to more than five hundred quid, and that's before today's ticket money and donations have been added in. Everything will go direct to the hospice who should have benefited last year.

We did something good.

It's just a ten minute walk to my budget hotel and I notice there is a police car parked outside it. As I walk in a policeman is in discussion with the guy behind the reception desk: '...and so camera three is just the hallway on the second floor, and four is the lift? We've done six and seven haven't we?'

'That's right,' says the receptionist. 'That's all of them.'

The policeman ticks off a couple of things on his clipboard. 'Well, I think that's all I need. If you can just get those discs with the last three days on over to me...'

As I wait for the lift to arrive, I say to the receptionist, 'Has something been stolen?'

He watches the policeman leave. 'No, it's just...normal. You know. This country.'

## 15th June BAD HERSFELD

Here's the plan: *Die Toten Hosen* play a stadium gig in Kassel, Germany. Andy and Michy, two people I know who run a little photo studio there called Fotomania, will be going with a bunch of their friends. After the show in the stadium, which is already sold out with 30,000 people, they want to invite about forty of them to the photo studio for an intimate private concert by me. To finance my trip over they'll charge a small entrance fee, and Steffen, another friend of ours, will organise a gig for me in nearby Bad Hersfeld the night before so I may even make a small profit.

And here's what actually happens.

I tell Vom, drummer with Die Toten Hosen, about the Fotomania show a few weeks before and he immediately says he wants to play it with me. Word gets out and Andy and Michy start to worry about loads of people turning up to their studio, which is in a residential block and would lead to problems with the neighbours. They decide to move the event to a bigger club called K19 and make it an official gig open to everyone. Vom tells the Toten Hosen I'm going to be in Kassel and they mention to him the idea of me guesting on a couple of songs with them. I'm going to be at the stadium anyway because Pil, the singer I met in Argentina a few months ago, is playing one of the support slots with his new band and wants me to sing Immortal Rich with them. Before I went to Argentina I'd never even heard of Pil and the last time I was at a Hosen gig was about five years ago, so as far as coincidences go this is up there. The Hosen also recently asked Vom's son Jez and his friend Meg to come on stage at two of their gigs and play a version of my song Lion And The Lamb—and they've been invited back to do it again at Kassel. Could be an interesting day.

But first, Bad Hersfeld. I'm picked up from Frankfurt airport by Niko, who lives in nearby Mainz but is coming to Bad Hersfeld to see the gig and also visit his parents, who live there. His father is the local priest, and many years ago when Niko still lived with them and I was on tour with Garden Gang we all stayed in their house, which is right opposite the church, and we even made a memorable visit to the top of the church tower the next morning. Before going to the venue, Niko and I drop in to see them. They've just got back from a festival in the medieval ruins in the town centre which featured musicians from many cultures and religions to celebrate the concept of 'tolerance.' I could quite happily sit and chat with them a bit longer, but Niko gets a call from Steffen to say we need to be at the club as soon as possible—the sound man is just leaving.

It's a five minute walk down the road. The club is a youth centre and, it has to be said, not really run in a completely professional way. Steffen has had to organise a small PA to be brought in, which is already set up, but the soundman has to leave soon and won't be around this evening for the gig. It actually doesn't sound too bad on stage at soundcheck considering the monitor box is about the size of a peanut but I am slightly worried that everything will change later after the six piece acoustic ska band going on first have played.

Despite the fact the club refused to put the gig on the website because it was an independent promotion, I'm gratified to see a few people turning up. One couple arrive and see me standing outside and say, 'Oh, so it really is happening then?'

By the time I'm supposed to play we have a grand total of thirty paying customers, plus ten or fifteen people from the support band and their friends. At the last minute, as the sun sets outside, I realise there are no lights on the stage. There's a huge lighting rig hanging from bars across the ceiling but no one knows where the switch is to make it work so I end up playing in almost complete darkness. You never quite realise how important stage lighting is until you try and play guitar in the dark for an hour and a half, but nevertheless the gig is enjoyable and the small audience try and make up for in enthusiasm what they lack in numbers.

Afterwards Steffen drives me back to Kassel, to the house where his girlfriend Marion's parents live. I used to stay at Steffen and Marion's place when I played in the area but since they got the two cats it's an allergy no-go zone. The parents have an en-suite attic room for guests though—I've stayed there once before and it's ideal. Steffen helps me up to the top floor with my bags and then sets off back to his place. Time for some sleep—I'll need to be at the stadium early afternoon for soundcheck with Pil, and I won't get on stage in the K19 with Vom until well after midnight.

## 16th June KASSEL

At breakfast I mention how good the honey is and Marion's father Eduard tells me that it comes from his own bees. After we've eaten we take a walk to the bottom of the garden and he lifts the covers from a few of the hive boxes and shows me the bees crawling methodically around on the honeycombs inside, fanning their wings to control the temperature. We're not wearing any protective clothing but the bees don't bother us. I ask if it's true what I've read about the bee population being under threat, and Eduard says they are having a lot of problems with poisoning by pesticides and infections of mites. The pesticide problem is particularly serious: there are many rapeseed fields around which are being heavily sprayed because the crop is only being used for bio-fuel rather than human consumption. He tells me how heartbreaking it is to open up one of the hive boxes and find the whole colony dead. When I mention that a swarm went over my garden in London last year and stayed for a couple of days on a tree he tells me that what I should have done is contact a local beekeeper to catch the swarm. Beekeepers are desperate to have them, and these days swarms can't survive in the wild.

We wander back up the garden to the shed where Eduard keeps his beekeeping tools: racks of new wooden honeycomb frames, the mask and smoke puffer for when they get agitated. I'd always assumed there was some kind of chemical in the smoke to quieten the bees down, but he opens up one of the canisters and shows me it's just a few stalks of straw. When the bees smell the smoke their instinct tells them that it's a forest fire and they all go back into the hive and gather round the honeycomb to protect it. Eduard also shows me a piece of irregularly-shaped natural beeswax honeycomb with its thousands of identical perfectly-formed hexagonal indentations. He tries to get the bees to make their honey in his neat stacks of prepared racks, but they always end up finding a spot in the hive to make their own as well. 'Typical women,' he says, 'minds of their own!'

Bees
(Kassel)

At two, Steffen drives me over to his apartment near the town centre. From there it's walking distance to the back entrance to the stadium, so we park and go the rest of the way on foot. We wander around for a while trying to find the entrance, then someone opens one of the fence sections for a delivery and we slip in. No one tries to stop us, which is handy as we don't have any passes yet. Carrying a guitar is a great way to get in to a gig for free, though it might not work so well if all thirty thousand people here tried it. The band haven't arrived yet, but we bump straight into a couple of members of Pil, who take us back to their dressing room so I can leave my bag and guitar and pick up passes from Mariano, who's working on his computer there. Strange to think we waved goodbye to each other just two months ago in Buenos Aires.

There's no sign of soundcheck happening yet, so I go off to the catering area to get a coffee. Soon the Toten Hosen bus pulls in and I wander over to say hello. Vom casts an eye over the vast empty stadium. 'Whew, pretty big,' he says.

'You could hold a football match in here,' I say.

'Tim, it's a football stadium.'

I'm excited to hear that he's arranged with Pil to play drums with me on Immortal Rich instead of their regular drummer. In the backstage room, Pil plays me the version we recorded in Argentina and tells me that he wants to trade choruses, with me singing some as usual, and him singing the others in Spanish. Then we get on the massive stage and practice it and everything sounds fine. Still no word from the Toten Hosen about playing any songs with them though. The rest of the band have disappeared into their dressing room so I can't ask them, but I've heard a rumour that they've invited a famous local singer/songwriter from the sixties to play a guest spot, so I suspect I will be one guest too many. Vom's son Jez and his friend Meg, on the other hand, are still scheduled to come on stage to perform Lion And The Lamb. When they see me they come over and politely say hello, and seem remarkably unworried about the size of the crowd—who are now streaming in to the stadium—they'll be performing in front of. The first couple of times they played with the Toten Hosen they were invited on as a surprise for the encore, but then they were told that the German child protection act forbids minors to do any kind of work after ten at night, so now the band invite them on in the middle of the set instead.

Showtime. Pil and band kick into their set, then Vom and I are announced and we walk on to a big—goodness me, that's BIG—cheer, and three minutes later we're finished. Playing one song in front of thirty thousand people is a bit like a roller coaster ride: short and thrilling, and when you get off the first thing you want to do is get back on again.

But for me it's now going to be a six hour wait until my own show in the K19 later. I decide to get something to eat now to keep me going, and in the catering area sit down next to Meg's parents, who I know quite well now as we've met round at Vom's place a few times. I tell them about my experience with the bees earlier. 'So, will you be doing any bee-related songs today,' asks Meg's dad with a grin.

I think about it. The Lion and the Lamb...and the Bee?

Just before nine the Toten Hosen take the stage and the place erupts. Forty minutes later singer Campino introduces Jez and Meg, and the band leave the stage while they launch into Lion And The Lamb. While I'm watching them from down in the crowd Vom's wife Mary comes over and grabs my arm, a big proud smile on her face. For me it's a peculiar feeling to hear the enormous crowd singing and clapping along to one of my songs, the accolades directed over my head at two people with a combined age of only slightly more than half of mine. It's even odder when the next song they play is Call Of The Wild, a Toten Hosen song for which I also wrote the lyrics. After that Jez and Meg leave the stage and the Toten Hosen come back on and start the second half of their set with a song called Pushed Again. Which I wrote the lyrics for.

At eleven the gig finishes and half an hour later Vom arrives in Pil's dressing room, packed up and ready to go to the K19. One of the crew whisks us out through the throngs in a minibus and it's only then that we realise none of us has the address and there's no GPS signal. We get into the general area but the club is somewhere behind a huge building site and all we can find are groups of punks roaming around who are lost too. Eventually a dirt track leads us to the building, which not surprisingly is still almost empty. Vom and I start to set up on stage and the sound man tells me he hopes it's all right if he puts a microphone in front of the guitar instead of using a D.I. box as he doesn't have one. That's a blow, as it means I'd have to stand motionless in front of the microphone for the whole gig—or, even worse, sit down—and it will sound terrible. There are some urgent phone calls made and half an hour later we have a D.I. box—and an audience. At twelve-thirty we're ready to start and have a great gig—the three hundred people in the crowd full of alcohol and in a good mood, and the two people on stage not far behind. Nearly two hours later Vom and I stagger backstage exhausted, then I head straight back out again to set up the merch across the front of the stage. I'm there for a while, and by the time things quieten down, a taxi has been called and Vom has to leave—it feels like it's been a long day for me but he's spent around four hours on stage, incredible stamina.

As the crowd ebbs away I pack up the merchandise, and by the time I get outside with Steffen to go back to where I'm staying the sky is getting light.

Sleep isn't long in coming, but just before it takes over I suddenly start thinking of song titles again.

No Time To Bee 21…

True Bee Leavers…

Expensive Beeing Poor…

Gary Gilmore's Bees…

# 18th June LONDON

Out of my shed and into town for an interview with BBC Wales to promote the upcoming gig in Penarth. 'I'm sorry, you've got the broom cupboard,' says the guy at the desk, showing me into a tiny studio. 'It's the only one free.'

It is small, but when he takes the spare chair out there's just room for me to put my guitar case down. The interview is going to be done remotely, with me on my own in the broom cupboard talking to the presenter who is in a studio in Wales. There's only thirty seconds before we're due to start so I whip on the headphones and adjust the couple of microphones on the table, one pointing down to the guitar, the other up towards my head.

Happily the presenter knows his stuff and we have an interesting chat, and the songs seem to sound good too. Things are pretty hot in the broom cupboard when I leave half an hour later and head back to my shed—which on reflection isn't a lot bigger—to carry on with the new album.

## 28th June IPSWICH

How nice to be back in the Steamboat in Ipswich, one of the friendliest pubs in the country. I try and get here at least once a year and we've established a routine: landlady Val picks me up from the station and lets me stay in one of the cosy bedrooms above the pub so I don't have to worry about finding accommodation. I once walked over from the station because I didn't want to bother her and I got such a telling off!

About fifty people are there for the gig, which is enough to fill the area in front of the stage nicely, and as I scan the faces in the crowd I realise that I know almost everyone here by name so there's a very warm and welcoming atmosphere in the room, plenty of chat going back and forth, and most of the setlist is decided by people shouting out names of songs. Towards the end of the set there's a request for Runaway Train Driver, which almost inevitably means the audience will start a conga dance. The idea of the Runaway Train conga was initiated by someone—this means you, Rikki Red Flag—many years ago at Ipswich beer festival and has become something of a tradition around these parts. What happens is, whenever I play that particular song the audience form a line which then winds its way around the pub, and usually out of it too. On one occasion I was left playing the song to myself while through the window I could see the entire audience conga-ing along next to the harbour wall in the snow. Before I start the song tonight I mention that if the conga goes through the Gents toilets, as it often does, the crowd could take a good look at my merchandising stand as they go past, as I've set it up right next to the door. I've only got a few T-shirts in odd sizes left over from the Subs tour earlier this year though. 'I need small men and extra large women,' I say.

'Don't we all?' someone shouts back.

So off goes the song and off goes the audience, round the room, into the Gents, then somehow they have got outside and are all waving at me through the window as they go past, big smiles on their faces, but are back inside in time for the final chorus and the big finish.

I sit around with Val and Rikki and a couple more of the crowd for a final drink then grab my bag and guitar and make my way through the kitchen and round a tight bend to the narrow staircase leading to the bedroom upstairs. Right in front of me there's another steep stone staircase leading precariously down to the cellar. 'Don't want to accidentally fall down there,' I joke to Val, who's just behind me.

'The only person who has actually done that,' says Val, 'was the Health and Safety inspector.'

## 29th June SHEERNESS

The local scooter club meet up at the Steamboat for tea and coffee at nine, then get back on their bikes, which they've parked up next to the harbour wall below my window, rev up dramatically and peel away in formation for the morning ride up to Lowestoft, honking their horns as they go. That saved the batteries on my alarm clock.

Val gets back from an abortive shopping trip in the town centre to drive me to the station. She wanted to get the weekend's produce in the market to support the local traders, but the council have brought in a new one-way system which meant she got stuck in traffic and couldn't get near it. They've also put cones down in the entire area so you can't park. 'I would love to be able to do it by bike,' she says as we head towards the station, 'but I needed about eight bags of fruit and veg. I know all the lads on the stalls and have been giving them my custom for years but I can't spare the time to sit in a traffic jam. Now I'm going to have to go to the supermarket.'

Although it's only a few miles across the Thames estuary, the only way to get to Sheerness by train is via London so I take the opportunity to pop home briefly. After a freshen up and a quick turnaround I'm at St Pancras station at four for the trip back out East.

Sheerness-on-sea, on the Isle of Sheppey. Most of it is below sea level. The only link in from the mainland is over the one bridge and rail crossing and once you get there there's nowhere else to go. Unemployment is high. Immigrants from Eastern Europe wash up here along with a lot of English disenchanted and dispossessed. They've closed down the funfair, the houses are sinking. It's different here. On the train I hear no less than four arguments, three of them shouted down mobile phones, two of them involving some kind of physical threat. 'Your f*cking boyfriend is going to get *rodded.*

WHY?? Because HE'S A C*NT!!

It's never been one of my favourite gigs as it's often beset by technical problems and poor attendances, but there are a handful of people here who I consider my friends so once a year or so I come back and play for them. I'm sitting with some of them in the garden behind the pub enjoying the last rays of the evening sun and one guy, Ian, tells me my T-shirts on the merch table look really good and asks what sizes I have. I explain that I've only got small men's sizes left, then look him up and down. 'Might fit you.'

He looks slightly affronted. 'I'll have you know I've lost three stone in the last three months.'

'*Three stone*? How?'

'I just cut out bread and potatoes.'

I think about that for a moment. 'How much bread and potatoes were you eating?'

Another guy tells me about the most fattening meal he's ever heard of: one of his friends wanted something to eat in a hurry when he got home after a night out drinking and made himself a pie sandwich.

Yes, all good fun, but I'm a bit concerned about the gig—most of the people from the previous three bands have already left and the room is looking worryingly empty by the time I'm ready to start, hindered only by the lack of soundman. Eventually he rushes in from outside. 'Sorry! I was getting right into one out there!'

It is kind of disheartening to stand on stage in front of fifteen people whose applause often finishes before the song. Soon into the set I notice that there is an unpleasant reverb on my vocal and ask the soundman to take it off. But the soundman has taken himself off. Dave, the guy who asked me to come and play here goes behind the mixing desk and finds the reverb control. There's still a strange irregular thumping sound coming through the speakers though. Exasperated, I ask, 'What *is* that noise?' and someone in the audience says without hesitation, 'that is the dysfunctional beating heart of Sheerness'— which wins my award for *Best Audience Comment Of The Night*. Although later in the set it almost gets beaten when after yet another groaning silence at the end of a song one youngish guy in front of the stage catches my eye and shrugs his shoulders. 'Sheppey,' he says. And he was in the local support band.

But as befits an island within an island the people here take a sensibly sideways look at what goes on in the mainstream and when I get back to Dave's place I have an interesting few hours sharing a few beers and getting the view of the world from Sheppey.

## 2nd July LONDON

You wait years to play at the Tabernacle with Tom Robinson then two come along at once. Well, within a few months. In January I was here guesting at his fan club gig, now barely more than six months later he's going to perform the entire 'Power In The Darkness' album live and has asked me to sing lead vocals on the title track. Although I'm not too bothered about fluffing my own lyrics now and again I feel under a lot of pressure to make sure I get Tom's right and have been running them round my head in odd moments over the past weeks. It's a strange feeling standing on stage in front of a packed crowd who all know the words better than I do and a big relief when I get through it without making any mistakes. In fact I'm so relieved I get carried away and launch into an extra chorus where there should be a guitar solo. 'Sorry about that,' I apologise to guitarist Adam afterwards. 'That's alright,' he says. 'It made it interesting. I'd just started going *wheee-eee* then I pulled it back and went *whooo-ooo* instead.'

## 6th July PENARTH

I don't usually drive to gigs, but today is an exception. I leave London with a map book on the passenger seat and the words 'Penarth' and 'Junction 33' fixed in my head. Unfortunately along the way the number '33' somehow becomes the number '35' and I'm almost in Bridgend before I realise something's not right. It's lucky I have the emergency GPS on my phone otherwise I might still be driving around South Wales now.

But I'm at promoter Karl's place by six, only two hours later than my initial estimate, and there's still time for his wife Susan to make us a luvverly cup of tea before we need to go to the venue, which is handily just a short walk away.

It's a room at the back of a pub, more decorative than some, with fake flowers in pots festooning the front of the stage. Karl apologises and says he tried to move them out of the way but they're cemented down. I tell him I like them. A couple of guys from Manchester arrive, and for a while we're the only ones in the room as the unusually warm summer weather means most people are hanging around outside. One of the Manchester guys suggests I should be all punk rock at the end of the gig and kick the flowers over the stage and I point out to him that it would break my foot. What actually happens at the end of the gig is that as I step off stage a girl who was been enjoying the show stops me, says she wants to give me something to say thank you, and reaches down to one of the flower pots.

'No!' I say.

'NNRRGH…!' she grunts.

It takes quite a tug, but after a moment's effort she presents me with a delightful bouquet of plastic flowers, a crumbling lump of concrete clinging to the base of them.

## 15th July ZÜLPICH

I'm flying to Germany for five days to do some recording in a studio belonging to my friend Jon Caffery, who I first met when he was producing records for Die Toten Hosen. He has since produced quite a few for me. He picks me up from Cologne airport and drives me to his place out in the country, a seventeenth century farmhouse with a mixing studio installed in one of the outbuildings, a former bull stall. He calls the studio, logically enough, the Bull Room. A concrete water trough still runs along the length of it and the cast iron tethering rings stud the walls. The bulls aren't here any more, fortunately, but Jon still has his pet dogs, two lovely-natured Retrievers called Zita and Bubba. I first met them when I was here working on another record six years ago, and that was also the first time Jon and I discussed the idea of making a solo acoustic record to try and capture the sound and atmosphere of how I play on stage. I was nervous about the idea then but in the meantime I've played hundreds of concerts and honed the songs to as good as they're ever going to get so finally I've decided to— er—take the bull by the horns and do it.

Jon shows me my bedroom upstairs then we wander across the courtyard to the studio and start setting things up. It's a daunting idea, knowing that you have to perform the definitive version of a song, but I end up recording around twenty of them, playing most of them two or three times so we can pick the best version. Finally around midnight I feel my voice and energy waning and we call it a night. In truth, there's no need to get so much done on the first day but I want to capture the urgency of a live gig. There's also another reason: I've spotted a few cats around the place and it's also high season for hay fever so I need to get as much singing done tonight before any potential allergies start affecting me. The definitive versions of the songs I have in mind don't include sounding like they are being sung by someone with the flu.

We go over to the house and have some cheese on toast and a quick wine club then get some sleep.

## 16th July ZÜLPICH

Apparently the bedroom door doesn't close as securely as I thought because I'm woken by a gentle nudge and turn over to find a pair of friendly brown eyes staring inquisitively at me, and a wet nose pressed against mine. Ah, just like home. (Joke).

I usher Baba out and shut the door, but he soon barges it open again and has a hopeful attempt at getting into bed with me before I decide it's time to get up anyway.

One of the great things about this studio is that, untroubled by neighbours, Jon can switch the volume up and open the studio doors and when I'm not needed I go and listen in the sunny courtyard. For the first time ever the phrase 'a studio tan' is actually going to mean 'a tan.'

During one coffee break Bubba leans up against me and keeps staring up pleadingly into my eyes. I have no idea what I'm supposed to do.

'He wants you to take the shell off,' says Jon.

I look down and see that he has got half a walnut shell stuck on to the pad of one of his paws so I reach down and ease it off. It's a bit of an *Androclus and the Lion* moment.

'It's happening all the time,' says Jon, gesturing at the mature walnut tree behind the farmhouse. 'Once he got two stuck on different paws and when he came walking across the yard it sounded like someone with a wooden leg.'

When we go into the studio in the evening to record some more songs we let the dogs in with us. At the end of one particularly intense take Jon removes his headphones and says, 'Very nice. Just at the end as the music faded away you could hear Zita snoring in the background.'

We have wine club, then just before bed I grab one of the rubber wedges from the downstairs doors to use on mine. I have a feeling that now Bubba has learned how to open it, and since we have bonded with the removal of the walnut shell, he may be a frequent visitor if I don't take preventative measures.

# 17th July ZÜLPICH

I forget about the wedge when I get up to go to the bathroom but the door slides open effortlessly anyway so obviously Bubba decided not to visit this morning. Downstairs he greets me happily and becomes rather insistent that I repeatedly throw a ball for him, even though I clearly told him that I would only do it once. Jon tells me about a friend who taught his dog to throw the ball for itself and it would happily amuse itself for hours on end.

Early in the evening we take a break from the studio to drive nine kilometres to the nearest supermarket as otherwise there will be no wine club tonight. It's the only place I've been apart from Jon's house and courtyard for three days and finding myself under the bright lights among the methodically stacked ranks of shelves of ReWe feels like walking into a stage set. Still, the wine was real as we prove later.

Convinced that Bubba will try and break in tomorrow morning, I pull out a heavy folding chair from the side of the wardrobe and lay it across the door.

## 18th July ZÜLPICH

I didn't need to worry about Bubba waking me up as some time in the night my cat allergy finally kicks in and I wake up all by myself at around five, wheezing like a steam train. I get up and take an anti-histamine and read for an hour or so until my breathing eases up, then try for a couple more hours sleep. I only fall into a light doze so later I clearly hear Bubba giving the door a few exploratory nudges only to find it mysteriously won't open.

The last day in the studio and we're well on schedule. By one in the afternoon we have narrowed the choice of songs down to twenty-one and Jon can start on the mixing, which means I can spend quite a bit of time in the courtyard topping up my studio tan. In the evening we take the dogs out for a long walk though the surrounding countryside. The sun has been down for a while and the stars are starting to twinkle in the darkening sky. We walk along grassy paths through the wheat fields, silvery under the light of the moon, here and there in the undergrowth the pinpoint sparkle of a glow worm. After a while Zita is having trouble keeping up. Just two weeks ago, Jon tells me, she would have been bounding along ahead of us, but the vets have found an inoperable tumour inside her which is slowing her down. Sometime soon, maybe any day now, it will burst and kill her. The poison in the tumour will send her to sleep first so it will be a painless death but watching her panting away trying gamely to keep up, knowing that when I leave tomorrow it will be the last time I see her does give the walk a somewhat melancholy air. When we get back to the house she's so exhausted that Jon has to lift her over the front step to help her in.

Back in the studio Jon does some final work on the recordings and everything sounds great. He'll carry on with the mixing over the next few weeks and I'm happy knowing that it's in a safe pair of hands.

## 22nd July PÉNESTIN

The offer I received on the UK Subs tour to play a street festival outside a shop called *La Mer Bière* in a small town in Brittany called Pénestin has come to fruition. Shop owner Frédérique's original idea was that I should do the gig—'Hundreds of people! Lots of CD sales!'—and combine it with a week long holiday—'Big apartment! Swimming pool!'—but in the end I couldn't spare the time to come for the whole week and will just be staying for four nights.

I take a budget evening flight to St Rochelle airport, a three hour drive from Pénestin, and Frédérique is there to meet me. She didn't trust her ancient Renault 4 to make the journey and came with a friend of hers called GG, a wiry 64 year old with a twinkle in his eye who has borrowed his girlfriend's spacious and sporty car. GG calls Frédérique 'Fred'—a bit confusing—and both pronounce Pénestin as 'Pénetin,' without the 's'. When I ask about that, Fred tells me, 'Only the tourists pronounce it Pénestin,'

Well, I wouldn't want to be thought of as a tourist, particularly when during the journey she tells me how she and GG spend most of the mornings sitting outside the café opposite the shop gently mocking the summer visitors as they pass: *they're wearing socks—with sandals!*

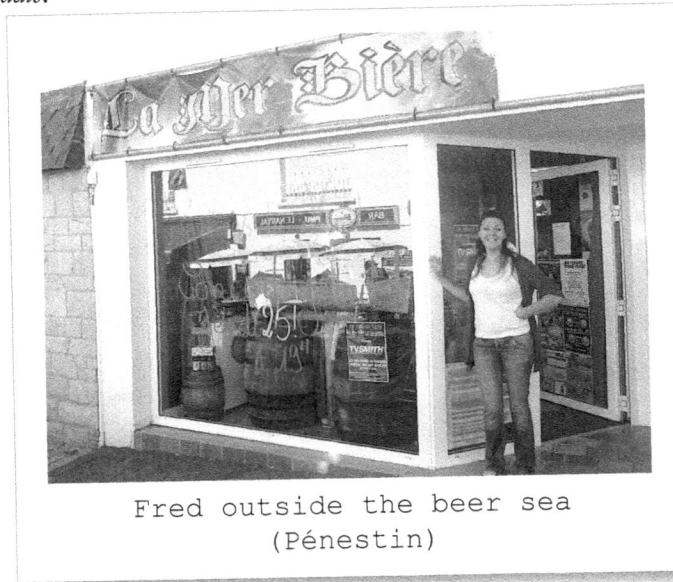

Fred outside the beer sea
(Pénestin)

*La Mer Bière*, Fred explains, sells beers imported from more than twenty countries, as well as wines and whiskies. My kind of shop. She lives in the apartment in the same building with her husband Lio, three children, a sister-in-law, and also a dog and a cat. The eldest son Tristan, she tells me, absolutely loves *grenouilles*.

'To eat?'

'No, he just likes them. There are frogs everywhere. You're not scared of snakes are you? He's also got a snake.'

It's only now dawning on me that I'm staying with the family. I'd been under the impression that the promised big apartment and apartment were going to be my own. Still, it will be interesting to be immersed in a French family and will hopefully give me a chance to improve my grasp of the language. I've already decided to not speak any

English on this trip and so far I'm not doing too badly and have only accidentally used German words about half of the time.

Close to Pénestin Fred suggests GG makes a small detour to show me a neighbouring town which she assures me is very pretty. It's a port on a small creek emptying into the estuary. We drive slowly around the harbour, where boats are moored and the slack water reflects the sunset. As we pass a bar where a few people are sitting outside enjoying the balmy evening weather, Fred winds a window down to say hello to the owner. They have a bit of a chat and then we are invited over for a drink.

'Shall we?' Fred asks.

We had been intending to go straight to the apartment and get something to eat, but when in France...

'Ça commence...' I say as I get out of the car.

Before I know it we've all had a glass of wine and I've agreed to come back here and play an acoustic gig in a couple of days.

Then it's back in the car, his *piège de filles*, as GG calls it—which I suppose would loosely translate as *babe magnet*. As we reach the town Fred suggests we stop to have a look at the sea. We park at the top of the cliffs and take the steep path down to the beach, lit only by the full moon and the torch on Fred's mobile phone. She points towards the horizon. 'No more land between here and America.'

Although the cliffs are too dark to really make out, they're renowned for their golden colour and the area is called *Le mine de l'or*—the gold mine. 'People say they used to dig for gold here,' says Fred.

'They say it? Or did they really do it?' I ask.

'They really did,' says GG. 'When the sun shines on the beach you can still see the traces of gold glinting.'

I'll be down here tomorrow with my bucket and spade.

Back in the car and finally on the way to the apartment, Fred tells me that a local brewery is going to brew a special beer for the street festival. She tells me the name but I can't understand it, though one of the words is *loup*: 'wolf.'

'Ah, *something* of wolf,' muses Fred. 'What's the word GG?'

He doesn't know either.

'Maybe it's Company Of Wolves?' I suggest. 'Like the film?' Funny sort of name for a beer.

No time to ponder over it any longer as we have arrived at the shop. GG takes the car on to his place and Fred invites me in and introduces me to Lio and those of the kids who are still awake. Out of the back door there's a large garden but the only thing close to a swimming pool I can see is a small paddling pool with an inflatable frog in it. I casually mention it to Fred and she explains that the swimming pool is actually at a friend's place fourteen kilometres away. So far things aren't turning out quite the way I was expecting, and when I'm shown up to where I'll be sleeping on the third floor I find out that it is a bed set up in a cramped landing between the children's bedrooms, right opposite the wide stairway. If I roll off the bed in the night there's a good chance I'll go straight down it. There's not even room to put down my suitcase, and the children will all have to edge past me when they get up in the morning—if I'm not lying in a crumpled broken heap on the ground floor by then. It doesn't sound like a recipe for much sleep over the coming four nights. I brood about this for a while downstairs while Fred and Lio prepare some bread and cheese, and finally decide to say something. I'm glad I do, because Fred and Lio are shocked that I'm not happy—'we don't usually put on gigs and we didn't know what you need'—and immediately set about moving the youngest daughter out of her room, settling her in the bed on the landing and preparing her room for me.

Feeling guilty, *moi?* Well, yes. But at least I'll be able to get a good night's sleep, and the daughter doesn't seem at all upset about having been displaced. I even manage to get the door shut despite the thick astro-turf carpet, so the cat won't be able to get in.

## 23rd July PÉNESTIN

Fred has been up since 6:30 as usual to prepare the shop for opening, and drops into the house to suggest I join her and GG outside the café opposite, from where she surveys the passers-by and runs over to assist any potential customers.

We sit for a few hours. Far from mocking the tourists, GG charms them all as they go past, shouting out jokes and comments to complete strangers as if they are old friends, and all the locals stop to chat and exchange *bisous* with him and Fred. I get pointed out to everyone as the guy who will be playing the concert on Thursday.

I just hope the weather will be good as the gig will be in the street. There was a rainstorm this morning breaking the recent heat wave and the skies are still cloudy. I mention this to GG and he shrugs it off: 'The sun is ordered for 12:00.'

A few of the regulars join us at the table over the course of the morning, including a sprightly 84 year old in a casual white suit, who after I say hello says, *'J'ai remarqué un petit accent Belge...'*

Fred explains who I am and the guy tells me that fifty years ago he used to present a live variety show with magicians, jugglers and fire-eaters among the acts. That was before television when you had to really know how to entertain people.

In the afternoon Lio takes me and Charley, the youngest of the family, for a trip around the coast in the old Renault 4, which starts after a few tries. There are plenty of people parked at the top of the cliffs now. Lio and Charley have their swimming trunks on but the stiff breeze blowing off the Atlantic puts me off the idea of a swim and I go down to the beach in a T-shirt and shorts. Good job I had the shorts as it's nearly high tide and after we've sat on the fast-shrinking beach for half an hour we have to wade through the surf to get back to the path up the cliffs. There's not even enough sand for me to go panning for gold. Lio tells me that tourists are always getting cut off in the summer. Another reason not to be a tourist: it's bad enough pronouncing the name of the town wrong, even more embarrassing having to get the rescue helicopter in.

There's gold in them thar cliffs
(Lio and Charley in Pénestin)

Abandoning the idea of lazing around on the beach—currently there is no beach— we take a drive around the coast. Pénestin covers a huge area despite its small number of inhabitants and the main employment here is *mytilicultur*—mussel cultivation and collection—which its two vast shallow bays are perfect for. The rest of the work in the area is mainly geared around serving the summer tourists who swell the population eightfold, pronounce the name of the town wrongly and get cut off by the tide. We stop at a headland where the cliff's erosion by the sea is clearly visible: one of the concrete wartime bunkers has been so undercut that it is in danger of toppling into the ocean.

When we get back to the car Charley absent-mindedly taps a pebble against the bodywork of the Renault. 'Don't break it,' says his dad. 'It's already broken.'

We drive back to the town, park the Renault, and then as we walk to the apartment someone from a group of people sitting outside the café opposite shouts out 'Great trousers!'

I say *merci!* and she says, 'Aha, I hear an accent from the East...' I say I'm English and they all look impressed and Fred hurries over to the table to tell them about the gig.

A few minutes later she comes rushing in to the kitchen, where I'm sitting with Lio and Charley. 'Testicles!' she shouts triumphantly. 'The beer is called *Wolf's Testicles!* *Couille de Loup*.

In the evening we take a half hour drive down the coast to visit a family, old friends of Fred, who are keen to meet me. They have prepared some food, there is champagne on ice, and in the garden there's a swimming pool heated to 31 degrees, warmer than the air temperature. As soon as we arrive the kids get straight in, and I although I had been considering it myself I decide that sitting in the back garden with the adults and a glass of champagne is the more mature option.

The wife, Anne, brings out a plate of locally caught *langoustines* and everyone pronounces them the best in the world. When Anne sees that I'm not eating, Fred has to explain that I'm vegetarian and hurriedly adds, 'but he *loves* cheese!'

'An Englishman who likes cheese—that's unusual.' says Anne. I don't think she's being ironic. Her husband Oliver goes indoors to look for cheese. He has to be a bit careful moving around because a lung disorder means he has to breathe through an oxygen tube which runs into a central tank somewhere in the house. Often it gets tangled up. Anne says, 'We have wi fi throughout the whole house—if only we could get it for the oxygen.' Oliver returns with a plate holding a huge selection of cheeses and apologises that there's no bread. There is popcorn though. Emergency popcorn and cheese makes an interesting variation to the usual emergency cheese sandwich.

There's a distant rumble of thunder and I look up concerned but Anne tells me we'll be fine. This area has a micro-climate created by the wind blowing in off the ocean over the salt marshes, which means storms virtually never happen around here. What does happen around here is mosquitoes. Already one has had a good bite at my ear which has begun to swell up impressively. The Guy With One Big Ear was not the look I was aiming for when I play my concerts. Anne tells me that we are in a nature protection zone and the authorities aren't allowed to spray insecticide. Which is good, I suppose, but the mosquito population is booming and most of them seem to be heading for me.

'They should just destroy them,' says Anne, miming a machine gun spraying across the garden. 'They think the snakes will eat them!' she exclaims.

Blimey, how many snakes are out there?

'Or the bats...'

One of which just missed me, perhaps trying to pluck a mosquito off my face in mid-flight.

We discuss a cluster of coincidences. The reason I'm here begins with a fan from Paris, also called Anne. Because I rarely get offered gigs in France, she usually sees me in Germany. This year I finally got a couple of gigs in France thanks to being on the UK Subs tour. Anne came to the gig we played in Rennes and invited her friend Fred, who was impressed and invited me to play here in Pénestin. Fred knows Anne because Fred and Anne's husband Pascal are both fans of a French singer called Daniel Darc and became friends after they'd bumped into each other a few times at his concerts. The *other* Anne, whose garden we are now in, has a son who works for a cigarette wholesaler. He recently made a delivery to a café *tabac* in Paris, got chatting to the owner and happened to mention that he comes from a little town in Brittany called Pénestin. 'I know someone in Pénestin,' says the guy, who turned out to be Pascal, and they realised that they had a friend in common—Fred. It's a small world despite the length of this anecdote.

Ironically, there's been a staff shortage at the *tabac* so Anne has to stay behind and work, but Pascal will be arriving tomorrow.

Eventually after a few hours it's time for the kids to get out of the pool and dry off, and for us all to head back. As we leave, Anne tells me that next time I'm in the area I'm welcome to stay with them—they have a big guest apartment at the other end of the garden but there was a flood and it's currently out of use. I'm finally piecing it all together: *this* is where Fred intended me to stay when she first discussed the idea of a gig.

As we get back to the town, Fred mentions that tomorrow is market day and will be very busy. 'What time does it start?' I ask.

'Ah, yes. Make sure you close your window. They set up at around 5:30 right below your room and it's pretty noisy.'

## 24th July PÉNESTIN

Not noisy enough to bother me as I sleep off the champagne. I wake myself up with a few coffees with Fred and GG outside the café then take a walk around the market with Lio and Charley. The stalls of local produce and general tat spread out over most of the town, and soon Charley gets hot and dehydrated under the blazing sun and we go back to the apartment. In the shop, Fred is loudly abusing her new beer distributors because they have only bought half as many bottles of BrewDog as she ordered, nowhere near enough for the concert tomorrow. Luckily the Wolf's Testicles will still be coming.

In the afternoon Lio suggests I take a walk with him around the head of the estuary to where the golden cliffs start. We set off on foot from the town in the fierce sun and just ten minutes later can see the broad expanse of the estuary across the fields. 'Just one word of warning,' says Lio. 'If you do see a snake, don't approach it.'

A somewhat superfluous piece of advice actually, because if I do see one I shall be swiftly moving off in the other direction.

As we walk Lio points out the strange cigar-shaped clouds that elongate in the wind so that all the tourists think they are aeroplane vapour trails. I'd hate to be thought of as a tourist, but the one he's showing me clearly *is* a vapour trail. 'No, no,' he insists. 'All the local fishermen will tell you. When they see this type of cloud they know the weather is going to stay fine.'

I'd better believe them. The fishermen around here clearly know what they're doing. They've certainly found the right spot for shellfish anyway. As we round the headland to face the ocean the beach underfoot gradually changes from fine sand to banks of crushed shell. We crunch across the bleached white remains of mussels, oysters, whelks and countless other varieties. Here and there a balloon-glob of beached jellyfish oozes across them. A sandy path shaded by cypresses leads from the beach up to the cliffs, grasshoppers chirp around us. We reach the road and tramp back to Pénestin, shirts off, arriving on the outskirts just as Fred phones to ask where we are: it's time to head off to the bar gig in La Roche-Bernard.

I get in the Renault with Fred and the eldest son Tristan and we rattle along the country lanes, the steering groaning at every bend. The rest follow behind with GG. The late afternoon sun is beating in through the window. 'I'll put the air conditioning on,' says Fred, and pushes a button. Two vents on the dashboard open and the lids flap up and down a bit, depending on how fast we are travelling. 'There is a sun visor if you need it,' she says. 'It's somewhere down on the ledge there by your knees...'

With all the other unnecessary bits that have broken off: rear view mirror, etc.

La Roche-Bernard looks even prettier in the sunshine than it did at night but as we approach the bar I can't help noticing that there are just the same ten people there as when we dropped in on the way from the airport. Never mind, with Lio and the kids and GG, plus a couple of locals, we have a grand total of around twenty by the time I start. It's certainly one of the most beautiful locations I've ever played—outside the café, right by the water's edge of a tiny port where myriad boats are anchored, the sun setting behind the two potted palms flanking me. The only thing spoiling the otherwise idyllic setting is—well, me, as I growl out my songs for an hour to the obvious surprise of the tourists who are taking their evening pre-dinner walks around the harbour.

Even the original twenty don't stay the whole course. After the first song, little Charley turns to his mum and says, rather loudly, 'Is it finished yet? I want to look at the boats!' In fact he says it after every song until someone from the bar takes him away for a stroll up the pontoon. Shortly afterwards Fred has to leave to pick up Pascal from La Baule train station, a thirty minute drive away, and she takes Tristan with her otherwise there won't be enough room in the other car for the rest of us to get back to Pénestin. A couple of bikers roar off thirty minutes later, drowning out the song I'm playing but giving a friendly wave as they go.

After the show the bar owners thank me and present me with two bottles of local red wine. Unfortunately my suitcase on the flight here, stuffed with CDs and vinyl for the promised sales, was already at the absolute weight limit. I've sold absolutely nothing today, so unless there's a big difference tomorrow I won't be able to take the wine back with me. There's only one thing to do with it really, and when we get back to Pénestin and Fred arrives with Pascal that's what we do.

## 25th July PÉNESTIN

It's Pascal's first visit to the town, and I sit outside the café with him for a few hours explaining the comings and goings of the locals, most of whom now come over and shake my hand as they go past. Pascal seem impressed that they all know who TV Smith is—but of course they don't. They just know I'm the english guy who's been around a few days and is staying with Fred and Lio. I'm virtually a local myself.

Lio plans a trip for the three of us to the *marais salants*, the famous salt marshes further down the coast near the medieval town of Guérande, but first he insists on a quick repeat tour around the local bays for Pascal's benefit. It's fascinating for me to see them again at low tide: what was all water when I made this trip a couple of days ago is now a vast expanse of sand bristling with rows of black wooden stakes. The stakes have been wrapped with nets to trap the mussels, and a few small cranes are out on the sand lifting the old poles and planting new ones. Tractors and trailers, even a few cars, are parked haphazardly across the whole bay and for a short few hours until the sea returns the place is a hive of industry.

On to Guérande. We leave Brittany behind and cross the border to Loire-Atlantique, where within a few miles we see the first of the salt marshes, most of them now disused, but some with the characteristic pyramids of gleaming white salt piled up in the centre of them. The real working *marais* start a little further along, but before visiting them we stop for lunch in Guérande, working up an appetite with a walk through the narrow streets inside the medieval moated fortifications that surround the old town.

Almost every shop in the old town is selling salt-connected produce: there are little cloth bags of salt, pottery salt cellars, salted caramel (the speciality of the region), salted ice cream, chocolates. There are also other temptations for the sweet tooth: we get waylaid outside a nougat shop by a salesgirl offering some pieces to try. Lio and Pascal and I chew thoughtfully and have to agree that it's the best nougat we have ever tasted and make a beeline into the shop, where a hundred varieties line the shelves. The salesgirl follows us in and takes Lio's order. While she weighs and wraps it they chat and Lio explains about the gig tonight and how I've come all the way from London to play it. By the time she's taken Pascal's order she's decided to come. As we're leaving Lio asks why I'm didn't get any nougat to take home and I explain that my suitcase is completely full and up to the top of the weight limit. Even 200 grammes of nougat could tip it over and I'd have to pay an excess baggage charge. It could be the most expensive nougat I've ever bought. (Actually it would be anyway.) On the other hand, I've never tasted nougat like this in Britain, and if I do actually manage to sell a few CDs tonight there'll be room… I turn back and buy some. I can always throw away a few CDs.

We wave goodbye and say 'see you tonight!' and stroll out of the town walls towards a café we see on the other side of the street. As we step onto a pedestrian crossing, Pascal marvels at the waiting cars. With wonder in his voice he says, 'They *actually stop…*'

He's from Paris.

While we sit outside the café waiting for the food Pascal phones up Anne, and she puts in a complicated order for more nougat. At that moment the girl from the nougat shop turns up and orders some lunch too. We ask her if the shop is still open as we have to go back and get more nougat. She says that her friend has taken over from her now and she's told her all about us. She'll probably come to the concert too.

After a coffee we head back to the old town and back to the nougat shop, where the new girl greets us with, 'Oh, it's you!' Laden with our many bags of nougat we head back to the car and realise that there's now no time left to go and see the salt marshes— we have to get back to Pénestin for the concert.

Outside *La Mer Bière* Fred is overseeing preparations. She introduces me to the sound guy, whose car is parked just down the road with the equipment inside. 'I hope it will be alright for you,' he says. 'I don't usually do this sort of thing. I'm more of a dance guy.'

At six they shut the street to traffic and the sound guy starts to set up the two speakers on the pavements either side of the road. The cafe owner and his wife arrange plastic tables and chairs in the street with the help of some of the customers. Everything's looking good, but then we hear some distant music. 'The parade!' says Fred.

Everyone lends a hand to pull the tables and chairs back on to the pavements as a small group of people in Breton costume appear at the top of the street and slowly make their way down past us, the musicians playing traditional instruments: pipe, lute and bombarde, a lone drummer taking up the rear.

Then the street is ours. I soundcheck to the empty tables and chairs, as well as the occasional cyclist returning from the beach. The two guys from the brewery arrive and set up a beer dispenser on a table outside the shop, while I set up a table for merch on the opposite pavement. The sound guy has a couple of spotlights with him and bolts one to the fence above my merch table, then goes up to the apartment and bolts the other to the window ledge outside the living room on the first floor.

An hour later there are about fifty people sat at the tables, I've had my first taste of the Wolf's Testicles and it's time to start. It is an unusual feeling to play in bright evening sunshine to an audience of locals and casual tourists, but pretty soon I feel them warming to me and they tolerate my painfully awkward French between the songs with good humour. I have a three hour slot to play in, and after ninety minutes or so I call a short break and retreat to the merch table to warm applause. Soon people are coming up and chatting and a few buy CDs. I see Lio edging his way through the crowd towards me with an excited look on his face.

'Tim! There's going to be room for the nougat!'

Half an hour later I pick up the guitar for part two and am happy to see the audience has swelled even more to about a hundred. I play almost another ninety minutes, bringing it right up to the curfew.

Slowly the people disperse, the chairs and tables are carried back to the café, the sound equipment and the Wolf's Testicles are taken away and the street returns to normal. GG thanks me for the concert and makes his way home. Fred and I watch the last few people cleaning up, and I sip on my last beer of this trip to Brittany. Suddenly a guy wearing a uniform emblazoned with the words *Police Municipale* strides up with a very stern expression on his face. He stand in front of us, saying nothing.

'So what did you think?' asks Fred eventually.

The policeman breaks into a grin. '*Trop court!*'

Too short! A bit like my forthcoming night's sleep, as my flight from Nantes tomorrow morning means I'll have to wake up at six. Still, I've had a lovely holiday in

Brittany, made lots of new friends and very much hope to come back.

I wonder if the girls from the nougat shop turned up?

## 27th July ROBERTSBRIDGE—WOLVERTON

It's just over a year since my friend and long-time musical collaborator Tim Cross died, and his friends and neighbours in Robertsbridge, the village in East Sussex where he lived, are holding 'Timfest' to celebrate his memory. As well as performances from local musicians, the two 'pros' Tim worked with—myself and Dana Gillespie—are coming down to play too. I meet Dana at Charing Cross station at midday, and we're both in a reflective mood. For both of us this journey used to mean a day of creativity to look forward to—and more than that, the anticipation of spending some time with one of the funniest, most effervescent human beings you could ever hope to know. Tim could have you in fits of laughter while you were working, but there was never any doubt about how seriously he took music, or his knowledge of it. As Dana reminds me while we're waiting for the train, he'd hear a car horn in the distance and say, 'B flat.' I used to arrive at Robertsbridge station to find Tim waiting, one of the 'lovely fags' that eventually killed him on the go, Mozart playing in the car stereo. Now the trip ends at an empty platform and is just a reminder that he's gone.

Tim's death hit the local community hard as he mentored and encouraged all the young local musicians, often inviting them in to record at his home. His greatest friends from the village, a family called The Hilliers, have spent months planning the festival and suggest Dana and I come down a bit earlier than the guests so we have a chance to reminisce before it all kicks off. Inevitably, the conversation isn't the happiest. We were all shocked when the diagnosis of lung cancer came, but Tim seemed to take it on board. The scan showed tumours all over his body—'the doctors said they'd never seen anything like it...'—far too advanced for any hope of a cure, and Tim spent his final few weeks receiving visitors with a kind of regal splendour, stretched out on his divan in the living room surrounded by all his beloved musical equipment and a steady stream of visitors who he kept entertained with his wickedly dark sense of humour, never once showing a trace of self-pity.

The Hilliers have made wristbands with the words *TIMFEST: missing you already!* printed on them, and there are Bacchanalian amounts of food and drink on tables all over the garden, where three large gazebos have been erected; one for the bands to play under, the others for the guests in case of the forecast storms. At the top of the garden there is a huge banner with three blown-up photos of Tim grinning down at us. Tomorrow would have been his 58th birthday.

Last year after the funeral we all gathered here and the rain came down in torrents all afternoon so it seems somehow fitting that the storm breaks just as the first band starts. I sit sombrely in the conservatory while the Hilliers rush around in the pouring rain, covering the sound desk with sheets of plastic to protect the electrics and poking the gazebo roofs to release torrents of water.

It's what he would have wanted!

Unlike last year the rain soon stops, the sun reappears and the band are able to start again. Things are now running late though, and I can't help glancing at my watch and worrying a little. I need to leave at five, missing the evening festivities here, because I have a gig in Wolverton, just outside Milton Keynes, this evening and have to be at the station at 5:10 at the absolute latest. Even then I have a three hour journey and will miss soundcheck.

The schedule slips even more when Dana steps under the gazebo to sing a few songs because the CD she's bought with her to use as a backing track won't play. She fills with a few anecdotes about Tim and finally the CD is working and she can start. As soon as she finishes I take over and play right up until the last possible minute.

Rushing out of the house to the station, I find Pauline standing at the front door worriedly scanning the road. As we hurriedly exchange goodbyes, she tells me that while I was playing there was a casualty at the top of the garden: someone collapsed and she's worried that it might be a heart attack. As I reach the station platform I see an ambulance speeding over the level crossing, blue lights flashing.

It's what he would have wanted!

By the time I reach London and change trains at Euston the skies have darkened and the rain is belting down again. I get to Wolverton and trudge through the downpour to the pub I'm playing in, which proves to be further away than it looked on the map. The rain hasn't diminished the oppressive heat either, so by the time I get to the pub my clothes are drenched inside and out.

Apparently another band has just played as the stage is currently being cleared. In fact, to my surprise there's time to do a quick soundcheck and still an hour to go before I play. There are only about thirty people in the pub, plus a few others who wander through to a back room where a thrash metal band are playing. As my gig is free entry I'm rather hoping some of them might wander back and swell the numbers a bit. Jon and Sophie are here and offer me a lift home after the gig, which I gratefully accept rather than risking the room above the pub. At the bar a guy with SKINS tattooed on his arm talks to me about the first world war poet Wilfred Owen, who we both agree was a genius.

I've more or less dried out by the time I start to play but it's a hot and sticky gig and

by the end I'm soaked from head to foot again. I go over to the merch table and one guy buys a CD then looks down at it and says, 'With sweat.'

I change into a dry T-shirt, but as we head out to the car the rain starts again and I'm drenched for the third time today. Jon tells me that they have their dog in the back of the car and gives me some instructions: 'Don't touch her for a while and don't try and rub her face. A friend of ours did that recently and she got a bit snappy. But she'll be fine once she gets to know you.'

She seems to get to know me quite quickly because once I'm installed in the front passenger seat she attempts to wriggle over from the back and sit on my lap.

Jon and Sophie will be returning to Jon's native Florida at the end of the year, and we discuss plans they have to invite everyone they know to a leaving party in December, which I'll play at. We have many mutual friends and it should be a fine way to finish off the year.

At one-thirty I'm back in my favourite hotel: home.


## 30th July LONDON

An email from Tom Robinson yesterday: do you want to come and save Legal Aid tomorrow afternoon?

There's a rally being organised outside the Old Bailey, London's central criminal court, to protest against the government's planned cuts. Tom was invited to play it and immediately thought of my song 'Straight And Narrow' so we're going to perform that together.

A couple of hundred people have gathered for three hours of speeches and the occasional musical interlude. There's only really room for one person at a time on the narrow platform where the speakers are holding forth but Tom and I manage to squeeze on when our turn comes. 'Straight And Narrow' goes down well, then I retreat to the back of the platform while Tom performs a song he's written specially for the occasion, someone on the ground below him holding up a sheet of paper with the lyrics he's only just scribbled out. There's a big cheer when he finishes and one of the organisers afterwards tells him it's already 'their anthem.'

It feels good to be doing something positive to protect the concept that justice should be available for everybody regardless of how much money they have. After all, a few mistakes, a bad decision or two—it's a short step from appearing outside the Old Bailey to in it.

## 10th August BLACKPOOL

What a way to start the Rebellion punk festival—bumped out of my slot by a ukulele workshop. I'd been invited to play the open mic up in the Spanish Hall as a warm-up for my proper headlining gig on the acoustic stage tomorrow night, but was already suspicious when I went up there last night to get some details and found the stage manager didn't know anything about it. Sure enough this morning it turns out there's been a double-booking and the room is chock-a-block with would-be ukulele players. I retreat back downstairs and set up a merchandising table instead, next to Yuko who's selling the UK Subs stuff as usual. Luckily my friends Coppo and Linda came here by car and generously offered to bring a couple of boxes of my merch with them, as well as some of Gaye's artwork which she's displaying upstairs, as there's no way we would have been able to carry it all on the train. For ten hours I man the table, chatting to people, selling CDs and T-shirts and books. There are six stages and hundreds of bands playing, and I don't see any of them.

At eight I pack away, and go into the town to look for something to eat with Gaye and Charlie Harper and a few friends. Charlie fancies a curry so we end up in a dubious Indian restaurant near the sea front, where the waiter looks like a bouncer and I get served an alarmingly bright 'saffron rice' where the chef seems to have mistaken the word 'saffron' for 'red food colouring.' I think I must be allergic to it: after I've eaten my fatigue transforms into a peculiar state of hyper-alertness and I spend the night staring at the ceiling unable to sleep, the sound of the night club across the road shaking the walls.

## 11th August BLACKPOOL

After a night awake, doing the merch for another eight hours is an even more surreal experience than yesterday.

One of the items I have on the merch table is a vinyl edition of my first ever band, Sleaze, who I formed when I was in art college, two years before starting the Adverts. The records consists of just five lengthy, fairly slow, prog/glam tracks and I've always hesitated to recommend it to people in case they think it's going to be some gritty garage pre-punk record. When one guy asks for a copy, I warn him: 'It doesn't sound like the Adverts, you know…'

He gives me a *duh!* expression and takes the record from me. 'Even The Adverts didn't sound like The Adverts,' he says.

Another guys buys an Adverts CD and tells me that we were his younger brother's favourite band. He confides in me that his brother wasn't the brightest kid in the world:

he spent a long time decorating the back of his leather jacket with studs and paint, then proudly showed it to his elder sibling. He didn't have the heart to tell him it said BORED TENAGERS.

Early in the afternoon my friend and occasional co-guitarist Leigh Heggarty wanders past. He played a triumphant gig with Ruts DC last night, which of course I didn't see, and tells me that he's been chatting with Jennie, one of the festival organisers, who explained that the guy who was supposed to play before me on the acoustic stage this evening can't come—so maybe I could do a longer set and Leigh could join me for some songs. Apart from the fact we haven't rehearsed and Leigh doesn't have an acoustic guitar with him, this sounds a great idea.

At eight I pack the mech away and make my way over to the acoustic venue. People are already staking their places at the tables and on the floor in front of the stage. Leigh has borrowed a guitar and we work out a setlist so that he can join me halfway through the set. By the time I start I'm thrilled to see that the room is absolutely rammed with people—a great compliment considering I'm up against a lot of other big bands in the same time slot on other stages. As I'm last on this stage I don't have to worry about the length of my set and play a full ninety minutes, with Leigh joining me for the last forty of them. Another great gig in the greatest punk festival in the world.

Afterwards people leave the room rapidly to go and see other bands, until just a hardcore of friends and fans are left. Coppo and Linda come up to congratulate me on the gig, and I suddenly remember that I haven't given them anything towards their petrol money for driving my merch up. 'Linda and I have been thinking about that,' he says. 'We don't want any money for it. All we want is a mention in your next book.'

Done!

I'm now so shattered that I can barely make it up the stairs to the after-show. Rebellion is an endurance test for even the most hardy, and hardly any of the bands have turned up for the party. Even the party hasn't turned up. There's some easygoing reggae playing from the DJs, three or four people on the dance floor, everyone else seems to be in a state of shock. I'm quite shocked too when I look at the time and see it's already three in the morning. Gaye and I gather our things, walk out into the gale force wind blowing in off the Irish Sea and head to our hotel. Another Rebellion survived.

Can't wait for next year!

## 24th August BISKIRCHEN

I switch on my phone at Frankfurt airport and the text message reads: *Welcome to Germany! We're going to be paddling for another two and a half hours, then we'll pick you up from the hotel.*

Some months ago Jan emailed me to ask if I would come and play the stag party he was organising for his friend Christian on a camping site next to the river Lahn somewhere in the middle of the German countryside. I'd never met either of them or any of the people coming to the party before, but Jan came to one of my gigs to explain in a bit more detail. Every since he'd known Christian, he told me, all he ever listened to was TV Smith, so it would be a great surprise for him. There would be about thirty guests, they'd take a boat trip during the day then build a big campfire for everyone to sit around in the evening while I played unplugged in the open air. It was so obvious that I would never agree to such a ridiculous idea that I said yes. I always do.

Jan mailed me yesterday to say that only sixteen people instead of the expected thirty had come. And according to the weather forecast I looked at, it will only be sixteen degrees instead of the expected thirty, and pouring with rain as well. Jan told me they haven't had any sleep because they have been erecting a large army tent so everyone can keep dry.

He's hired a car and driver to take me from the airport to Biskirchen, a town of just fifteen hundred inhabitants. Once I've been dropped off at the hotel I wait to hear from Jan again. As I'm only staying one night I travelled with just hand luggage, which got me through the airport quickly but means there's not much to do while I'm waiting—I couldn't even fit in a book. No merchandise either, and just a few items in my wash kit. There is a disposable toothbrush and mini-tube of toothpaste that I saved from a previous transatlantic flight but I soon find the toothpaste has become solid as cement and won't come out of the tube. I squeeze it to try and clear the nozzle then force a little water in from the tap in an attempt rehydrate the paste. After shaking it for a few minutes I manage to achieve a thin drizzle of minty liquid that almost does the job. I didn't really need to clean my teeth but it passed a little time.

After a couple of hours I get another text: *Still paddling!*

Outside the rain is hammering down and inside the wi fi doesn't work. The television is totally uninspiring although as I flick through the channels I hit on a programme called 'The Perfect Wedding.' I can only hope Christian's won't be much like that one because it was so perfect it was depressing.

After a while, Jan calls to say someone is waiting for me at the hotel entrance to drive me over to the campsite. He clearly isn't, because I'm on a sofa right next to the entrance trying to pick up a wi fi signal. Eventually I find him at the entrance to the restaurant adjoining the hotel. When I walk through the packed restaurant to get there, everyone stops eating and looks at me.

There is just room in the back of the car to fit in the guitar on top of the two crates of empty beer bottles, then after I've tactfully established that my driver doesn't drink alcohol himself, we set off for the campsite. He is a little unsure of how to get there. 'I've never been here before,' he apologises.

'Me neither!' I reply.

He explains that everything is running late because the boat trip took much longer than expected. They had a six kilometre stretch of river to paddle down. Unfortunately, of the sixteen people on board only eight were paddling, the other eight were just drinking beer. I ask him what kind of boat it was, and he points at a large black inflatable dingy on the back of a trailer being towed behind a car that is just coming out from a side road ahead of us.

'It was just like that,' he says. 'Hang on, that *is* our one!

After a few wrong turns we find our way back to the campsite and I see Jan approaching me as I get out of the car. He points out a guy looking my way with an *I don't believe this is happening* expression. 'That's Christian!'

I go over and introduce myself. 'So no one gave away the secret?' I say. 'Not even your future wife?' Jan had told me she is a fan also and had really wanted to come too.

He nods thoughtfully. 'This explains *a lot* about some things that have been going on over the last few weeks.'

As luck would have it, the sky has just cleared over to the west revealing a sensational cloud-fringed sunset and against the menacingly dark clouds across the other side of the sky a bright rainbow is appearing. We have our photo taken in front of it.

The campfire is just getting going and I stand by it chatting with the guests. I notice quite a few of them ask me if I have a cigarette lighter on me. One guy grabs a large piece of wood and plunges one end of it into the fire for a few moments then lights his cigarette from the glowing embers. 'How come no one here has a lighter?' I ask him.

'On the boat trip everyone had to go into the water at least once. None of their lighters are working any more.'

'Even I went in, and I wasn't drinking,' says my driver.

'There was a big tray of matchbooks back at the hotel! I could have set up a merch stand and made a fortune!' I say.

The driver laughs. 'Great idea!'

'Any chance you could drive me back so I could get them?'

'Cut me in?'

'Ten percent.'

'Deal.'

But we don't.

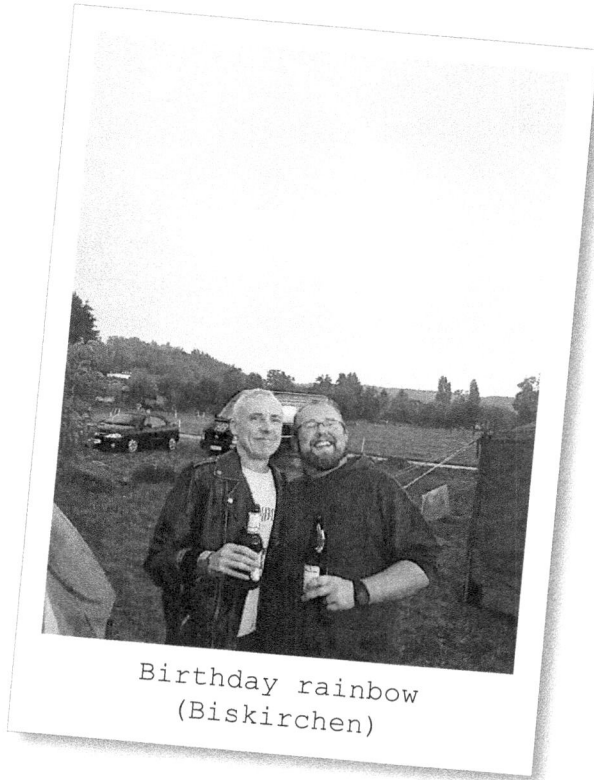

Birthday rainbow
(Biskirchen)

There is one other group of campers at the site and they start up a peculiar game where one of the group issues commands and everyone else follows them. 'Arms out! Thumbs up! Bums out! Wiggle them about!' I'm sure it's great fun, but in comparison to our bedraggled bunch of punks drinking beer, lighting cigarettes from hunks of wood and wolfing down barbecued meat it looks faintly ridiculous. God knows what they're going to think when I start the gig.

Although they might not even hear it. Suddenly the rain starts to slam down again and we retreat into the tent. 'Is it waterproof?' I ask Jan.

'It is so far,' he replies.

He and some helpers drag the big table and benches out of the way and suddenly everyone is looking expectantly at me and it's apparently time to start.

Although Jan had been looking forward to a campfire concert, I'm rather glad that the rain has forced us into the tent. With an audience of sixteen sitting around me on benches there's a great intimate atmosphere which it would be hard to create out in the open. There are frequent stops for beer and chat between the songs and after about ninety minutes we have a break. Christian seems overwhelmed by the gig so far. One of his friends tells me, 'He's so excited he's not going to sleep for ten days after this. He's not going to *wash*!'

Maybe I should apologise to his wife now.

As I start playing again, Jan mentions that the rain has stopped again so we could go outside now. I say I prefer it inside, but as I play I find myself hatching a plan. As I reach the moment for the big three Adverts songs at the end I stand up with the guitar and walk out of the tent towards the fire, playing the intro to Gary Gilmore's Eyes as I go. Everyone follows, and we finish the gig out there, the fire blazing away in front of us.

By the time I get to the end, the other group of campers have arrived, curious to see what's going on, and are also cheering and applauding. 'New fans,' says Jan in my ear. 'Now you have to play more!'

I welcome them, and explain who I am, and then for a joke I say, 'Thumbs up! Bums out!'—and they all do it. Then I play another five songs.

I hurry off to the tent to pack my guitar away and retreat from the calls for more encores. I've already played two and a half hours and that seems enough. Also, I left my beer in there as I couldn't carry it when I walked out with the guitar. Jan follows me in after a while. 'All those people from the other camp wanted to know who you are and said they are going to look you up on YouTube,' he says. 'You could have sold a hundred CDs!'

The one time I come without any.

We go back out to the fire and drink more beer, until I'm feeling quite in the stag party mode myself. I have to get up early tomorrow morning for my flight back though, so after a while I start saying my goodbyes. I want to say goodbye to Christian, but no one has seen him for a while. When I go back to the tent to pick up my guitar I find him wrapped up in a sleeping bag under a bench, out for the count. So much for not sleeping for ten days!

When I get back to the hotel my toothpaste is just right.

## 30th August TAMPERE

Two days until the meteorological last day of Summer, so what better way to spend it than heading far north to Finland for a few gigs. The first date is a festival and I have to fly out the day before because I have no chance of getting there in time otherwise. Even by leaving home at three in the afternoon I won't get into Tampere until past midnight and after that it's still a two hour rail trip to Jyväskylä, where the festival is being held. I'll take the train in the morning, first staying the night at my friend Jukka's place. He owes me one: the last gig of the tour will be in his living room for his birthday.

'It's not my birthday party, though,' he says as he drives me in from the airport. 'It just happens to be on my birthday. If you say that it's my birthday party people might bring me presents and—you know how Finnish people are—that would be embarrassing.'

As we enter the house he points to the area on the right leading to the bedrooms and says, I thought you and the others could play here.'

'The others?'

'Ah, well, I have also asked a young girl singer and a Clash covers band to play.'

'So it's a festival now?'

Jukka wrote me an email a while back that said: *the first time you saw my living room you said, I've played smaller clubs than this. So then I started thinking, what about a whole tour in people's living rooms?* His plan was that he would contact all our mutual friends in various towns throughout Finland and suggest they each put on a gig in their living room, just inviting people we know. It was such a typically Finnish ridiculous idea that I said I'd do it, but somehow it never happened and the idea slipped away. Then when tour agent Harri booked me for the Jyväskylä festival and was looking for a few dates to go with it he phoned up Jukka out of the blue and said, *that idea about having Tim play your living room? It will be on the 6th September.* Jukka was a bit surprised but, as he tells me, 'It was my idea in the first place so it's my own fault.'

Not only that, it coincided with his birthday. Five years ago I played his fiftieth birthday party – I might as well play his fifty-fifth too. Not that it's a party.

## 31st August JYVÄSKYLÄ

A ninety minute train journey to Jyväskylä, and I can see the festival site on the other side of a dual carriageway next to the railway tracks as we pull into the station. There is supposed to be someone to meet me and take me over there, but after I've hung around by the station entrance for a while and no one comes I decide to go and check in to the hotel instead as it's only just up the road in the other direction. The festival doesn't open for another half hour and I'm not due on until mid-afternoon so there's plenty of time. I spend an hour in my room and when I come out I walk straight past a taxi, only realising at the last minute that the driver is gesturing at me. 'Are you Mr. Smith?'

I see the flyers for the festival stuck on his car. 'Are you here to pick me up?'

He says he is so I put my guitar and bag in the boot and get in the passenger seat. Just out of curiosity I ask him how long he has been out here waiting and he says he's just arrived.

So now I am doing my tour managing by telepathy.

I'm driven to the back entrance of the festival and met by the promoter, who shows me around and introduces me to the stage manager. Sandwiched between a lake on one side and the road and railway track on the other, the festival is being held in a large gravel-floored yard next to Jyväskylä's best-known music club, with a second stage inside. It's the only old red brick building among the surrounding clone-town glass-fronted office blocks.

Just about an hour later at 3:15 I find myself on stage. There are a couple of hundred people out there, oddly segregated because the Finnish alcohol laws require the bar area to be fenced off and manned with security, so that from where I'm standing it looks as if the people with a drink are penned in like cattle. Anyone who wants to get near the front has to leave their beer behind.

At first there are only forty or so up near the stage. During the opening song a horribly familiar crunch of high volume interference starts up every time I stamp my foot, which rather dampens the excitement of my big entrance. I plough on, then at the end of the song go and have a word with the sound technician at the side of the stage.

'I think you need to change the D.I. box,' I say.

'I think you need to change your guitar cable,' he says.

I unplug my cable from the D.I. box so that the guitar is no longer going through the P.A. and stamp again, setting off another explosion of noise. 'I think you need to change the D.I. box,' I say.

This really isn't the start I'd hoped for, and the audience are understandably getting a bit restless, so I stand at the front of the stage and play a song acoustically, which has the double advantage that the people at the front enjoy it and the people hanging back can't hear it so they have to come forward too. And then everyone's at the front and the D.I. box is working again and we all have an excellent forty-five minutes.

The only problem is, now it's only four in the afternoon and I'm already done. I wander inside to check out the club venue and one woman who I noticed at the front enjoying the gig calls to me as I pass. 'Every time I see you play you put a big smile on my face,' she says.

'That's my job,' says the guy next to her.

'He's my husband.'

I see her again while I'm hanging around the merch area, and she hands me a little origami bird she has made. 'It's not much, but I wanted to give you something to say thank you,' she says, and shows me how to make the wings flap.

That bird is going with me on the rest of the tour. It may sound silly, but these things are important to me.

After that I wander out to watch a band or two, get some reasonable vegan food in the backstage area, stand watching another band for a bit... To be honest, most of the bands are playing the grind, thrash and grunge style of punk which I don't much like, and I'm beginning to wonder how I'm going to get through the next six hours. Then a girl called Maria who I recognise from previous gigs in Finland taps me on the shoulder and accuses me of looking lonely and says I should come into the bar area where she'll buy me a beer and introduce some of her friends. Suddenly there's conversation going on and I'm starting to enjoy myself. 'Let's go outside and meet the rest!' Maria says.

Outside, those who can't afford the festival ticket, or just can't afford the beer prices, are drinking cheap booze and making their own entertainment. They're all sitting around on the curb of a side road feeding the offices, next to the main road and railway. We are metaphorically and actually on the other side of the tracks. Maria introduces me to Jyväskylä's 'godfather of punk', who 'educated everyone here about punk music', and then to 'my greatest fan', who is unfortunately already too drunk to seize the opportunity to say hello. I sit next to her friend Heiki, who is collecting empty cans to get the refund. She has a hard time getting enough money to live and has to keep shouting at the other can collectors who frequently come past stealing her business. She shows me a photo of her dog. Someone else comes over to say hello to me and collapses on top of her two plastic bags of cans as he tries to get near enough to talk, splitting them open so that some of the cans roll across the road. Heiki looks very annoyed and he offers her a couple of euros to make up for what she's lost. Suddenly she starts sobbing, so he offers her five more euros, but then she starts to cry even more.

'What's the matter with her!' asks the guy. 'Life's not about money!'

'It is when you haven't got any,' I point out.

I gather some cans back into the plastic bags and try to reassure Heiki that she hasn't lost any but she is inconsolable. At that moment someone spills a full can of beer on the pavement behind me and before I can get up it has soaked right through my jeans. It's time for me to go back inside.

'Are your leaving us?' says Maria.

'My arse is soaked with beer,' I reply.

I grab some paper towels from the kitchen, and in the backstage toilet I get to work and soon my trousers and underwear are acceptably dry. It's not a good start to a week on tour though. Many hours later, when I finally do get back to the hotel, those jeans are going in the sink. I only hope they get dry by the morning—I don't want a 'Trouserless in Jyväskylä' incident.

## 1st September TAMPERE.

The first day of Autumn and it's pouring with rain. But my trousers are dry.

Harri couldn't find gigs for the Sunday and Monday so I now have two days off and will take the train back to Tampere to spend them at Jukka's place. I'm also going to use the time to have a rehearsal with Punk Lurex tomorrow in preparation for a short tour of Russia being planned for later in the year. As well as playing our own sets, the promoter has asked us to play a few songs together.

Jukka lives a little way out of town and had offered to pick me up from the station, but I have time on my hands so I try the local bus service, which works flawlessly, gets me there in fifteen minutes and only costs two and a half euros. Jukka seems surprised to see me so early.

We while away the afternoon, then Jukka cooks for us. In the evening we have a sauna, then go out onto the terrace in towels and drink a beer, then go back in the sauna, then go back out onto the terrace in towels and drink another beer. After that we're quite mellow. I grumble a bit about all the bands I endured last night and Jukka tells me there is a bit of a revival in '77 style punk bands starting in Finland. He tells me a few of their names, of which the most memorable one translates as *Urgent Need For A Shit '77*. The '77 tag at the end being the master stroke.

Jukka and his wife Teija go to bed fairly early as they both have to get up for work tomorrow, and at a bit of a loose end I have an early night myself, getting my head down soon after midnight.

## 2nd September TAMPERE

I take the bus into the town, passing the grand Tampere Hall on the way, which proudly boasts that it is the biggest congress and concert centre in Scandinavia. A poster outside announces that it's currently hosting the '16th International Conference on Diseases of Fish and Shellfish.' I bet that's exciting.

I visit the cathedral for another look at Hugo Simberg's visionary murals then go for a stroll around the harbour, breaking off after a while to drop into a coffee bar. As soon as I walk in someone says, 'Hey, TV Smith – I saw you in Jyväskylä the other day! Great!'

'Thank you!' I say. 'Will you be coming to the gig here?'

'When is it?'

'Thursday.'

'Hmm...probably not.'

Back at Jukka's place, Tiina comes to pick me up for rehearsal at seven. As we leave she says to Jukka, 'So, see you on Friday for your birthday gig.'

'It's not my birthday gig,' he says. 'It *just happens to be on my birthday.*'

Rehearsal goes well and we soon have four songs ready for the Russian tour. I'm still not sure if the tour will actually happen—there are only six weeks to go and still no word from promoter Denis about how to get visas. Tiina also tells me there is now a new date booked in St. Petersburg, which I didn't know about. We retire to the pub to discuss.

I'm actually quite nervous about what conditions will be like on a low-budget-no-profit tour of Russia, even if it happens. Tiina tells me that Denis organised some dates for Punk Lurex a couple of years ago and he was quite reliable, but the tour involved brutally long journeys and the sleeping places were pretty basic. At one of them she got so badly bitten by mosquitoes that she had problems with her joints when she got home afterwards. 'Oh, and there was one time we were in this alley in St Petersburg next to the venue and all these big rats were running around us.'

'You're not helping,' I say.

Coincidentally, the manager of the big Tampere venue Klubi is in the bar and comes over to talk about the show planned there with the UK Subs and me next year. Inevitably the talk turns to Russia. 'You have to be very careful there, especially at the moment,' he warns.

'You're not helping,' I say.

Back at Jukka's place, there's an email from Denis with the visa application form.

## 3rd September VIRRAT

I spend a lot of time on the internet fighting two frustrating battles: one, to figure out the complexities of the visa application—which will in any case require a visit to the Russian embassy when I get back to London, so I leave it for now—and, two, attempting to obtain something called an ISRC code, which has to be imprinted on the master of my next record before I can get it pressed. I had applied online to a rights company called the PPL for this code before I left for Finland but neglected to take my password for their website with me and have been unable to access it to find out what's going on. They seem unable to grasp this. Despite my attempts to explain the situation to them I have a number of emails in my inbox saying, *your case 01826740 has been updated*, with a link to the website, which is completely useless as I can't log in. I had hoped to have the record ready as a surprise for my fan club gig in Germany in one month but that is looking increasingly unlikely. Just before I'm due to leave the house mid-afternoon I get an email from the PPL telling me how to change my password. I quickly dream up a new one and then I'm in. I hurriedly fill out a couple of pages of forms, and by the end of that it looks like I will get the code in the next 48 hours. I'm not absolutely sure though. The forms were almost as complex as the Russian visa application and I have a suspicion I may have applied twice or not at all.

I take the bus into Tampere and walk up to the imposing Finlayson building—once a textile mill employing most of the town, now tastefully renovated to become a cultural centre with bars and restaurants. Tour agent Harri, who teaches at the music and media college in a town called Virrat has arranged for me to meet one of the other tutors here so he can drive me to the gig there tonight. It will be the third time I've played Virrat, and I'm not expecting too much as the audience is usually made up exclusively of kids from the college who know nothing about me. When the tutor, Timo, arrives he admits he doesn't know much about me either, but Harri sent him a few clips from YouTube yesterday and he's had an idea. 'You don't have to leave until two tomorrow,' he says. 'How would it be if you came into the college in the morning and had a chat with the students about your career and maybe even recorded a song, solo or with a band?'

'I don't mind having a chat with them,' I say. 'I could even record a song if you like, but it would have to be solo—I don't have a band.'

'The students would be the band,' Timo says.

'I wouldn't have time to teach them a song, I think solo would be better.'

'They will learn the song before you get there.'

I have the feeling I'm being steered into choosing to agree to something that's actually already been decided.

Ninety minutes later we reach Virrat. We stop off at Pub 66 so I can have a quick soundcheck then drive on to where I am staying the night, which turns out to be a small wooden cabin on the edge of a lake, part of a holiday complex. Very idyllic, but I only have a few minutes here before I'm supposed to meet Harri and I can't get the door key to work. Timo has already driven off to the hut he is staying in further up the hill. Eventually I head up after him on foot, and he comes back to see what the problem is. He twists the key and the door opens effortlessly. 'The doors are new,' he says. 'You have to push them.'

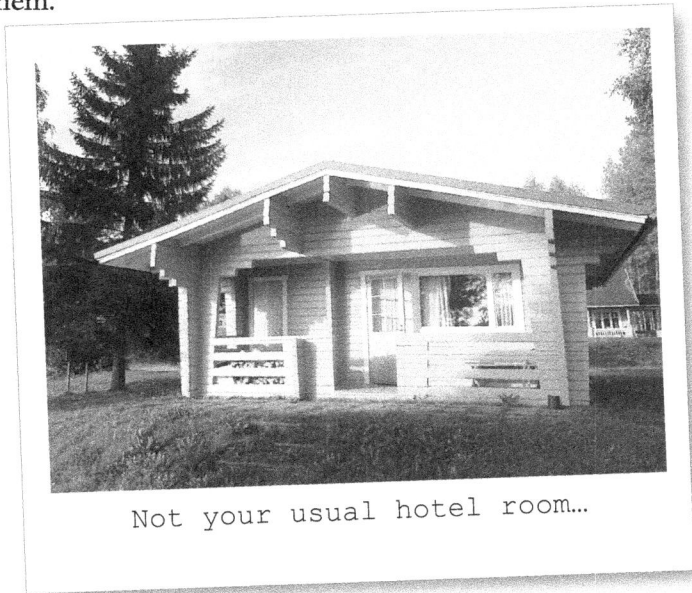

Not your usual hotel room...

'Then they should have a sign on them saying, *PUSH!*' I complain, in a bit of a bad mood. 'Then I wouldn't have had to stand here like a c*nt for ten minutes.'

I'm a musician. I can't be expected to know how to open doors as well.

I drop off my suitcase, then Timo drives me back into town where we meet up with Harri and have a snack in a falafel cafe. 'Will you be coming to Jukka's gig on Friday?' I ask him.

'I am not sure yet,' he replies. 'It's his birthday party isn't it?

No! It *just happens to be on his birthday!*

Then Harri drops me back at the cabin until it's nearer show time. It's certainly a nicer place than a bar to while away a couple of hours—though a bar would have beer and possibly even wi-fi. For the moment I will simply have to forget about my visa and my ISRC codes and watch the sun set over the wooden jetty where one could relax and feel human if one weren't about to get on stage. Don't want to get too mellow. After all, I may be staying in a holiday cabin but I'm not *actually* on holiday.

```
...or the usual view from it
     (Virrat, Finland)
```

Everyone else here is though, and the idyllic peace is soon interrupted by a gaggle of excitable children who gather at the lakeside outside my hut for a lesson in night canoeing. There are a lot of shouted instructions, then the kids don life jackets and launch their canoes, paddling off in the gathering darkness towards a beacon flashing on the far side of the lake. Peace then descends again and I am left to reflect on the fact that, satisfyingly, this is the second 'paddling event' in two consecutive trips.

Harri picks me up at ten, and half an hour later I'm ready to start in Pub 66. The audience aren't quite ready though. I chat with the few who are in and most of them seem quite surprised that I'm playing Virrat and even more surprised that I'm chatting with them. 'I can't believe you're sitting with us,' says one. 'When I saw you earlier getting out of the sub I was so excited I took a photo and sent it to my girlfriend.'

'Sorry?'

'This afternoon. I saw you getting out of a sub.'

I'm sure I would remember that.

Then I get it. A *Saab*. Timo's car.

It seems to be the standing joke that nothing happens here. 'If Elvis played Virrat,' another guy says, 'Only twenty people would come.'

Someone else tells me he has lived in Virrat for nineteen years and finally moved out last weekend. To Jyväskylä. He went to the festival on Saturday but somehow missed my performance so he's come back to Virrat one more time to see me here. One other guy tells me he saw me last time I played here and bought the Useless CD afterwards. He steers me over to the merch table and proceeds to buy a copy of everything else I have on display, seven CDs and a vinyl. I'm not in such a bad mood when I start the gig at eleven, and the response is so good I play for ninety minutes.

On the way back to the cabin Harri tells me there were 44 paying customers.

That's 24 more than Elvis would have got!


## 4th September TURKU

Oddly, these cabins don't have any mirrors, which makes having a shave a bit random.

Harri picks me up at eleven and drives me over to the college. I use one of their computers for a while and have just found an email with the ISRC code I've been waiting for when Timo comes to tell me the class is ready. 'We'll have a chat then maybe record something,' he says.

'Have they learned a song they want to record?' I ask.

'No...'

'I won't have time to teach them anything before I have to leave.'

'Maybe just record something solo then. Let's see what happens.'

I hurriedly send off the ISRC code to Jon, who is mastering the CD, then grab my guitar and go to Timo's classroom in the college recording studio upstairs. All the students are sitting waiting, and when I've sat down too Timo asks the class, 'So, who was at the gig in Pub 66 last night?'

Everyone puts their hands up. The only one who wasn't there was Timo, who was too tired after a five in the morning start yesterday and had to get an early night. I point out one of the students. 'I recognise him. He bought me a beer.'

For about half an hour Timo asks me about punk rock and the music business and how I came to be doing what I'm doing now, and then the students ask some questions themselves. When they finally fizzle out Timo says to me, 'So...would you like to tell us a story now?'

A story? 'Uh—I don't do *stories*.'

'Okay then, let's call it a day.'

The students get up and start packing their chairs away and no more mention is made of recording anything.

I get in the car with Harri for the drive to Tampere, and say, 'So this is probably the last time I'll ever come to Virrat.'

'I think that is certainly true.'

From next year the music college moves to Tampere, and it's hard to imagine me playing Pub 66 without the students around. Harri says, 'Actually the pub will probably still put on gigs at weekends, but it will be Finnish rock and cover bands.'

And no one will come.

Harri drops me off at Tampere station, where I take the train for Turku, arriving just before six. Unusually for Finland, the train doesn't have wi-fi, which is unfortunate as I don't have a map of where the club and hotel are. I think I have a pretty good idea from last time I was here but just in case I cross the platform and stand next to an inter-city train for a couple of minutes and check on the internet using their wi-fi signal. I find the hotel without trouble and when I get to the room there is a nice personal greeting on the television screen: Welcome Dear x Tv-Smith.

Klubi looks different somehow. I remember quite a wide low stage and a big P.A. but now I'm crammed into a corner on the floor next to the table football with speakers on stands either side of me. The soundman says, 'Probably you were in the upstairs room last time. Tonight we have a lot of metal bands up there. I'm doing the sound for them. We'd better get you done quick, I have to be up there in ten minutes.'

I'm done in five and it sounds brilliant—I just hope that there are no technical problems later as from now on I am the soundman.

Probably I can do without a soundman, but an audience would be good. Twenty minutes before showtime at eleven there are about ten people in, much less than last time I played here. I recognise someone who comes to quite a few of my gigs so go and sit at his table. He tells me he has driven five hundred kilometres for this gig and will have to leave straight afterwards as he has to get up at seven in the morning. I'd better start then!

I go upstairs to the dressing room to get my guitar, and just out of curiosity follow the stairs up one more flight to see what's going on in the main room. There is a six piece Russian metal band on stage giving it their all...and six people in the audience.

After seeing that I feel a lot better about my own gig when I go back downstairs, and actually there are a few people arriving now. If the people outside smoking also come in and everyone moves to the front it could actually be okay. It's time to start but not only is there no sound man, but no one else to help me either, and it seems to be up to me to switch off the background music from the unmanned DJ booth. I ask one of the women behind the bar about it. 'It must be something here,' she says, gesturing at the DJ's mixing desk. 'I guess you would know better than me how these things work.'

'Maybe this one,' I say, twisting one of the knobs that looks like it might be the master volume. Nothing happens.

'How about this...?' says the woman, pulling down a fader, and the music stops. She gives me a look, and goes back to the bar.

I'm a musician—I can't be expected to know how to work a mixing desk as well.

Luckily the mixing desk in the corner where I'm playing still has all the same settings as at soundcheck and when I plug in everything still sounds great. Even better, there are now around sixty people in, and they've all gathered at the front and give me a huge cheer when I finish the first song. One woman is dancing all the way through the songs. Slightly worryingly, she is also dancing all the way through my introductions between the songs as well, but after the fifth song she shouts out, 'You are the perfect man!' so she clearly has good judgement. As I get near the end of the set I start to get requests for some quite obscure songs from my back catalogue and before I know it my scheduled sixty minute set has turned into a ninety minute set, something I really hadn't expected on a Wednesday in Turku.

I chat with some of the audience afterwards and have a few beers with them. When I pack away my merch I notice someone has left a marigold on the table for me. I put it in my bag. It may sound silly, but this sort of thing is important to me. It's now got very late, but it's a good feeling to know that whenever I want to leave it's just a five minute walk to my hotel, a very comfortable Holiday Inn. Even though I'm not actually on holiday.

## 5th September TAMPERE

Back to Tampere for the final official date of the tour before the unbirthday gig. I check in to the hotel, which has at my disposal, according to the poster in the lift, 'a refreshing cool water pool'—I don't think so—then I go for a walk around the town. Despite it being so late in the year and so far North there is a cloudless sky and the temperature is in the mid twenties so I spend a few hours sitting on the grassy bank of the river in the town centre, just soaking up the sun, listening to the sound of the Tammerkoski rapids, people-watching, and gradually becoming enveloped in a peculiarly Finnish sense of melancholy. Who knows how many days like this we'll be able to enjoy before winter comes? It's a question that has even more resonance to the Finns than to me.

When I arrive at the Telakka club there are quite a few people out on the terrace enjoying the last of the sun and absolutely no one inside. I wait out the time to the gig worrying about the lack of audience arriving, but one guy explains it's always like this because of the Finnish alcohol laws—it's so expensive to drink in a club that most people stay at home and drink cheap alcohol there, only coming out at the last minute.

He tells me he used to be in a band himself, and their name was 'The Fucking World.' 'We were the only punks in Lempäälää!' he says. 'Imagine how often we used to get beaten up!'

For me, used to feeling the atmosphere gradually build during the course of the evening before I play, it's an unsettling feeling being almost the only one in a club for so long, but sure enough in the final half hour before showtime people start to arrive, and in the last ten minutes there's suddenly a queue at the door. By the time I start we have a reasonably full house and a great gig. As I finish a woman comes to the front of the stage and hands me a rose. That's going up on the table in my hotel room next to the marigold and the origami bird.

## 6th September TAMPERE

When I become king I will introduce a law that requires vacuum cleaners to be fitted with a device that disables their motors if anyone tries to start them up at 7:30 in the morning. Especially next to my room.

There's a good breakfast buffet at the hotel and I'm able to stock up on lots of salad and fruit that has been lacking from my diet in the last few days. 'Salad' in Finland usually means 'shredded cabbage,' not great news for vegetarians.

I don't need to be at Jukka's place until late afternoon and I'm sure he'll be busy organising things at home for his party—not that it's his party—so I leave my suitcase and guitar in the hotel luggage room and head out to the town. If someone had suggested to me before that I could spend three hours captivated by the history of the Tampere textile industry I would have laughed in their face, but that's exactly what happens in the Finlayson museum which is not only packed with fascinating old looms and fiendishly complex spinning machines but tells the history of the factory and its workers in such a wealth of detail that my head is, aptly enough, reeling by the time I get out. Then I go into an adjoining building to see the vast steam engine that powered the factory, and after that I happen to notice that the media museum has free entry on Fridays so I have a look around there too. I suddenly realise the afternoon is slipping away and I should get over to Jukka's place. I'm not *actually* on holiday.

Jukka has changed his mind and decided I should play in the corner on the other side of the room than where he suggested the other day, which makes sense as there's more space—but he has to take the flat screen television out of the way first, and asks me to make sure I don't swing my guitar over my head as there is a mirrored ceiling above me. I'll have to be careful to hold back a bit when I'm playing. The other thing that will be a bit odd, I suddenly realise, is that it's Finnish custom never to go into someone's house with your shoes on so I will presumably be doing the gig barefoot.

I tell Jukka about my trip to the Finlayson museum and he says, 'Did you know that this factory had the first electric light in Scandinavia?' I did know that, I tell him. In fact there is *nothing* I don't know about Finlayson after three hours in there.

He tries again. 'Did you know that there was a huge water tank on the roof that fed a sprinkler system and if there was a fire the tin in the pipes would melt and release the water to flood the entire factory?'

Damn. I *didn't* know that.

At six a sound guy arrives and sets up a small PA system and we have a quick soundcheck. The Clash covers band aren't going to make it for soundcheck, but Danny, the girl singer arrives and sets up. Then we wait for the guests, who slowly trickle in, including the Helsinki crew Tommi, Berjia and Janne, and past and present members of Punk Lurex. Quite a few of them bring cards and gifts for Jukka. How embarrassing.

While the room fills I go to the end of the garden, where I have noticed Danny and her two friends are sitting on their own. 'We don't know anyone here!' she says. She tells me that this is only her second ever gig. No wonder she looks nervous. She's leafing through her songbook of the '77 punk covers she will be playing. I sympathise and tell her I'm sure it will be fine, though actually I'm nervous myself—these private gigs are often harder than a normal gig. As it's nearing time for her to start we wander back up the path to the house where Jukka is waiting for us. I realise I have made a bit of a blunder—I didn't put my shoes back on when I went out. 'I'm sorry Jukka,' I say. 'I suppose now I will have to take my socks off when I go in. And if I do it again I will have to take my feet off.'

I feel myself getting more and more nervous as Danny and then the Clash covers band play. As they finish Jukka comes up to me and says, 'That's it for old '77 punk rock. Now it's time for you to play some new '77 punk rock.'

I'm aware of the expectations in the air as I plug in. I introduce myself by saying: 'I've been playing gigs for nearly forty years but this is the first time I've *ever* played... without shoes.'

It gets a good laugh, and I steam into the first song and the nerves instantly evaporate—though I soon find I really do have to make a conscious effort not to stamp the way I usually do while I'm playing because I am seriously in danger of breaking my foot. Ninety minutes later it's two minutes before midnight and I announce I will play just one more song and after that Jukka's birthday party is over.

Not that it ever was his birthday party.

## 7th September LONDON

Home again, I open the passwords program on my computer to write in the new password I thought up for the PPL site only to find it's the same as the old one I forgot. At least I'm consistent.

## 8th September LONDON

I spend quite some time trying to fill out the Russian visa application online but it's extremely detailed and demands a lot of information that I simply can't give them: every job I've had since I left school, for example, with dates of starting and leaving and the phone numbers of my bosses. 'Punk rocker since '77' is not really what they're after. Unless you complete every box on each page the system won't let you advance to the next section so after a couple of hours I find myself stuck and still only halfway through the application. Increasingly frustrated at the waste of time and aware that so far there are only two gigs in Russia actually booked I write to Denis and tell him that I can't complete the form and can't afford to spend any more time on it. I'm really feeling like giving up on the idea of going to Russia.

## 9th September LONDON

Denis writes back to say it's 'really not cool' to think of cancelling the gigs now, and he'll give me any advice I need about filling in the forms. I brace myself for another day online and go back to the visa application site, where I start again and quite by chance I find that if instead of writing 'none' in the 'employment' section I just leave it completely blank I am allowed to proceed to the next page. I continue like this on to the end of the form, and print out a copy, almost completely blank except for my name and address. I send a scan of it to Denis by email and he writes back to say it 'looks pretty good.'

## 10th September LONDON

I'm quite surprised to find there are only a few people in the queue ahead of me at the agency that processes the visa applications, somehow less surprised when the woman behind the counter leafs through the 'employment' section and shakes her head. 'If you're self-employed we need stamped bank statements.'

*Here we go*, I think. Then she looks through the rest of the form and hands it back to me with my passport. 'Apart from that everything looks fine,' she says. And smiles. She points at the date I'm leaving. 'You have plenty of time.'

My only problem is that I need to get the application in today: the visa takes seven working days to process and they keep my passport in the meantime. This is the only seven day period I have coming up where I don't need to be abroad, but I leave for a tour of Spain just after that. I find the nearest branch of my bank, Lloyds, and walk to it to request a copy of my statements, but when I get there I find it's been changed to a branch of TSB in the Lloyds break up that happened only last week. The next-nearest branch is a thirty minute walk away and I get there to find there is a computer breakdown and they can't access anyone's accounts. 'It could last ten minutes or all day,' they tell me. I give it thirty minutes and return to find the system is back up and running and I'm at the end of a long queue. Eventually I have the stamped statements and hurry back to the visa centre where I hand over the forms just before the office closes for the day. The woman takes the payment and says, 'You can come back and pick up your visa in a week.

Blimey. In the end that was easier than America.

## 17th September LONDON

I'm at the visa office at 4:30 in the afternoon as instructed and the visa is waiting for me. When I get back home I take a photo of it and send it to Denis. He emails back, 'HOORAY!'

## 18th September LONDON

My new CD is delivered from the pressing plant, two weeks before the deadline. HOORAY!

## 22nd September BARCELONA

Jonathan is at Barcelona airport to meet me with Mateo and Marky—my new band for a short 'Best of The Adverts' tour here in Spain, to be followed by a longer one in Germany later in the year. I'm a bit sad not to have the Valentines as my backing band but drummer Mone decided to retire from music and guitarist Mars and bassist Massi couldn't guarantee finding and rehearsing another drummer in time. Instead I turned to my old friend Jonathan, bassist from Suzy & Los Quattro, to put a new Bored Teenagers line-up together. 'Just make sure their names all begin with M,' I told him. (Joke)

They've been rehearsing on their own for some weeks, and we now drive to the rehearsal room for one more run through with me. Ninety minutes later we're out of there, very happy with the way it's all sounding.

When we get back to Jonathan's flat I take off my shoes and notice there's a sticky patch of chewing gum on one of my socks. I can only assume there was a wad of gum on the floor of the airplane, as that was the last time I had my shoes off. Not a big problem, but you can only take so many socks on tour and that's one of them gone.

We have something to eat with Jonathan's wife Suzy—singer of Los Quattro— then Jonathan and I walk over to the Barbara Ann bar, where I once played a solo gig many years ago, to have a few beers.

When we get back to Jonathan's place at nearly three, I'm disappointed to find that the new sock I put on earlier is now covered with chewing gum too. It's only then that I realise the gum must now be inside the shoe—transferred from the original gummed up sock when I put my shoe back on at the end of the flight. That's two socks gone now and I go to bed obsessed with the thought that somehow I have to get that residue gum out of my shoe first thing tomorrow. If I don't remember I'll be three socks down before the tour even starts.

## 23rd September URRETXU

I do remember about the gum, because Donna barges into the bedroom, grabs my sock in her mouth and leads me out to my shoes.

(Donna is Jonathan and Suzy's dog.)

I feel around but can't find any chewing gum in the shoe. Presumably it has all been soaked up by the two socks.

We drive down to the rehearsal room to meet the M&Ms and load up the van, then we're on the road to the first date of the tour, way up to the North in the Basque Country. It's a beautiful hot day and a great feeling to have a return to summer when Britain has had cool rainy weather and leaden skies for a few weeks already. It's just a shame I will be spending seven hours of it sitting in the van.

Soon after we've left Barcelona Jonathan points out an oddly-shaped mountain on the right hand side of the motorway which is famous for its black Madonna housed in a monastery on the summit. Less well-known is the fact that Hitler visited the monastery thinking it might be the location of the Holy Grail. 'There was a programme about it on Catalan television a few years ago,' Jonathan tells me. 'They spoke to the last surviving monk. He had actually been the one who showed Hitler around, and told the documentary team he didn't know what had disappointed Hitler most: the fact he didn't find the Holy Grail or the fact that the Madonna was black.'

Nestled in the mountains of the Basque country is the small town of Urretxu, where we'll play tonight. The place has a special significance for Jonathan, because it's the home town of his best friend Hank, who was murdered in a street robbery in Barcelona a few years ago. Shortly after his death, when Jonathan and I were on tour in Spain in a three piece small band format, we took a detour to a farm up in the hills nearby and played a few songs for Hank around the tree he is buried under. Since then, a bar has opened in the town called 'Hankie Hankie' in honour of him. We attempt to head there when we arrive in Urretxu, but it's the last day of the town festival, many of the streets are blocked off and there are crowds everywhere. After we've circled the area a few times, Jonathan's friend Burja comes out to meet us and jumps in the van to guide us in.

After a beer in the Hankie Hankie we walk to the place we'll be playing tonight, a low tented structure in a car park just up the hill. The marquee has a big stage erected at one end of it, but it turns out that we're going to play on the floor at the other end next to the bar. It looks rather unpromising: a small area of the concrete floor marked out with a couple of lengths of metal fencing with a drum kit precariously balanced on some beer crates behind. I think I might leave my stage clothes in my suitcase tonight. Never wear stage clothes when there isn't a stage.

The rest of the band will stay at Burja's place, but Jonathan has booked a room for me in a *pension* and walks me over there. The festival is in full swing on its final day and we weave our way past street musicians and through crowds of kids throwing firecrackers. When we reach the *pension* Jonathan points out an ancient section of wall on the opposite side of the square where the traditional Basque ball game, an early version of squash, was once played.

We get back to the car park to find that the two support bands have unloaded their equipment next to ours but there's no sign of anything else happening yet. All of the band members and bar staff and crew now sit around long wooden tables and many bags of meat-filled baguettes are delivered. One foil pack is rescued from the rest and handed to me. There are no visual clues as to what the filling might be but Jonathan tells me that it's that stuff, er, what's it called, that grain you give babies for their first solid meal.

Mmm, baby food! Who says it's hard to be a vegetarian in Spain?

I ask Burja what kind of music the two support bands play, and he asks around and then tells me, 'Post-core. I have no idea what that is.'

Me neither, but when the first of them finally play, some hours after the scheduled start time, I find that I quite enjoy it. There are about thirty people watching, nodding along and applauding politely. After a while I go and sit on the big stage back in the shadows out of the way, thinking about my coming performance. Even though this isn't the explosive start to the tour I'd imagined—playing to a handful of people in a car park—I focus on the fact that it is the start of a journey that should eventually bring us to play in front of two thousand people at the Rebellion festival next summer.

As it gets near to showtime the band and me gather at the van and formulate a plan: we will play the whole set non-stop, no gaps, no talking between songs, no stopping for tuning or technical reasons unless absolutely unavoidable. Even though it's only a small crowd we intend to be an irresistible force.

And that's what we do. The only break comes from Marky, who stops playing briefly after I accidentally tread on his plugboard and switch off the power to his amp.

We finish the final song to cheers from the small crowd then I go and stand by the bar, sweat dripping off me. An attractive woman turns to me and says, 'That was great! Can I buy you a drink? I'm the town mayor!'

We're leaving the van in the car park overnight so load the big speaker cabs in there but for safety carry the guitars and smaller bits of equipment over to Burja's place—which is on the fifth floor, lift not working. 'I can feel an entry in your diary coming on,' says Jonathan, as we wrestle the gear up the narrow staircase. Then we walk down to Hankie Hankie to celebrate our first performance with a few beers. As three in the morning approaches it's finally time to break up the gathering. We arrange to meet for breakfast at 10:15 tomorrow then I set off towards my *pension*.

'You're sure you know where it is?' asks Burja. 'You'll find it with your GPS won't you?'

'I don't have GPS,' I tell him. 'I'm old school. I'll find it no problem.'

I start off quite well—definitely recognise this street, and there's that shop with the ugly pottery vase in the window that I noticed when I walked back to the gig earlier. Then I go past *Bar Restaurante Ezkiotarre*, which I've seen before, and then a rather grand porticoed building I also made a mental note of, with the square opposite with a statue in the middle. Should be able to see the square that has my *pension* in it up the hill on the left soon. But gradually I start to get the feeling I'm in new territory. None of the streets going off to the left look familiar and now I'm at a main road with a railway on the other side of it and I have definitely not been here before. Suddenly it occurs to me that I didn't pick up a card for the hotel and don't know its address. Or name. There was just a sign saying *PENSION* above the door. There's no one else about at this time of night and if I do see someone the best I could do would be to ask them if they know where to find a *pension* somewhere near that old bit of wall where people played the original version of squash. I might have to ask them in Basque.

I turn around and start back down the road, hoping to find something I recognise, and glancing up a short side street I notice that although it looks like a dead end, in fact the road narrows at the top and makes a dog leg off to the right. I go up to investigate, turn the corner and and sure enough there's the old wall and there's the square and there's the door with *PENSION* above it.

And the key even works. But once again there is chewing gum on my sock.

## 24th September URRETXU

I throw away a sock then I'm at the café by ten. Jonathan arrives just as two men on the opposite side of the street start cutting a slab of marble in half with an angle grinder. He looks at me and says simply, 'Noise attractor.'

With some difficulty I'd managed to make myself understood in Spanish when I ordered my first coffee, a *cortado*—now Jonathan teaches me how to order one in Basque. The woman behind the counter seems slightly confused to have me speaking to her once in bad Spanish and the next time in bad Basque. All the same, I am pleased to have made myself understood with '*ebakki bat*'—though not so pleased to hear Jonathan quietly breaking into sardonic applause at our table.

Bit of a change now—after spending the last two days only playing songs from the Adverts, today Jonathan is going to be recording bass parts for my new album. We had a day off anyway, and he found a studio fifteen minutes drive away that offered a good rate so we decided to use it. It's in a beautiful location out in the countryside and high up in the hills with a view over the valley, but most importantly it's really well equipped and has a great recording engineer. By the end of the day Jonathan has recorded all his parts.

We drive back to Urretxu intending to reward ourselves for a good day's work with a beer in Hankie Hankie but it's shut. We find Mateo and Marky in a nearby bar and sit down at an outside table with them and discuss where we might go to eat tonight. Jonathan takes a phone call then tells us, 'Seems like we don't have to look for anywhere. Burja has booked us a table for 10:30 in a restaurant right nearby.'

When Burja arrives we all get in the car and after we've been driving along the switchback road up the mountain for five minutes Jonathan turns back from the passenger seat and says, 'There may have been some misunderstanding about it being right nearby.'

There's been some misunderstanding at the restaurant too: when we get there the place appears to be shut, there is just one guy sweeping up inside. He unlocks the door and has a short conversation with Burja which Jonathan translates for me.

Burja: 'We made a reservation for ten-thirty.'

Guy with broom: 'We close at ten.'

So we go back down the mountain and find a place that officially stopped serving at nine but is happy to serve us now, at nearly eleven, and the food is excellent.

And I'm even nearer my *pension* than last night and don't get lost. And there's no chewing gum on my sock.

BB on bass for the new album
(Nr. Urretxu, Basque Country)

## 25th September VALLADOLID

We meet in the café again and Jonathan teaches me Basque for 'two *cortados*,' and then the men start cutting up the marble again so we go up the road to the van and leave for Valladolid. The GPS leads us up the switchback mountain road where we all boo at the restaurant at the top, then we wind our way back down the other side and soon find ourselves back in Urretxu a couple of streets away from where we started. But then we're off to Valladolid!

It's my first time in Valladolid so I take a few hours on my own to wander around in the sunshine and get a feel for the place. Maybe it's just the sensational weather—the temperature is still in the mid thirties and the sky a perfect blue—but there's no sign of the *malaise* caused by the economic depression I hear so much about in the English media. People seem happy, they're well-dressed, the cafés and restaurants are full and the streets are clean and litter-free.

I go to the venue by foot and meet the band there. I'm pleased to see that it's a proper club with a good stage and PA, so tonight we'll be able to give our first real performance. After soundcheck the promoter takes us on a lengthy walk to a small restaurant where he has booked us a table. The chef comes out of the kitchen to explain the menu and when my vegetarian moussaka is brought to the table, rather than the greasy stomach-liner I'd feared it turns out to be a dainty tower of perfectly baked aubergine and bechamel sauce, thin fries balanced on top of it and drizzled with various sauces. The meat options for the rest look equally succulent, and we applaud as each dish arrives. We all take photos of our food and after we've eaten the chef comes out to have his photo taken with us. He tells us he'll be coming to the show tonight.

Although the meal wasn't too rich, we're still all glad of the walk back to the club, and when we get there a few people are hanging around out in the street even though the doors haven't opened yet. I remember Jonathan saying on the way in from the airport when I first arrived that we'd probably 'get sixteen in on a Wednesday' so it's a comparative triumph that by the time we start there are sixty-five paying customers in the room. Once again we play straight through, and it goes down a storm.

Now it really feels like we're on tour.

## 26th September BURGOS

We arrive in Burgos by midday and decide on a walk into the centre for some sightseeing. As we near the the cathedral we pass two street musicians, a guy sitting on the floor playing acoustic guitar and a girl standing next to him playing violin. As we pass she stops playing and runs up to me to ask if I'm the guy she saw in the paper. She says they wanted to come to the gig tonight but, well....she gestures at the almost empty box for donations in front of them. We put them on the guest list.

I walk on with the band to a restaurant Mateo and Marky recommend and we have lunch at the counter, in my case a spectacular salad with carrots and peppercorns, strips of marinaded beetroot, dressed lettuce, cheeses, blackberries, melon and pineapple. What's going on? Spain used to be *the* danger country for UMMs but on this visit I've had some of the best vegetarian food I've ever eaten on tour. UMM has become YUM.

Although I had been intending to look around the inside of Burgos's huge cathedral this afternoon the weather is simply too good to spend hours inside and instead I sit lazily with the band in one of the town squares and drink coffee. Then we wander back to the hotel and head off in the van for soundcheck.

It's a nice little club and everything sounds good but the place doesn't open until ten so we drive back to the hotel when we're done. On the way I ask Jonathan if there have been many advance sales for tonight and after a short pause he says mysteriously, 'Let's just say, it's not looking good.'

Oh dear. When we return to the club I'm encouraged to see there are a few people hanging around outside, but as it turns out they are just about the only ones in front of us when we start, though the crowd does swell by two when the street musicians turn up. It's a big show for forty people but we give it everything anyway and they love it and even demand an encore. We're on the road to Rebellion.

Afterwards we hang around for a while and chat with the audience, including the two street musicians who kindly say that if we need somewhere to stay the night we could sleep in their squat. Another guy tells me that he annoyed me last time I was here by trying to get me to drink some herbal spirit that I didn't want. 'This time I am going to annoy you by making you drink my favourite coffee liqueur!' he announces.

Actually I'm quite tired, hoping for a reasonably early night, and have been timing my forthcoming sleep/coma quite carefully by rapidly chucking a few beers down while the band have been packing their equipment away. The last thing I want now is to get more drunk and woken up at the same time by a coffee liqueur so when the guy returns waving a glass of it insistently at me I make my excuses and head for the backstage. As I go through the door I hear him exclaim loudly to the room: 'TV Smith—you used to be punk! But now you are *nothing!*'

```
Bored Teenagers on the
road to Santiago - and
Rebellion (Burgos)
```

## 27th September MADRID

Marky arrives in the hotel breakfast room where I'm toasting a Bimbo (it's a brand name for sliced bread) and tells me that after we got back last night he and the other two decided to go out again to have a drink with the boss of the club in another bar he owns. 'It was a bit sad,' he says. 'There was only him and the sound man in there.'

So let's leave Burgos to the pilgrims. On to Madrid, where there's sure to be more action.

When we finally make it through the traffic we're lucky enough to find a parking space right outside the hotel, which is almost opposite the venue. The wi fi doesn't reach my room up on the sixth floor so I go back down to the lobby. While I'm sitting there on the settee working my way through my emails, a woman comes out of the lift and tentatively asks the guy behind the desk if there is any toilet paper. He goes through a door behind him and after quite some time reappears with about a third of a roll which he proffers to the woman on the end of one finger. She looks at it.

'Is there any more?'

He gives an apologetic shrug.

'Will there be any later?' the woman continues, then glances over at me listening in and raises her voice a little. 'I mean, *there are three of us.*'

There's a good crowd in the Wurlitzer by the time we get on stage soon after midnight and they're pretty wild, dancing at the front and trying to grab the microphone from me so they can sing with—or to be more accurate, *instead of*—me. At one point I get forcibly crowd-surfed. With most bands this happens with the collusion of the singer, but I actually didn't want to leave the stage: a few people grabbed my legs and sort of wrestled me up and carried me off on their shoulders. They could at least have delivered me to the stage at the end of the song but in fact they dumped me halfway down the club and I had to walk back. The crowd might be a little *too* wild if the truth be told—just as we start 'Gary Gilmore's Eyes' proceedings are brought to a grinding halt when someone spills a glass of beer over the plugboard on the stage and all the electricity to the amps shorts out. So much for non-stop. It takes ten minutes to get the electricity back working, but then we power on though the rest of the set and the crowd reacts as if there had never been a gap.

Afterwards we sit for a few minutes dripping with sweat in the tiny cockroach-infested dressing room feeling pretty pleased with ourselves. I drink a litre of water then go out to meet the crowd.

Unfortunately we have an early start for the seven hour trip to Barcelona tomorrow. Jonathan told me earlier that to make sure he is fit for the drive he has set himself a curfew of three here tonight, so it's a bit of a shock to find that by the time we're loading the van it's already 2:55, nearly four by the time we finally get to bed. Where did the time go? Madrid steals the night.

## 28th September BARCELONA

As we blearily drive off at 9:30 we notice that the Wurlitzer is *still open*.

We make it to Barcelona with ten minutes to spare before the club's load in curfew of 4:30, then after soundcheck face the long wait to a planned 11:30 stage time. Marky and Mateo head home and I take the Metro with Jonathan up to his place. He stops at a shop on the way and when we get in he cooks up a light dish of omelette with fresh vegetables. We're both exhausted after the last few days and food is now a delicate balancing act between eating just enough to give us the energy to play but not so much that it sends us to sleep.

Jonathan and Suzy take the dog for a walk, then we take the Metro back down to the club. It's my fourth time at the Sidecar and proves to be the best so far. There are more than a hundred people in and they seem to know the words to all the songs, singing along and dancing throughout the whole set. We collapse backstage afterwards, simultaneously elated from the show and saddened that it's the last one of the tour. I drink 1.3 litres of water, then a beer, then top up with another bottle of water.

Jonathan has arranged for someone else to drive the van with the equipment back to the rehearsal room, so all we have to do now is gather at the Barbara Ann for a final beer and look forward to meeting again in two months in Germany for part two. We're ready.

## 2nd October DÜSSELDORF

I'm at the airport with Gaye but we're taking different flights: she's heading to South Germany to organise the hanging of her artworks at a music and art festival called ACUK (Augsburg Calling United Kingdom), I'm going to Düsseldorf to play a private wedding party and do some recording with Vom. After that I'll take the train to Augsburg to meet Gaye and play a couple of gigs at the festival.

I arrive at Vom's place to find he's ill and is going to have to cancel plans to join me at the wedding gig tonight, a shame as we'd been hoping to do a TVOM show. The newly weds are a couple of young punk rockers who come to all my gigs so when I turn up at the party I'm surprised to find it's a formal dinner with everyone dressed in suits. I'm in my normal gig clothes. Resisting appeals to come into the dining room for the meal, I slip out onto the balcony with a few other reprobates and down a few beers. After the dinner there are some traditional German wedding games where female guests are 'auctioned off' to raise money for the bride and groom—pretty dubious if you ask me—and speeches are made and the cake is cut. The evening drags on and I don't get to play until well after midnight, by which time I've been out on the balcony quite a lot. During the gig people finally start to let their hair down, and afterwards there's even a DJ—although there is only one record deck so all he plays is a punk compilation LP—and people start dancing. Finally the party is kicking off, but personally I've been partying for some considerable time already and now it's time to leave.

## 3rd October DÜSSELDORF

Having successfully avoided the wedding party and the potential subsequent visit to his bar last night, Vom is looking fitter than me this morning. Still, I'm not the one that has to play the drums. Actually there are just two songs left from the new album for him to record, and when we get into the studio—actually his rehearsal room with some strategically placed microphones—he gets everything down in a couple of takes and we spend the rest of the day working on percussion.

## 4th October AUGSBURG

It's a five and a half hour train journey to Augsburg. Luckily I booked a seat; every single one is occupied and people are standing in the aisles and corridors. Eventually, going stir crazy, I decide to stretch my legs and go to the buffet car. I ease my way down a couple of crowded carriages, looking down as I go to make sure I'm not treading on anyone's feet, and finally I'm at the counter, where I order a coffee.

'Would you like to drink it here or take it back to your seat?' enquires the guy as he reaches for a cup.

I look around for a table, and see that the entire buffet car is crammed shoulder to shoulder with uniformed *Polizei*. And they're all looking at me.

'I'll take it back to my seat,' I say.

I find my way to the hotel in Augsburg and see Gaye for just ten minutes before I have to leave again for soundcheck. Down in the lobby I find Spizz—he of 'Where's Captain Kirk?' fame—who played a short set after the opening of the art show yesterday and has some work in it himself. Spizz is not known for being a shrinking violet, and I'm not really surprised that here in this rather conservative southern Germany hotel lobby he has on heavy eye make-up and is dressed in full leather stage outfit with hi-vis decorations mostly saying 'SPIZZ,' even though he hasn't actually got a gig today.

Gerhard, who organises the festival picks us up and drives us to the old gasworks complex where it's all taking place. The official venue for the music is right below the old gas container, but Gerhard has appropriated another room where I can hold my fan club gig this evening. It's the *Kühlerhaus*, the old 'Cool Room'—still pretty cold actually—three storeys high and big enough to hold a couple of hundred people. When I get on the stage and try the microphone the sound reverberates around as if I'm in a cathedral.

Not the most intimate setting, and I'm a bit concerned because I'm not expecting a big turnout. All the english fans cried off when they realised how difficult it is to get to Augsburg, leaving just a handful of people likely to attend. Still, soon they start to arrive: Uli, who lives nearby and whose idea it was to try this area, PamP from Garden Gang who'll be playing a solo support slot, René and Mariann from Switzerland, my website manager Klaus with a small group who've travelled all the way from Aachen... It's starting to look like quite a decent crowd. The other venue is even bigger and even colder so nearly everyone coming to the festival has ended up in this room, including the bands. The only problem is, it's nearly time for them to play so now they have to leave, and we are in a situation where approximately fifty people are split between two huge venues.

A small audience in a large room is not really what I originally had in mind for my album launch and annual fan club get-together, but on the positive side I don't feel under too much pressure while performing the new songs. Afterwards it's time to unveil the brand new album at the merch table. I sell three copies and give away six.

Everyone from the main venue has now made their way back to the Kühlerhaus, the bar is still open and the only thing missing is music. Spizz comes to the rescue by plugging in his MP3 player, which by an extraordinary coincidence has a few backing tracks of some of his own songs on it so soon he's up on the stage singing along. Afterwards he sells more merch than me.

## 5th October AUGSBURG

Today it's the official gig in the big room. But first there's time to be a tourist. Gaye, Spizz and I head out in the pouring rain towards the cathedral, arranging to meet up there with fellow Englanders Jowe Head and his band, who will be playing tonight. They were supposed to play yesterday, but there was a mistake in the spelling of the name of one of the band members on the air ticket and Ryanair refused to let him on the flight.

Gerhard picks me and Spizz up from the hotel at 4:30 and drives us over to the festival so I can soundcheck. I ask Spizz if he has a gig today and he says enigmatically, 'not officially.' I would bet any money that he will be on stage by the end of the evening.

I didn't get time to go and check out the main venue yesterday, but walk in now to find it's just as cavernous and cold and unwelcoming as everyone has been telling me. It would make most underground car parks seem cosy. Nevertheless, there's a large stage and PA at one end, Garden Gang have already soundchecked, and Jowe and his band are now up there taking their turn—not the speediest process in the world when one of your band members plays a theramin, a teapot and a saw.

My soundcheck is over quickly, then I head to the dressing room to get a coffee. It's on the first floor in a distant building beyond the *Kühlerhaus*, but worth the effort because there is at least a semblance of warmth up there. Julia, one of the people helping with the festival, is preparing some snacks and laying them out on a long table. Spizz is chatting to her and liberating a few beers from the fridge.

Back at the venue, I set up a merch table against the back wall but no one buys anything. Soon the first band of the evening starts. There is a great sound, a stunningly sophisticated light show—and fifty people in the audience, huddled in their coats. I take the long walk back to the dressing room to grab a beer and have a quick warm up. There's just Julia and her boyfriend up there. 'Where's Spizz?' I ask.

'He said he was tired and was going to go back to the hotel,' she says.

'I was sure he would get on stage later...'

She points at the portable CD player on the table. 'He did plug in to that and sing us his song,' she says. 'He did all the movements and everything.'

I go back to watch Jowe and then Garden Gang, then get on stage myself and am so relieved to finally be warm under the lights that I play for two hours, untroubled by the threat of an oncoming Spizz.


## 6th October AUGSBURG

We all have the day off in Augsburg before our flights home tomorrow and have made the decision to go to the puppet museum. In Spizz's case, via the pub. Gaye and I leave him there while we drink a coffee on the terrace of a café just around the corner, looking across the square to the historic town hall. Spizz soon joins us and orders another beer, then I hear a shout and see Klaus approaching, with a couple of friends in tow. They join us at our table but say they won't be able to come to the puppet museum because they have to start on the long drive back to Aachen. Gaye gets a text to say Jowe and band are on the way and will meet us at the end of the street. We say our goodbyes to Klaus then head off, leaving Spizz to catch up later—he's just going to have one more beer—and almost immediately bump into René and Mariann, who were in a café just around the corner and are coming to the puppet museum too. At the end of the street, Garden Gang arrive, along with Jowe and band, and soon we are joined by Gerhard and his wife Dag who live right nearby, along with a member of Gerhard's band *Generation N*. We have a punk puppet museum posse.

It takes a while to get a posse moving but finally we start on the trail, arriving at the museum to find Spizz already there. He's had a quick look inside and has decided the puppet museum looks pretty much for children—surprise!—so he's going to the Irish pub around the corner instead.

That's where we find him when we've finished our visit. Everyone settles down with a drink for a while but soon the posse is on the move again, heading for a restaurant which claims to serve 'the best pizza in South Germany!' according to Gerhard.

A few more of Gerhard's friends arrive at the restaurant at the same time as us, and we all sit at a long table in a back room. Unfortunately I am seated opposite Gerhard's band companion, who is not only very drunk but also repeatedly taking snuff. He blows his nose loudly and often, and as the brown stain spreads further and further over the handkerchief he is clutching against his face the looks of disgust from those of us on the opposite side of the table increase. I notice Spizz move off and strategically position himself as far away as possible. Another member of Jowe's band arrives and sits at the end of the bench, forcing their guitar player in next to me. 'Oh no,' he says. Across the table the snuff guy finishes noisily blowing his nose yet again and looks up, blood and snuff dripping down across his upper lip. I am rapidly losing my appetite.

The food arrives, and we doggedly try and get it down despite the rising nausea as our friend across the way lets half-chewed pieces of food fall out of his mouth onto his plate as he mumbles away to himself.

So there it was: the best pizza in South Germany with the worst dining companion.

Next stop is a touristy cellar bar with a reputation for a very good local beer, where we sit around a table chatting and getting increasingly raucous until Katherine, the theramin and saw player from Jowe's band, notices that we are getting some black looks from the diners at the other tables. For them, we have become the equivalent of snuff guy. 'The reputation of the British takes another nosedive,' I say.

Katherine and her boyfriend Tim discuss their problems getting on the plane yesterday. They were refused because Tim's name had been booked as 'Brown' instead of 'Bowen'—the old terrorist trick. She mentions that she once tried to take her saw on board in her hand luggage. When Security found it she explained that it was a musical instrument and they just laughed at her.

We're about to order another round of drinks when Gerhard jumps up and says he knows a much better place we should go to. Actually we're all enjoying ourselves here, but he's already heading for the stairs so we gather our coats and follow him. Katherine writes the word 'sorry' on a cardboard coaster and leaves it on the table.

The next bar is indeed a music bar, as Gerhard promised. It is also tiny and currently hosting a performance from an acoustic duo who are possibly the quietest musicians I have ever heard. You could hear a pin drop in the room as we shuffle around the seated audience to the bar, but Gerhard and Spizz seem oblivious to the circumstances and carry on chatting at full volume to the embarrassment of the rest of us. When the duo take a break, I see Spizz heading towards them, eyeing up the stage. 'He wouldn't!' says Katherine.

He would. Five minutes later he's up there playing guitar quite badly on an extended—some would say over-extended—version of one of his songs, with lengthy comedy asides in a style somewhere between Eric Morecambe and Tommy Cooper. I lean over to Tim and say, 'The reputation of the British takes another nosedive.'

To be fair though, the audience are quickly won over by this sudden unexpected burst of energy and humour. Spizz spins out the three minute song with audience participation sections and singalongs and manages to make it last nearly fifteen. Afterwards as the acoustic duo start the second half of their set a reverential hush descends on the room once more, apart from the sound of Spizz loudly blagging free drinks from the bar owner.

Punk rock tour guide prepares us for the puppet museum (Augsburg)

## 7th October AUGSBURG

Before the drive to Munich airport for our flight home, there's just time for a quick trip to the local food market, where Gaye and I buy some *Steinpilze* mushrooms from the Bavarian forest and a wedge of Pecorino cheese laced with truffle, while Spizz and Gerhard take the opportunity for a farewell beer. In the car Spizz sits in the front passenger seat and when we get to the Autobahn presses his hand on Gerhard's leg to try and make him drive faster, then looks round with a cheeky expression at Gaye and I to see if he's managed to successfully wind us up.

On the plane the three of us are seated in the Exit Row, which gives Spizz an ideal opportunity to pretend to fool with the emergency release lever on the door, the kind of joke which could have other passengers screaming with laughter, or in some cases just screaming. 'I'm keeping my eye on you,' says the stewardess. It would be hard not to.

In half an hour he'll probably have found a spare pilot's uniform and a way to plug his MP3 player into the public address system and be running up and down the aisle singing 'Where's Captain Kirk?'

Gaye and me on the plane with the irrepressible Spizz

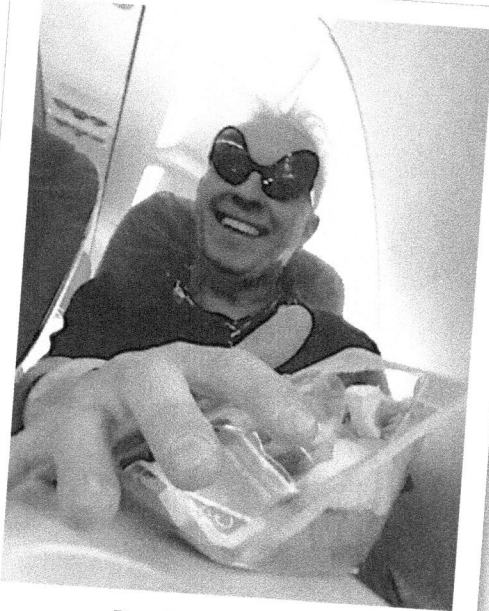

In-flight meal

In-flight feel

# 12th October CANTERBURY

Late leaving the house and only get into Canterbury station at 6:30, the same time soundcheck is planned. I'm slightly held up at the Travelodge, where the receptionist greets me with the news that they've 'had a problem with some of the rooms' and she has had to put me in a very small one on the third floor, no lift, and before I can even say 'I don't mind' she offers me a complimentary breakfast.

On the way to the venue I lose my bearings going under the complicated subway system and emerge to find I no longer know which side of the road I'm on. I'm working on memory anyway as I left the map in the room. I set off in a hopeful direction towards where I think Watling Street is and ask a few people along the way, but none of them know it. There are a bunch of young chavs hanging around outside Tesco Express and when I ask them they don't reply, just give ironic wolf whistles at the way I'm dressed. Further along I ask someone else and he walks on rapidly, shaking his head. Twenty paces on I see a sign that tells me I'm already in Watling Street and twenty paces after that I reach the pub I'm playing, the Three Tuns.

It's an *Olde Worlde* style of pub, with a warren of small rooms with low wooden-beamed ceilings, and when I eventually find the back room where the gig is being held it's soon clear that I needn't have hurried. The room has three levels, stepping up to some french windows at the back, and a band is setting up in front of them. There are cables and equipment all over the place, and people push past the musicians to get to the outside smoking area through the french windows. No one seems to be in charge and it's immediately obvious that there's no point in me attempting a soundcheck so I dump my merch at a table at the lower end of the room and wait to see what happens. Pretty soon I see a couple of guys I know from my Sheerness gigs. Dave is drumming for one of the two support bands and has also had to supply the PA because the people organising the gig had a problem with theirs. He couldn't bring his usual one, he tells me, so he's had to bring this old one and he's not sure if it works. 'I hope you brought your own microphone,' he says.

I did. My secret weapon. As I listen to the muffled feedback-riddled sound from the stage as the band attempt to try a song, this is all I have to cling on to.

At the bar, a guy introduces himself as Karl and tells me his is the person who emailed me and invited me to play this gig, timed to coincide with him and some of his mates celebrating their fiftieth birthdays. Originally I'd told him I was nervous about playing Canterbury because I've had bad turnouts here in the past, but he assures me there will be a good crowd in tonight. 'This is just early doors,' he says, gesturing at the already-crammed bar. 'They'll all be in later.'

I go back to the other room and start setting up my merch, not very confident I'll sell anything tonight but at least it gives me something to do. Actually, quite a few familiar faces come past and say hello, and at one point it occurs to me that there are more people I know here than at my fan club gig last week. The room is quite full by the time the first band play, even more so for the second band, and the only thing worrying me as I get up to the stage area myself is the atrocious sound. 'You might want to try and find out how to take that reverb off the voice,' says the singer from the band who have just finished. That would be a start.

While the other band pack away behind me I grab the only microphone stand that's not broken and plug in my secret weapon. I find the control to take off the reverb, add in some high frequency and take off some mids on the EQ but the vocal sound is still muffled and distorted and I realise that the PA is completely, to use the technical term, knackered, and no amount of twiddling with knobs on the mixing desk will save it. Not that there are many knobs—most of them have broken off. There is a monitor, but it either produces no sound at all or just feedback, so I switch it off and angle the front speakers in so I can hear a bit from them. I'm just trying to get the guitar working when a guy from the support band comes up and asks if he can take the microphone stand—he brought that one himself and needs to pack it away with the rest of their gear. That leaves me with a stand that is broken at every joint and impossible to screw tight, which means it will inevitably swivel away from me mid-song. I attempt to tape up the joints with gaffa tape but don't feel too confident. Well, the sound isn't going to get any better so I guess it's time to start.

Tell it to the people who want to smoke! The trouble with free entry gigs like this is that you get quite a few people who just aren't interested in the music, and during the first song a steady flow of them continue to try and get across the stage area to the smoking area behind, while others come in through the french doors and edge their way past me to get back into the pub. As I sing on, trying to ignore them, the clasp at the top of the microphone stand – the only bit I didn't tape up! – gradually swings down under the weight of the microphone until it is pointing at the floor and I have to bend my knees and sing up into it like a dwarf Lemmy. Luckily my friends Jon and Sophie are in the audience, and after the first song I hear Jon shout, 'Sophie has a Swiss Army knife!'

I get her to pass it up. 'Don't lose it!' she says. 'It's got my car keys attached to it!'

I open up the nearest thing I can find to a screwdriver, then the singer from the support band jumps up the step and holds the stand while I attempt to tighten the clasp. We both look in awe at the screw that is holding the thing together, bearing a head with a mysterious and arcane indentation that no screwdriver known to man could fit. I hand the knife back to Sophie, beaten.

The singer from the support band has now formed an empathetic bond with me, and stands in front of the step to stop the smokers going past, as well as jumping up every time the microphone droops and straightening it up again. Curiously, after a couple of songs, people stop trying to get across the stage and the microphone stops drooping and for the next ninety minutes we all have a very enjoyable gig.

## 13th October CANTERBURY

I'm in the breakfast room having my complimentary breakfast, unfortunately accompanied by News 24 blaring out of the big screen on the wall. There's a report on a Grand Prix race yesterday: Hamilton had a puncture and was forced to retire.

*I thankyew.*

## 15th October LONDON

What happened was: when I played the gig with Tom Robinson at the beginning of July he told me he'd interviewed Neil Gaiman on his radio programme recently, and as well as being complimentary about my records Neil had also said some nice things about my books of tour diaries. I was just preparing to publish the fourth volume of the books and it occurred to me that it would be handy to have a quote from such an eminent author on the cover so I checked out a recording of the programme, picked out a couple of relevant quotes and asked Tom if he could get Neil's permission to use them. Not only did Neil give permission, he also wrote a completely new endorsement, and so did Tom. In the email Neil also had a question for Tom and I: *would you like to be my special musical guests at an event I'm doing on October 15th? I'm reading all of FORTUNATELY, THE MILK, my really silly book for kids (and adults) and it might be fun to get a song or two...I may draft you in to make alien/pirate/vampire/aztec/dinosaur cast noises as well. Interested?*

Of course I said yes, though I was surprised when the song he chose for me to perform at this 'very silly' event was 'The Day We Caught The Big Fish,' one of my most melancholic.

I'm also surprised to turn up at the enormous Westminster Central Hall, fully expecting the reading to be held in a side room, to find out that it is actually taking place in the main hall and is already sold out with an expected audience of two thousand people.

There are quite a few other guests taking part in the evening, including comedians Andrew O'Neill and Lenny Henry. When Neil arrives we all go into a function room and have a read-through of the book, with Neil assigning parts for each of us. I get a few lines as a pirate and a short appearance towards the end as a dancing dwarf shouting 'Oi! Olay!' and 'Pertung!'.

The song goes better than I could have expected. It's an overwhelming feeling standing on stage with the warm applause of two thousand people washing over you, on and on and on.

Not so sure about the dancing dwarf bit though.

## 17th October TALLINN—18th October PETROZAVODSK

I've been looking forward to and dreading this trip to Estonia and Russia in equal parts since it was first proposed, but recently the dread has been getting the upper hand. I know other bands who have played low budget gigs in Russia and they've come back with nightmare stories of vast distances and no sleep, so when promoter Denis first approached me I told him I wasn't worried about making money, all I wanted him to guarantee was somewhere private to sleep each night. I finally received a schedule from him yesterday and it's not looking quite that way. Straight after the first gig in Tallinn we have to leave for the next one which is way up to the north of Russia in a town called Petrozavodsk. The following day in St Petersburg we leave after the show to take a nine hour night train to Moscow. One of the reasons this information is so late in coming is that Denis has been desperately trying to find a van for the tour. I'll be playing the gigs with my friends Punk Lurex from Finland and the plan had been that we would travel in two cars, but over the last couple of days both of them, according to the email, '*get crashed in accidents.*'

Both of them.

Then there's the political situation in Russia: Pussy Riot and Greenpeace activists thrown in prison, recent anti-gay legislation, neo-Nazis on the street. Things can change of course, but I'm already thinking, *never again*, and I haven't even left yet.

Denis and the local Estonian promoter Mart meet me at Tallinn airport and drive me into the town centre. We park in an underground car park which has the restored remains of the city's mediaeval walls in it, pushing it immediately to the top of my 'Historically Significant Car Parks' list. (It's not a very long list)

The club is ten minutes away, and as we walk there—my 23 kilo suitcase full of CDs bumping heavily over the cobbles behind me—Mart points out various buildings of interest. One from the Soviet era was allocated by the state for members of the Writers' Union, but thanks to its central location is now a highly sought-after apartment block that ironically only the rich can afford. There's still a bookshop on the ground floor. A quaint building on the corner of the main square is a fifteenth century apothecary, the oldest still-operating commercial enterprise in Tallinn. Up on the hill stands what was once the second-tallest church in Russia.

Punk Lurex are on stage in the middle of soundcheck when we arrive in the club. It's great to see them again, and even better to know that whatever happens over the next few days I will at least be traveling with friends. After soundcheck is done they suggest we have a walk around the town and find a bar, but just then Mart introduces me to a journalist who is keen to interview me and by the time we've done that Punk Lurex have gone. I think about going out to find them but Denis points out that I could get something vegetarian to eat here, and as I don't know what the food situation will be like in the coming days I have a look at the menu and choose a vegetable burger. The vegetable turns out to be potato.

The guy who did the interview sits at the table with me and carries on asking questions while I eat. Either he has his tape recorder still running or he's just very interested. Afterwards I say I'm going for a walk and he says he'll come with me, he knows a bar I should see. A couple of other guys say they are coming too. The journalist tells me that they are established figures on the Tallinn punk scene. One of them is called Villu, and is in a band called JMKE who will be supporting tonight. He's about the same age as me and chats with me knowledgeably about UK punk rock. The other guy joining us is called Lauri, has a band called Psychoterror and look quite psycho himself. He keeps staring at me and it's very unsettling. After a while I can't take it any more. 'Please stop staring at me,' I tell him.

'Sorry! Sorry! So sorry!' he says, then starts staring at me again.

Most of the bars in Tallinn have been smartened up and gentrified for the tourist trade, but the one we are going to is for the workers and has remained unchanged since Soviet times. The same clientele come every night, the journalist tells me, although a few tourists drop in to have a look.

We walk in to to find a small shabby room, bottles piled up haphazardly on shelves, people seated on stools around the U-shaped bar, some slumped with their heads down on it, others sitting staring into the distance, most with bottles of vodka in front of them.

There's just enough space to edge around the stools to find somewhere to sit at the far end of the room. On the wide window ledge an accordion and violin lay abandoned, and the journalist points out the two musicians who will usually strike up a song for a few rubles. We find stools next to a smartly-dressed couple who are sharing a bottle of champagne, a rather blatant display of wealth in such a downbeat place—obviously the token tourists.

Meanwhile some of the regular customers have roused to shout rowdy greetings at the two guys who came in with us, and some lurch over to shake their hands. At least it distracts that guy from staring at me. We order a beer and then it occurs to me that Punk Lurex might enjoy this place too, so I send a text to their singer Tiina to see if they are nearby.

I may have made a miscalculation about the couple next to me. The woman strikes up a conversation and it turns out she is Finnish and her husband is Spanish. They come to this bar every time they visit Tallinn and love the ambience here, particularly when the musicians play. Last time they were here, a couple of years ago, there were tangos all evening and the customers were up and dancing around the bar. The reason there is no music tonight, she confides, is that a very rich guy came in and said he would buy everybody in the bar a drink if the musicians *didn't* play. A strange request, but it seems he wanted all the attention to be focused on him.

'Did you get him to buy that?' I ask, pointing at the champagne, and she laughs and nods. She drains the last glass then orders a beer. We talk a bit more and it turns out she lives in London, walking distance from my home.

Just then Tiina rings back and asks where the bar is. 'I'm not sure,' I tell her, 'It's not far from the club though. Oh, hang on—I'll put you on to someone who can explain...'

I hand the phone to the woman next to me.

So, just to recap: I am in Estonia for the first time in my life and have sat next to someone who happens to almost be my neighbour in London but comes from Finland and is currently speaking in Finnish to one of the Finnish band who I am on tour with.

One of the songs I recorded with Punk Lurex when we first met was called 'The World Just Got Smaller.'

Back at the club the first of the two supports is playing, a young raucous three piece, and after that the red-haired guy who came to the bar with me gets on stage with his band. The audience seem to know all their songs and sing along with most of them. When they finish quite a few people leave, and by the time Punk Lurex begin there are only about half as many in the club as there were earlier, a sparse forty or fifty at a guess. The club is quite small though, so it doesn't look too bad and their performance goes down well. A few more people have drifted away by the time I get on at midnight but those who have remained gather at the front and give me lots of encouragement, even more so when Punk Lurex join me at the end for the four songs we play together. All the same, it's a bit of a disappointment for my first-ever gig in Estonia, and hanging over us all is the thought that after this we'll be getting straight in the van and driving to Russia.

I sell a few CDs from the stage and chat with a few people while the band pack away their gear around me. I commiserate with Mart about the low turnout but he says it's hard to get people out in Tallinn, particularly midweek. It could be worse though: he introduces me to someone who puts on festivals in Estonia. Two years ago, he tells me, he promoted one that had a couple of international bands playing in a big tent, but hardly anyone came and he lost six thousand euros. He's still paying it off now. 'It really hit me at the end of the night,' he tells me, 'when I was left cleaning out the festival toilets on my own in the dark, up to my elbows in shit.'

Not to be defeated, he tried again last year. The festival didn't lose money this time, but while they were packing up at the end some people stole the tent.

While I'm putting all the unsold CDs back into my suitcase a girl comes up with a few friends and says, 'What are your plans for the night? Will you be partying? Or are you hungry? I know a place where they have a great meat pie!'

Tempting as that sounds, upstairs our driver Alexei is waiting with the van. It has started to rain. Punk Lurex and I put our gear and bags in the back as fast as we can, trying not to get drenched, and we set off for what I already know will be the longest and worst drive of my life.

It starts off quite well: while Denis and Alexei chat in Russian in the front, a bottle is passed around the musicians in the back and we have a few laughs. But soon the mind-numbing effect of the road starts to take over, silence settles over us, and over the following hours the only sound is the rumble of the wheels. We make occasional roadside stops as the alcohol works its way through, some of us slump into disrupted sleep. By the time we get to the queue for the Russian border at around five in the morning the laughs are a long way behind us.

Ahead we see the stark lights of the border post. We edge along, moving forward a few metres then stopping again for an interminable time while documents are checked on the vehicles at the front of the queue. Drummer Marcus sighs and looks at the low wall running along the edge of the pavement beside us.

'Is that the Volga behind there?' he says, reaching for the door. 'I'm going to go and have a smoke and piss in the Volga!'

A few minutes later he is back. 'It wasn't the Volga. It was a tennis court.'

Finally we reach the first check point. We show our passports, then a uniformed figure comes around the van and opens the sliding door, shining torches in our faces. The border guard hands out some immigration forms for us all to fill in, tiny scraps of paper with the questions so small that they are illegible. We pass around torches, pens and reading glasses and attempt to fill them out. Then we have to get out in the freezing temperatures and queue up at a cabin where our passports are checked again, and then we are made to fill out the immigration forms again because we haven't done it correctly. We get back into the van and drive on a short distance where our passports and immigration forms are checked, and then just to be on the safe side they are checked once more as we finally cross the border.

Welcome to Russia.

We stop at the first rest station to fuel up with coffee and food, but the coffee machine is out of order and there is no vegetarian food—though the carnivores might like to consider a pack of dried horse meat chews. Alexei looks at his watch. 'We should go,' he says. 'We still have another six hundred kilometres.'

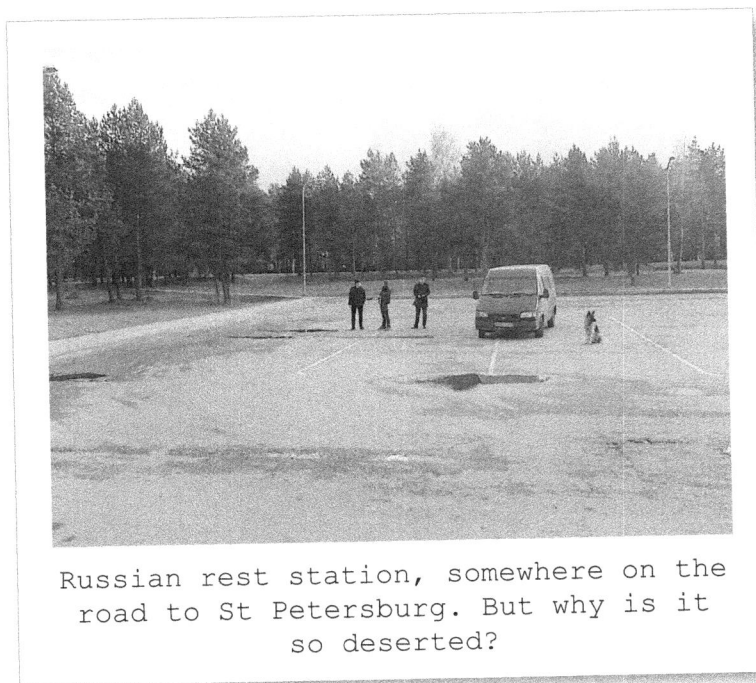

Russian rest station, somewhere on the road to St Petersburg. But why is it so deserted?

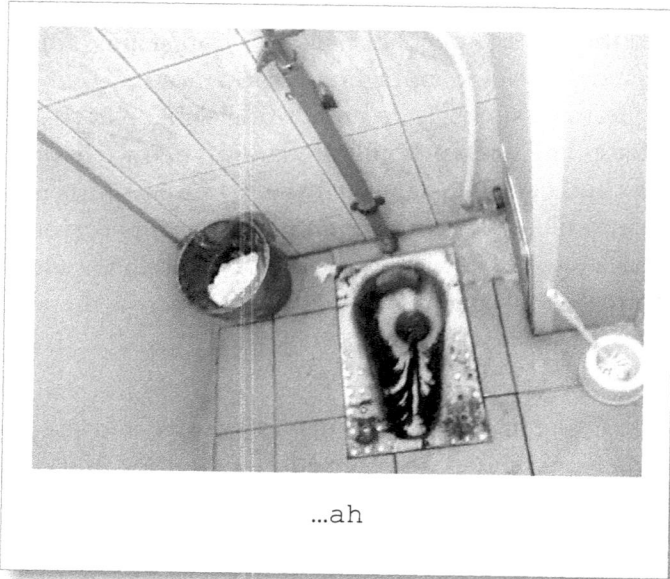

...ah

It's seven in the morning, we've been driving since two and we haven't even covered a third of the journey. And now we hit the Russian roads: pot-holed two lane highways where cars continually edge out to overtake the slow-moving lorries, swinging back in at the last minute as oncoming traffic approaches. The sky is gradually becoming light, revealing a drab brown landscape of scrub and trees. There is continual drizzle and the wipers slap away across the cracked windscreen of the van.

Nothing much changes over the next ten hours. The only thing of interest is when we get pulled over by the police—*Siberia here we come!*—but it's only for a minor driving infringement, and and after a nervous wait they let Alexei off with a warning. The only town of any size we pass is Saint Petersburg—where in a startling display of bad routing we'll play tomorrow—and after that the roads get even more bumpy and the landscape even more desolate. By the time we reach the outskirts of Petrozavodsk in the early evening we are cheering every miserable run-down roadside shack as a sign of approaching civilisation.

Tired and bedraggled, we troop downstairs into the club hauling our suitcases and instruments. We say hello to the people behind the bar and they look sullenly at us and don't reply. I go back upstairs to the single toilet and do my best to have a shave and clean my teeth in the tiny sink there. When I get back downstairs Punk Lurex guitarist Passi says, 'Don't forget that in Russia you should clean your teeth using bottled water.'

Too late.

After soundcheck a meal is brought in, the first thing we have eaten since a small pastry with a dollop of egg mayonnaise in it at a mid-morning rest stop. There's a bowl of salad, and another bowl with some over-cooked rice and a few vegetables in it. We're all starving and wolf it down, but—well, put it this way: no one is taking photos of their meals.

I hadn't dared to ask about sleeping arrangements for tonight, fearing the inevitable disappointment, but now Denis reveals that everyone else will be sleeping at a friend's house, but I really do have a hostel room as promised. After we've finished the food I am driven over there to check in. It's a perfectly decent room, warm and clean, and the bathroom has even got toilet paper—the first I've seen since I got to Russia. The emergency Wet Wipes I bought in Hammersmith before I left home can go back into my bag for one night.

Bed and shower both look incredibly tempting after nearly twenty-four hours awake and unwashed but Denis and Alexei are waiting downstairs for me so I just have time to drop my luggage and leave. There is now a freezing gale blowing outside, and even wearing my two T-shirts and two coats it seems like a trans-Arctic expedition battling the short distance from the van to the club, and a relief to be back indoors.

I order a beer from the bar and the girl serving looks like she would like to kill me when she realises I don't speak Russian. She snatches the receipt from the till and points angrily at the price: 120 rubles, which I dutifully hand over. Then the pump needs changing and I have to hang around for ten minutes until the beer arrives, while the barmaid scowls at me the entire time. Back in the dressing room, Punk Lurex guitarist Kukka tells me she refused to serve him at all.

There aren't many people in by the time the support band plays. I watch them for a while but then my glass is empty again so I carefully count out 120 rubles and go to the bar where I eventually catch the attention of the same barmaid who served me earlier. She pours the beer and I hand over the money. She says something in Russian and stabs her finger at the receipt. 80 rubles. How embarrassing. Only a stupid Englishman would think that if you go back to the same bar and buy the same beer it would be the same price.

Even though the attendance is low, the gig is good for both Punk Lurex and myself. The people all stand at the front and some even sing along even though they clearly don't know the songs. I've only played for about half an hour when I notice Denis sidle up to the stage and surreptitiously give me the 'two more songs' signal. It seems a long way to come for such a short set but I wind up anyway and invite Punk Lurex to join me for the ten minutes we play together. We're all so tired that there are a few mistakes, but no one seems to notice. There's even an attempt at stage diving and one audience member is carried off on the shoulders of his friends, not that easy as it's rather a low ceiling.

Tiina and I set up a merchandising table at the side of the stage and at the advice of the promoter offer our CDs and vinyl for much less than usual, almost cost price, but still no one buys anything. One girl comes up and points at one of the Punk Lurex albums and says to Tiina, 'Are these free?'

As we pack away, Tiina and I grumble about the situation: we've both got bags weighed down with merchandise and had hoped to offload some of it by now to at least make getting around a bit easier, but sales have been miserable. We're both looking forward to the next two days, when we'll get to the big cities and things are sure to improve.

At around midnight people start to stream in and the place turns into a karaoke bar. Somewhat incongruously after a night of punk, as I leave there is a girl on stage singing 'All That Jazz'. It's after two by the time I'm dropped off at my hostel and Denis says they'll come and pick me up at ten. That's a potential seven hours of sleep ahead of me—an average of three and a half per night over the last two days—but in fact I lie in bed for a while wide awake, worrying about tomorrow: a minimum six hour drive, a late gig, then the night train to Moscow, presumably another night without sleep...

I'm losing sleep about losing sleep.

## 19th October ST PETERSBURG—20th October MOSCOW

O travel sink plug from Exeter, I call upon your services again.

Denis and Alexei are waiting for me downstairs at ten along with the promoter from last night, and there's just time to get a coffee from the machine before we leave. The writing on the buttons for the different types of coffee is all in the Russian Cyrillic alphabet so Denis goes through them with me. When we get to the ones for Expresso and Americano, Alexei mentions that those two are actually the other way around as he pressed the one for Americano yesterday and ended up with an Expresso. I was thinking of having an Americano so I press the button for an Expresso, but end up with an Expresso, which I realise as I drink it was what I actually wanted.

We all squeeze into the van with Punk Lurex and drive to a modern pizza place for breakfast. Pizza isn't usually my idea of breakfast but after the lack of food recently I'll take what I can get. We sit under a poster of The Beatles on the Abbey Road zebra crossing, and Denis orders a giant size pizza for us all to share. There's a long wait. At one point the waitress comes and hand out some plates and I pick up mine and pretend to take a bite. 'Russian pizza!' laughs the promoter.

When the real Russian pizza eventually comes it is so large that—I was wrong about this yesterday—some of the band actually do take photos of it. It's also extremely thin and seems to have been steamed rather than baked. Despite the size of it, between the nine of us it's soon gone without really troubling our hunger.

Then we say goodbye to the promoter and get in the van, still in good time to be in Saint Petersburg for soundcheck at five.

Or so it seems. The first four hundred kilometres are much the same story as yesterday: the dull featureless landscape swishes past, the drizzle and wet snow falls, oncoming cars linger on our side of the road as they overtake then dart into impossibly tight spaces at the last minute. We take one rest stop at a roadside café where the only vegetarian food available is some small pastries filled with a stuffing of either apple or cabbage. I'm not sure which one I got. It's not the kind of meal you want to take a photo of, though I do take a photo of the toilet—stomach-churningly filthy. We drive on and on, and there are just forty kilometres to go when we see the red tail lights of the traffic ahead at a standstill.

The sun sets, the skies darken, people get out of their cars and smoke cigarettes. Metre by metre we edge forward, the arrow representing our position on the Sat-nav unmoving. Nobody knows what is going on or how long it will last. For the first time since the start of this epic journey Alexei begins to look tense. He reaches for a wooden frog on the dashboard, removes the stick it holds in its mouth and gently rolls it across its ridged back, producing a gentle ululation. *Urrurrurru.* My mind goes into neutral, my legs and stomach begin to cramp. *Urrurrurru.* I put my hood up to protect myself from the cold and to hide from the world as my spirits plummet. After the stress and lack of sleep and food over the last few days this feels like some kind of torture. When I get home people will ask, *what did you think of Russia?*—and I will tell them the truth: I don't know. All I saw was the road.

*Urrurrurru.*

Over the course of the following hours I have some very black thoughts. Punk Lurex talk amongst themselves in Finnish, Denis and Alexei in Russian, and I sink deeper into my bubble of despair and feel my life draining away. Time for soundcheck passes, time for the club to open passes, time to get a meal passes, time for the first of the two support bands to be on stage passes. I've been told that St Petersburg is one of the most beautiful cities in Russia. I'll never find out if it's true.

Four hours after we first reached the queue we have moved just three kilometres. Finally the problem comes into view: the road has been partly closed for resurfacing. We edge our way through among all the other cars jostling for the one available lane, and then the way ahead is clear and there is a half hour drive left to Saint Petersburg.

It's just after eight in the evening and it looks as if we will still make it in time to play.

Close to nine, we pull up on a deserted city street and Denis and Alexei get out. Further up the street I see a few people drinking beer on the doorstep of a nondescript building. They see us and I hear a shout, 'TV! TV!' followed by a drunken cheer. I pull my hood tighter over my head. Soon they are upon us.

I do my best to look sane. One of the guys says, 'You remember, we met in Puntala festival in Finland last year, I asked you to come and play in Russia.'

I do remember. I remember smiling and nodding and thinking, *never.*

But here I am. The guys help carry the instruments and the equipment and suitcases and bags and lead us into the *Zhopa* club. We head up to the stairs to a crowded room on the first floor, where a band are just getting on stage.

The guy I met in Finland says, 'this way,' and leads me through a side room with a table-tennis table set up in it and through to the dressing room, which is packed with people, coats, bags and equipment. Everyone is smoking. The guy pushes his way through the people and throws some bags off an old armchair in the corner. 'TV, please, this for you!'

It's a generous gesture but I am stressed and confused and have to urgently change strings on my guitar—I haven't had time to do that over the last two days and if I don't do it now there are sure to be multiple breakages on stage tonight, the last thing I want when the clock is ticking. Hanging over my head is the knowledge that we have pre-booked tickets for the night train to Moscow and have to leave straight after the show. I carry my guitar out to an empty area next to the table-tennis table and set it down, then kneel on the floor and start changing strings. Out of the corner of my eye I notice someone take my photo and I try and keep my temper. Usually I don't mind but right now I feel like I'm in the fucking zoo.

Timings have been delayed because of our late arrival and the second of the two supports are only now hitting the stage. I go into the main room to check them out and get a beer. The place is now shoulder-to-shoulder with people. Quite a few come up and ask me to sign photocopies they've made of the *St Petersburg Times*, which I did an interview for last week, and which I now see fills an entire page along with a big photo, which probably accounts for the good turnout. I spent three hours on the phone to various journalists that afternoon so I'm glad to see at least one of the interviews made it to print. I only wish I had time to relax and chat with some of the people who are asking for autographs. Instead I duck back into the dressing room where Punk Lurex are trying to get their gear organised for their imminent gig, desperately trying to find space among the other people here. Just as they leave the room for the stage Denis arrives with two pizza boxes. He gestures towards me but I wave him away. My stomach is gnawing with hunger but there is no way I can eat now, so close to show time. I follow the band into the other room, where the guy from Puntala finds me again and gets chatting as Punk Lurex plug in. 'TV, are you going to play seriously tonight?'

I look at him questioningly. 'Am I going to play seriously?'

I expect I will. I usually do.

'Yes. Will you play seriously? No...not seriously. I mean, probably. Will you play *'Probably'* tonight? It's my favourite song!'

I tell him I'll try, but I'm worried about how much time I will have on stage. It's already 10:30 and our train leaves in just over two hours.

The first song from Punk Lurex goes down brilliantly but I am so tense that I can't really enjoy the show, and go into the side room to gather my thoughts. After a few minutes Denis passes and I call him over. Timing is going to be down to the minute if we are going to catch the train so I need to know the exact time I have to finish my solo set and get Punk Lurex back up for the final ten minutes.

Denis thinks it over. 'Station is not far, just fifteen hundred metres. Alexei will drive. I think, you must finish 11:40.'

I look at my watch. It's 10:55.

'You mean my solo set, or the whole thing?'

'Everything finish at 11:40.'

'But that's ridiculous. I'll hardly get any time to play at all…'

'If you go onstage at eleven and play for half hour, then with Punk Lurex, finish 11:40.'

I look at my watch again. 'But I won't GET on stage at eleven will I? It's nearly eleven now and Punk Lurex are still on. I'll get on stage at the earliest at 11:15, then I'll have FIFTEEN MINUTES…!'

Suddenly I can't take it any more.

'Denis, what is the point of me coming all the way to here, not getting any sleep, driving for two days, not getting to see anything of the cities we're playing, doing three hours of interviews in England, getting a full page in the local paper so people pay their money to come and see me…and then PLAYING FIFTEEN FUCKING MINUTES! WHAT IS THE FUCKING POINT?'

I take a deep breath and check my watch again.

'How about this. Punk Lurex are just finishing now. I'll go on stage as soon as they come off, let's say 11:20. I'll play for thirty minutes, get them on just before twelve, we're offstage by 12:10. As soon as it's over we pack up straight away, no hanging around drinking or selling merch—just pack up and leave. We're at the station by 12:30 latest. Ten minutes clear to get to the train.'

It just might work.

I rocket through the gig, then get Punk Lurex on, and the crowd love it. They are the biggest and most excitable audience of the whole tour and there's nothing I'd like to do more now than hang around with them for a while and drink a few beers, maybe even offload some of my merch. Instead, still dripping with sweat, the band and I pack up our things at lightning speed and get our street clothes on over the top of our still-wet stage ones.

We run out of the club and throw our stuff in the back of the van. One of the promoters gives me a hurried handshake and says, 'The club name *Zhopa* means *Arse* so now you can say you have played in the arse of Russia!'

We slam the van doors shut with still twenty minutes to go and every chance we will catch our train. We speed off through the deserted streets but five hundred metres down the road the police wave us down and gesture at us to turn the van around and park. We all let out a groan, then sit in the back in disbelief while Alexei gets out to explain the situation.

'If you have tickets, police allowed to let you go...' says Denis quietly.

A couple of minutes later Alexei is back, jumps into the driver's seat and starts the engine.

'They could at least have given us an escort,' I mutter.

We park in front of the station and grab our things out of the back, hurriedly thank Alexei and run for the nearest entrance, only to find the gate across it is locked. Denis curses and points us to an alternative way in. We rush after him and hurry into the vast atrium of the station, ignoring the X-ray machines that we are supposed to put our luggage through. Denis shouts a query at one of the station staff, who waves us towards a platform where a train is waiting, the guards just closing the doors. It is 12:39.

We throw our luggage and instruments into the very last carriage, jump on board, the door slams behind us and the train moves off.

I look up and see a long narrow corridor. On one side are cramped sleeping compartments, every space full; on the other side a single row of tables and chairs, also with every place occupied. Our compartment is somewhere further up the train and we still have to get there. Denis moves ahead and Punk Lurex follow, hauling their gear with them. I have my guitar and shoulder bag, and the roller suitcase, unfortunately still full of CDs and weighing twenty kilos. I roll it as best as I can but have to keep lifting it because it's almost exactly the same width as the gangway and I can't get it past the bags that have been left there, or the legs and feet which people hang out from their bunks and chairs and stubbornly refuse to get out of the way as I try to squeeze past. I still have my heavy coat on from the journey here, and beneath it I am overheating and still dripping with sweat from the concert. I can't take the coat off because I have no hands free to carry it. I struggle to keep up with the rest of my party, every now and then stopping to distribute the weight of the luggage, apologising to other passengers as my suitcase wheels runs over their feet or as I accidentally elbow them while trying to lift the case over some new obstacle. Five long carriages in I feel like I want to end it all right now. Suddenly I come across the rest of the band. Tiina explains that the next carriage is locked and it looks like we won't be able to get to the sleeping compartment we have booked, but Denis is in discussion with one of the guards and eventually a key is produced and we are allowed through. Now it seems we are in the next class up because the sleeping areas are slightly more spacious, with just the corridor running down the side of the carriage, no tables and chairs in my way. There's even a thin rug on the floor, but that proves to be a bad thing as the wheels of my suitcase ruck it up as I roll along and soon I am dragging the entire length of the rug behind me and the only option is to carry the suitcase all the time. All around us people are preparing for bed, and they dart suddenly out of their compartments carrying towels or nightclothes, and give me dirty looks as they crash into me, struggling along and blocking the whole corridor. The band draw ahead again as we trudge up the next ten carriages—*how long is this train?!*—and as I step through the end door of one carriage my shoulder bag snags on the handle and drops down my arm, forcing me to drop the suitcase which lands with a crash.

'FUCK! SHIT!'

I weep tears of frustration, and give it a hefty boot, then I drop the guitar and kick that across the corridor too. I tear off my coat and throw it on the floor, defeated. I see some of Punk Lurex looking back worriedly from the compartment ahead. A couple of guys smoking cigarettes in the area between the two compartments step over and speak calm Russian words and pick up my things from the floor and gently hand them to me. I take a deep breath and trudge onwards.

Many carriages later I come across the band and Denis waiting outside the two sleeping compartments that have been assigned to us. The good news: they are the type of compartments that have doors, unlike the open ones in the first part of the train. The bad news: the two narrow bunk beds in each compartment are tightly packed together, and though we had been promised two compartments for the six us, leaving a couple of spare beds so we don't have to be too crowded, mysteriously two people are occupying the spare beds in one of the compartments so every space will be full.

I have to have THE TALK with Denis. The only time we've really communicated since I first arrived was when I shouted at him earlier and now I can't go on with this tour unless I know why it's happening the way it's happening. Why haven't I had places to sleep when it's the only thing I asked for? Why these insane drives? Why am I not getting to play a full set? Why hasn't he even kept his promise about little things like the spare beds on the train? We go out into the corridor between the carriages and discuss it over the clank and grind of the wheels beneath and the screech of the wind rushing past outside.

'Tim, I am sorry. You have to understand, nobody knows you here. I tried to get the interviews so that people would know who you are. I put on famous bands at the gigs so people would come. Normally they would be the headliners, but they all wanted you to come and they agreed to play for nothing. We had two cars crash before the tour and I had to pay for another one and driver. The drive to Petrozavodsk was a mistake. I didn't know the Tallinn gig would be so late, I thought you could have some rest in hostel first. I am sorry for that. And the traffic today, the other bands had to go on late. And I am sorry I only sent you details two days ago. I had troubles at work, I have to do construction work and shitty jobs, I just get eight hundred euros a month. I will lose money on this tour but I don't care about the money. I do it because I would die without music. But when two fans offered to buy the spare beds in the compartments from me I accepted so we don't lose so much money.'

I tell him I understand. We shake hands and the tension between us is over.

Well, at least someone's happy
(Night train to Moscow with Punk Lurex)

Back in the compartment, Punk Lurex are trying to squeeze their bags and instruments into any spare space they can find. Someone has brought one of the pizza boxes from the backstage. 'I had to hide it under the jackets in the club,' says Tiina. 'One of the drunk girls in the dressing room was trying to take it.'

We sit on the bottom beds around the narrow table and I eat two slices of cold pizza. It tastes like the best pizza in the world.

Then we head down to the restaurant car and squeeze onto high-backed wooden benches around another narrow table and have a few beers. We talk over everything that has happened in the tour so far and finally unwind a little and have a few laughs. I'm aware that we're all going through the same thing and I'm the only one to have lost his temper. I apologise for my bad behaviour earlier and explain that I just couldn't take it any more. For the first time since the 1980's there were moments today when I felt like giving up.

'I have *never* in my life kicked my guitar case before,' I say. 'I was so angry that I would have thrown it out of the window and be finished with it.'

'But the window wouldn't open,' says Pasi.

'No,' I admit.

Pasi smiles and says, 'Huzzah!'

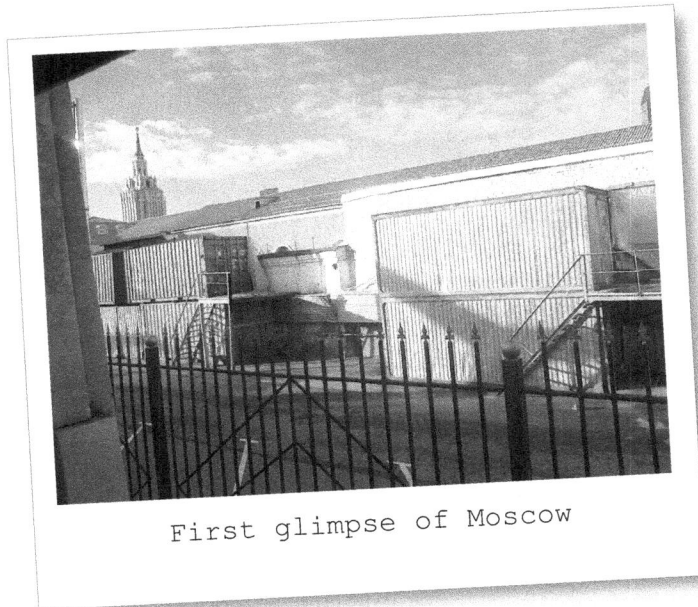

First glimpse of Moscow

Marcus points out that he is still in his stage shorts as he didn't have time to change after the gig. 'I was walking through Moscow in the middle of the night, in October. *In my shorts!'*

The restaurant car closes at three and there's nothing left to do but go back to the compartment and try and sleep through the next six hours until we get to Moscow.

The most you can do is doze, really. The train lurches and shudders, slows to a grinding halt, rattles and screeches. It feels like an earthquake from where I am up on one of the top bunks, and I hear the others tossing and turning restlessly around me too. After fitfully falling in and out of sleep for what seems like forever there's a knock on the door and a woman's voice announces something in Russian that must mean we're approaching Moscow. A glance at my clock confirms it.

We stumble out onto the platform blinking in the sunshine and I look back to see just how astonishingly long the train actually is. As we make our way to the end of the platform we pass what is obviously another band in a huddle with their bags and instruments and give each other a weary nod of solidarity.

The longest train in the world

Outside the station there are two cars waiting to pick us up. Punk Lurex have no accommodation tonight as they will be taking the night train back to St Petersburg after the gig and Alexei will drive them back to Finland from there. They are now to be taken straight to the club where there is a shower and something to eat for them. I'll be flying home tomorrow and have a hotel for tonight, and Denis has arranged for a couple of his friends to take me over there so I can freshen up and sleep if I want. I would dearly like to sleep, but this is my first few hours free since the tour started, and I can't miss the opportunity to have a look around Moscow. It's now nearly eleven in the morning so Punk Lurex and I agree to meet up again in an hour or so and take a trip to Red Square.

The couple driving me introduce themselves as Constantine and Katya, and take me over to their car while Denis goes over a few details with the other driver. Once I'm seated in the back, Constantine asks me how the trip so far has been.

'Awful,' I say. I explain about the lack of sleep and the long drives. 'Being vegetarian doesn't help,' I add.

'We are vegetarian too,' he says. 'Are you hungry?'

When Denis gets in the car they all discuss where to go for breakfast and we drive a short distance to a large dimly-lit cellar restaurant where we are the only customers. Denis hands me the menu, which thankfully has an English translation, and although there aren't a lot of vegetarian options I'm quite satisfied with the idea of an omelette with mushroom and tomatoes. The meal does however take quite some time to arrive, and I start to think that the waitress must be out the back somewhere begging the hen to lay. Meanwhile, a toasted sandwich arrives, which Constantine and Katya share. I see they are having some sort of issue with it, and after a while they call over the waitress and have a short discussion. The waitress takes the plate away, and a few minutes later brings it back and there is another discussion. When she has gone I ask what the problem was. Was the food cold or something?

'No,' says Katya. 'We thought there might be some ham in it. But she went and asked in the kitchen and they say it is only smoked cheese.'

Ah, how encouraging—the same old problems faced by vegetarians worldwide. The classic UMM that turns out to be a USCM.

Some years later my omelette arrives and is very tasty. Afterwards I feel quite revived from the stresses of the last couple of days and ready to enjoy a look around Moscow. I am aware that because of the long wait for the food it's already around the time I should be meeting Punk Lurex but there is no way I can continue the day without getting out of the clothes I was wearing on stage yesterday and all night and getting under the shower.

The hotel is out in the suburbs, just a ten minute drive on a Sunday when traffic is light. In the hotel lobby I hand over my passport to the surly woman behind the desk and she glances at it and says something to Denis. He turns to me. 'Tim, they need your immigration form.'

The immigration form? 'It was in the passport,' I say. 'The last time I saw it was when I gave it in to the hotel in Petrozavodsk. They must have kept it...'

It couldn't have fallen out of my pocket without me noticing. It just *couldn't* have. Or could it?

I go through all my pockets just in case, and with two winter coats on that's a lot of pockets. When nothing turns up I open my suitcase and take everything out item by item, scouring every possible place that could hide a tiny thin scrap of paper that has suddenly taken on an enormous significance.

Denis looks thoughtful. 'This is a problem. They won't let you in to the hotel without the immigration form. The other thing is, you need it at the airport tomorrow to leave the country.'

Suddenly I have to sit down.

Denis has another conversation with the woman at the desk and comes back to report. 'The hotel in Petrozavodsk will have made copy of the form when you checked in, so maybe they can fax it here. You might have to pay a fine at the airport, but a copy should be enough.'

'How long will it take to fax it over?'

'They think, around two hours.'

Goodbye shower. Goodbye walk around Moscow. But maybe...*maybe*...I will still get out of the country tomorrow.

The hands of the clock above the Reception desk sweep on and it occurs to me that I should just check the tool pocket inside my guitar case. I can't see any way the immigration form could have got in there, but I'm desperate now, and anyway it's been playing on my mind that I should check that I didn't break my guitar yesterday when I kicked it across the corridor in the train. I open up and am happy to see the guitar is in one piece, but when I check the tool pocket there's no immigration form. There is also no tuner or string winder which, I realise with still-further-sinking heart, I left on stage yesterday in the rush to pack up.

After about an hour Denis receives a phone call. He has a long talk with someone, then relays the conversation to me. 'It seems they have problem with fax machine in hotel in Petrozavodsk and can't send copy. They will keep trying, but if it doesn't work they will have to send from post office. Post office closed on Sunday so must do it tomorrow morning.'

'That's risky. I have to be at the airport at twelve.'

'Hmm, maybe we will have to go to embassy tomorrow to get you new form.'

'What time would we have to be there?'

Denis shakes his head worriedly. 'Traffic on Monday morning very bad…I think we just hope copy arrives.'

I think it over. 'Look, why don't we just go to the club. I can get a shower there and then there might still be time to have a look around the city before soundcheck. If the fax arrives in the meantime we can come straight back here.' I still haven't broached the subject of where I will sleep tonight if it doesn't come, or how I will get out of the country tomorrow.

Denis nods. He has a word with the woman behind the desk and she hands back the passport. I take it from her and open it…and there on the first page it falls open at is the immigration form. She didn't even check.

At least she has the decency to look embarrassed.

Upstairs, almost hysterical with relief, I have a lightning-quick shower and pack a small bag of merch for the gig tonight. I get in the car with the others and head back to the Plan B club, where Punk Lurex are waiting outside. They've now been hanging around for quite a few hours. They had a shower in the club but there were no towels and they ended up having to use their dirty clothes to dry themselves with.

We all head to the subway. There are still two hours left before soundcheck and the possibility to finally do one tourist thing. We emerge from the cathedral-like underground station and troop towards Red Square, stopping briefly to peruse the souvenirs stalls. Constantine and Katya buy a little Russian doll and present it to me to remember them by. It may sound stupid, but a little thing like that means a lot to me and when I get home it's going up on the shelf in the shed next to the origami bird.

Red Square turns out to be just as stunning as expected. As I look around in awe I realise that I am finally starting to enjoy myself. We have a plan to get some group photos in front of St Basil's cathedral at the far end of the square, and when we get there I notice a black and white striped walkway across the cobbles. 'Let's do the Abbey Road shot!' I suggest, and Punk Lurex line up on the crossing, Pasi out of step with the rest. I take the photo while humming 'Back In The U.S.S.R.' to myself.

We walk back through the glass-ceilinged arcades of the luxury goods-filled GUM department store housed in the huge neoclassical building that borders the East of the square, the opposite side from the Kremlin. Fatigue is creeping over all of us by now, and we decide to have a coffee before we return to the club. It's all tourist prices around here of course, so Denis leads us off through the neighbouring streets to a bookshop he knows with a coffee bar in it. On the way we pass the monolithic KGB headquarters and he says, 'There's a Russian joke that this is the tallest building in the whole of Russia. You can even see Siberia from the basement.'

The shop is a delirious jumble of old books with a coffee bar in the corner. I wander into a back room where there is a small vinyl shop and bump straight into a young dark-haired girl who looks up and says, 'Hey, TV Smith! My name is Natalie. I'm in the support band!'

Greg, who runs the shop, is in it too. They're just closing to go to soundcheck and invite me to share a taxi, so I wait out on the street with them and another friend of theirs while Punk Lurex and Denis head back to the subway. Greg and Natalie try to flag down a few taxis but it takes a while before one of them stops and by the time we have their equipment in the boot and are seated inside we are frozen from the icy wind whipping down the street. The driver maps the location of the club into his GPS system while taking a phone call then gets into some kind of discussion with Greg, who is in the front. Finally Greg gets out of the car and gestures us to follow. 'He got a better offer and now he won't take us,' he says.

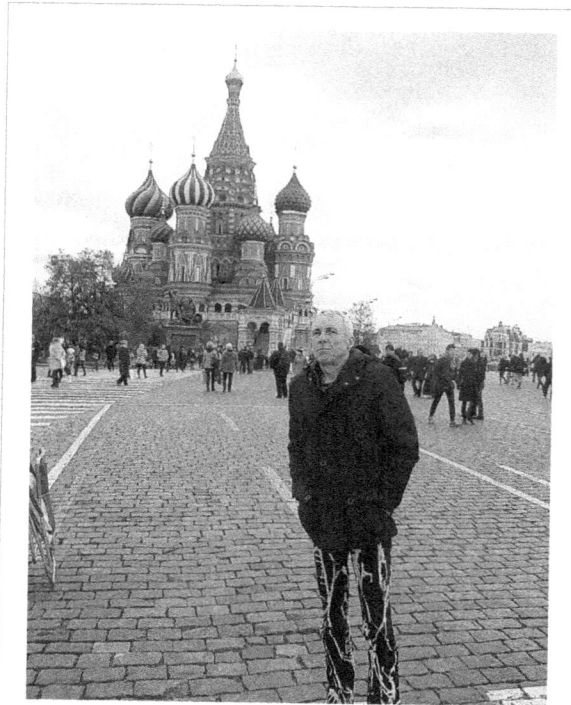

Red Square.
Trying to look sane

We unload the boot and put the stuff by the side of the road and wait until the next taxi comes along, another bone-chilling ten minutes later. This time we set off with no problems. Natalie translates an item on the car radio news as we go along: it seems there was an accident on the metro this morning when one of the drivers fell out of the cab. *While driving the train.*

I make it back to the club before Punk Lurex and set about changing my strings without the aid of tuner or string winder. Ah, just like the old days. Meanwhile the food for the nine musicians playing tonight is brought in and laid out on the dressing room table: a small sliced loaf, two thin packs of sliced processed cheese, a plate of sliced salami. One bottle of vodka.

Out in the club I can hear Punk Lurex starting their soundcheck so I go out to join them. There's a big stage, great lights and sound system and the club itself is large and very professional. Too large really, as I can't see my first appearance here drawing the thousand people that could probably fit in the room. All the same it's good to be playing in comfortable conditions.

Denis comes to tell me that there's someone selling merch out in the club and he's willing to sell mine too. This has a particular urgency today, not just because I would like people here to have my music, but also because I've sold almost nothing on the tour so far and am likely to face an extra baggage charge on my Easyjet flight home tomorrow if I don't get rid of some of it. I wander out into the club, where the first people are starting to trickle in, and find the merch table in a dimly-lit corner under some stairs at the far end of the room. The only light comes from some blue fairy lights hanging from the steps overhead. Luckily I have my torch with me and hold it up to light up the table as people peruse the CDs and books. When others in the audience spot me there's suddenly quite a brisk trade and I swap the torch to my mouth while I sign some autographs. People tell me how much they are looking forward to the gig and thank me for coming to play Moscow. This is what I'm here for!

As the only alcohol in the dressing room is vodka I go and buy a beer from the bar, then come back to the merch table where I'm disappointed to find that the battery in my torch has suddenly run out, effectively ending my sales as no one can see anything on the table any more. Why now, just when I needed it most?!

Back in the dressing room I find that I have no spare batteries in my bag, but when I look at the torch more closely I see that it hasn't run out at all—a perfectly-fitting coin that I was given as change when I bought the beer has become wedged over the lens and completely blocked it. As soon as I prise it off I'm back in business.

Greg and Natalie's band start their show to about forty people, most of them hanging around by the back walls. By the time Punk Lurex start there are another twenty in, which wouldn't be bad for a small club show, but doesn't have much impact on a place of this size. After one song, Pasi asks people to come forward and they all do, and immediately the atmosphere is much better. By the end of their set the band are being warmly received and even get demands for an encore. Backstage Tiina says to Pasi, 'I'm glad you told them to come nearer. It wasn't very Finnish though.'

Time for my gig. There are still three hours before Punk Lurex need to take their train, so no rush this time, and I've been getting a few requests from people in the audience while I've been hanging around with them watching the other bands. Songs I didn't think anyone here would know: 'We Want The Road,' from my long-since unavailable album 'Immortal Rich,' 'Eurodisneyland Tomorrow,' which I've never even recorded for an album, 'Useless,' 'My String Will Snap'... It's all very encouraging. I play them all and some new songs too, and the audience all stay down the front and sing along and applaud, and when Punk Lurex come back on we play the songs tighter and better than we ever have before, and it's just a shame we have nothing left to offer when the demands for an encore come at the end. Backstage, I listen to the cheers and applause ring on. This is how I want to remember Russia.

## 21st October MOSCOW

The alarm goes off at eight. I hurry into the shower, then pack my bags and am downstairs to meet Denis at nine. 'Monday traffic very bad,' he says. 'We get taxi to metro.'

Outside I can see the cars jammed up on the highway into the city centre, nothing moving. There are still a couple of hours before I need to be at the airport, but it occurs to me...*it's not over yet*...

Much later the taxi arrives and now I am really getting nervous about catching my flight. There's an airport train leaving from Central Station at 11:40, still an hour to go, but as we ease out of the hotel entrance we hit three lanes of solid traffic.

Obviously it's not the first time the taxi driver has come across this situation. He swings in and out of lanes, speeding forward to every gap, slamming on his brakes as he veers into them, animatedly discussing possible alternative routes with Denis. Driving in Moscow during rush hour is a game of bluff where only the most aggressive get to progress. It's not hard to see how the two cars we were supposed to use for the tour crashed. There's no seat belt in the back of the taxi. *It's not over yet*...

We're dropped within walking distance of the station with still twenty minutes to go before the train leaves. Denis carries my guitar and as we hurry along he tells me that yesterday outside the station he got surrounded by a gang of men who tried to steal his mobile phone. He has a very old and battered model—'more use as a bottle opener than a phone,' he says—and when he brought it out of his pocket and showed it to them they decided not to bother.

He leads me into the station, buys me a ticket and takes me up to the correct platform. He sets my guitar down and we stand watching as the airport train pulls in.

So this really is goodbye to Russia. I have mixed feelings. I met some lovely people, had some good times, saw some extraordinary sights and had a wealth of intense experiences that would never have happened if I hadn't come. I've also had far too little sleep, too little to eat, and spent far too long travelling. Sometimes it all got to me and I didn't behave as well as I would have liked. I don't want to be that person. I have learned a lesson which I need to bear in mind when I consider the conditions of any future tours I get offered:

You can push me so far. But only so far.

On the plane I'm seated next to a lady who is just back from visiting her family in Siberia. 'Such a wonderful place,' she says, 'the landscape so beautiful, the air so pure, the people so friendly…' She is an academic at Cambridge university, making studies in social anthropology, and has travelled to the far reaches of the Russian continent, staying with families and documenting the way they live. A few years ago she was allowed to stay at the house of a woman in Mongolia. Already in her seventies, the woman regularly travelled hundreds of kilometres on foot to buy goods from neighbouring China and bring them back to her community, where they were occasionally exchanged for money but usually traded for local produce or services, such as repairs to her hut or gathering or chopping wood for her fire. Not everyone could afford to pay her back, and when the academic asked her how much she was owed altogether, the woman calculated that over the years it was in the region of five thousand pounds. But it wasn't about the money. She considered her treks across the border and lugging back the produce a service to the community. As for what she is owed? 'Perhaps when I die, which may be soon, they will contribute to my burial.'

At Gatwick the automatic passport machine doesn't recognise me so I'm sent to one of the desks, where the female border official takes my passport.

'Have I changed?' I ask her.

'You look like you to me,' she says, considering the photograph, and hands back the passport. 'But sometimes the machine just isn't sure if you are who you are.'

Sometimes I'm not sure myself.

## 25th October HASTINGS

Down to the south coast for two nights in Hastings for the wittily-named Trash Cannes film festival. They will be showing Jamie Palmer's 'We Who Wait' documentary about The Adverts and myself tonight, with a Q&A with Jamie and I afterwards, then I'll be playing a normal gig tomorrow in a pub called the Brass Monkey. A couple of days by the seaside! I'm on holiday!

There's a storm blowing in from the South and I battle my way against the rising winds to the seafront hotel booked by the festival. I've bought more merch than usual thinking people might be wanting to catch up with my stuff after seeing the film, and it's a struggle getting up the narrow stairways to my third floor room. Unfortunately as soon as I walk in I know I've got the arse room. It's at the back of the hotel looking over the car park and has clearly had an issue with the flat roof leaking at some point because although the decor is smart enough the room stinks of damp.

After ten minutes in there I feel my eyes and throat starting to itch so go down to the lobby to see if I can change rooms. The Receptionist apologises. 'We take the comfort of our guests very seriously,' she says. 'All the rooms in your price bracket are full though and I don't have the authority to upgrade you. I'll have a talk with the manager when he gets back from his jog. Come and see me again in half an hour.'

I go back in half an hour and her sympathetic attitude has changed somewhat. 'He said it's a complimentary room and he's not going to change it.'

We take the comfort of our guests very seriously. But not if they're freeloaders.

Well, I won't be in there much. And at least it's not Russia!

I meet with Jamie in the lobby and we walk to tonight's venue, a grand porticoed building further down the seafront. Inside, about fifty people sit at tables scattered around the auditorium where some short films are being projected on the large screen behind the stage. I can't actually bring myself to watch 'We Who Wait' when it's shown and spend most of the time pacing around outside. The evening is running late and it's past 11:30 when the film finishes so there's only ten minutes left for the Q&A, a shame because there are plenty of questions coming up from the audience and it could easily have gone a lot longer. It's also a bit frustrating for me to spend only ten minutes on the stage and not even play.

The overloaded merch was a bit of a miscalculation too: I sell two items.

## 26th October HASTINGS

Despite the gagging smell of mildew I sleep late and arrange to meet Jamie for lunch in town before he goes on to a panel discussion about 'the state of the documentary.' The meal is also complimentary, offered by the restaurant in exchange for some publicity in the festival programme, so I'm hoping it won't be an arse meal to go with the arse room. In fact it's a very tasty vegetable tagine, though it does take an hour to arrive because our order 'fell down the side of the table.'

I accompany Jamie to the Jerwood Gallery with half a mind to listen to the discussion, but it's thrillingly wild and windy weather outside and I decide I don't want to be stuck indoors for the afternoon. Instead I head off on foot past the black clapboard fishermen's huts up towards the headland, then double back and walk along the shingle beach, the waves crashing thunderously beside me.

At the hotel, Jamie is just back from the discussion and offers to help me carry the merch over to the Brass Monkey. I'm running late after my walk but there's still time for a soundcheck before the first of tonight's films is shown. There are a number of shorts, then a full length feature about the Clash, concentrating on the period when they were breaking up. I thought I never wanted to see another film about The Clash in my life but in fact it's grimly fascinating. The band's final years of internal arguments and loss of direction are still resonating in my head when I get on stage, thankful to be solo and in control of my own destiny, as far as that's possible.

Not a bad turnout by the time I start, and a great atmosphere. Afterwards two people tell me separately that it was the best gig they have ever seen in their lives. This is exactly what I want to hear. Almost no merch sales though.

Outside the wind is so fierce it's difficult to stand upright and even harder to battle my way to the hotel, my guitar acting like a sail, my bag of merch the anchor I drop every now and then to steady myself. I have to tack my way up the road. In my room I go to sleep with the window open, letting the sound of the approaching storm in and the smell of the damp out.

## 31st October LONDON

Q: When is packing tape not packing tape?

A: When you get it from the Pound Shop.

It looks like packing tape, but as I'm preparing the merch for the Toy Dolls tour which starts tomorrow it doesn't actually hold any of the boxes together for more than a few minutes before it flaps off. Or maybe the boxes are made from some special non-stick cardboard?

I'm out in the street washing the cat shit off the bike when Olga pulls up in the van to take my stuff ready for the tour. I thought I'd cleaned it all off yesterday but when I got the bike out of the shed to go to the post office I was greeted with an unmistakeable acrid choking cloud that had built up to deadly strength overnight in the confined space. 'Mind those leaves,' I point out to Olga as he gives me a hand out with the boxes. 'It could be anywhere.'

He's leaving with the rest of the band for the first gig in Manchester a day early, I'll go up on the train and meet them there tomorrow. Later in the afternoon I get a text: *We are on the motorway now. I have that cat crap on me shoe, bah. What a stink.*

We're off!

## 1st November MANCHESTER

'We had to stop the van and try and get it off with a tissue,' says Olga. 'It was *that* bad.'

It was too. I felt it still hanging around me on the train all the way up. I got a double seat though, and the lengthy walk in a stiff wind up from the station to the venue seems to have finally blown it off.

Great to see Duncan and Tom from the Toy Dolls. We all got on well on the tour we did together five years ago and I'm looking forward to traveling with them again. They also have the same merch guy, Koan, and the same sound guy and driver, Merten, as last time as well as two new crew members, Koan's brother Johan and stage manager Keith. At the end of the Dolls soundcheck we try Gary Gilmore's Eyes together, which we plan to play as a surprise encore. It sounds great and we all get quite excited.

Then I go to the front of the venue to set up the merch stall but unfortunately neglect to pick up a pass so that when I try and get back in ten minutes before I go on stage I have to blag my way past the various sets of security. It's just like the old days! The first ones aren't too difficult: the woman looks me up and down, says, 'You look like you might be a musician,' and lets me through. Glad to know I'm giving it off. The second security woman at the curtain by the side of the stage is more troublesome. She only finally relents when someone leaning against the barrier at the front of the stage shouts over, 'He's the support!'

It's only eight in the evening when I start, but the place is already packed and it's a great gig. Only half an hour on stage though, it feels like it's over in a flash, and strange to leave not having played the 'hit'. By the time I get back on for it at the end of the Dolls' set the audience are thoroughly warmed up and it works a treat, just a couple of small mistakes. Tom admits afterwards that at one point he thought, 'this is sounding really great!'—and then immediately played a wrong note.

Afterwards in the van on the way to the Travelodge we are talking bollox about cover bands and come up with the concept of The Toy Dolly Partons. The Sat Nav takes us round some new housing estates which it doesn't know are there, and some considerable time later we realise there's an 'r' missing from the required street name on the itinerary. There is much grumbling about missing 'r's while Merten re-programmes the Sat Nav but soon we are in a more likely-looking area. 'Over there!' shouts Olga, 'there's the sign, *Tavelodge*!'

It's a slightly better than average one and the heaters have even been switched up for us already so the rooms are nice and cosy. I've got my emergency sandwich and my emergency beer from the dressing room. The window opening is restricted, as the sign says, *'for your own safety'* —even though I'm on the ground floor—so all is good. It's not Russia.

## 2nd November SUNDERLAND

A big one for the Toy Dolls, this: their first gig in Sunderland for thirty years. Olga was brought up in nearby South Shields and knows a lot of people in the area. The gig has been sold out since a few days after the thousand available tickets went on sale. In the van Johan writes out the 75 person guest list and Keith says, 'I just remembered, I need to put my wife on.'

'Sorry mate—full.' says Olga, deadpan. Then he relents. 'I'll put her on with a minus one.'

I'm a little bit nervous about playing in front of such a dedicated Toy Dolls audience but as people file past my merch table on their way in I recognise a lot of them, and quite a few come over and say hello and tell me how much they're looking forward to seeing me play. Even though I'm on stage thirty minutes after the doors open the room is nearly full and again I get a great reaction. I go back to the merch stand and chat with a few people while the Toy Dolls play, then make my way to the backstage ready for the encore song with them, which tonight we play flawlessly. After that I rush back to the front of the venue to man the merch stand again. When I pull the first of the CDs out of the case I realise something is wrong: it's wet. I look into the case and see the whole thing is swimming in beer. Quite a few people have been setting their drinks on the floor by the merch table while they go outside to smoke but the scenario I see before me now is the following: someone decides that rather than put their beer on the floor while they go outside it would be a better idea to rest it on my open case of CDs on the stool behind the table. Then afterwards when they arrive back and accidentally spill the contents of the glass into the case, rather than tell Koan so he can dry it up they run off without owning up to it, leaving me to find out much later when the beer has already been soaked up into the CDs and it's too late to do anything about it. As I angrily fling ruined CD after ruined CD onto the floor I feel dark thoughts—which haven't been too far below the surface since Russia—bubbling up again. And it had all been going so well.

Back at the hotel there's an Autumn storm coming in. I can hear a continual roaring outside and an intermittent tapping at the window. I look out to see the stand of young trees outside, planted to screen the Dulux Paint Centre, thrashing around wildly as if possessed. Thank goodness the window opening is restricted for my own safety.

## 3rd November GLASGOW

I wake up determined to be positive and not let little frustrations get to me—even when the little frustrations mean losing a hundred pounds worth of CDs from the merch stand that I spent nearly an hour building up and then all bloody evening manning while I wasn't on stage only to end up making a loss... Oops, there I go again.

While the band set up their gear in Glasgow ready for soundcheck I take all the CDs out of the merch case and spread them over the seats and tables in the club, then get out the emergency Wet Wipes from Hammersmith via Russia, clean them all off and then give the inside of the case a good scrubbing. By the end of that I have the most fragrant merch case known to man and am good to go again.

Perhaps there are some secret pheromones in Wet Wipes, because even before I get on stage I sell loads of merch and more than make up for my losses yesterday. I have to excuse myself to my potential customers and explain that it's time for me to start the gig. When I get on stage I'm in a very good mood and it's the best of the tour so far. As I leave I hear the audience chanting 'More Tim! More Tim!', which is awfully sweet. Mind you, five minutes later they have stopped that and are chanting 'Ol-ga! Ol-ga!' to the same rhythm. The public can be so fickle.

We will be staying in a Travelodge a couple of hours down the motorway to break up the journey to Birmingham tomorrow, so pack up quickly after we finish. The venue is throwing everyone out anyway so they can reopen for a club night shortly. Outside on the fire escape as we are loading out one of the security guys tells me about the wild weekend of Halloween parties they've just had. There were quite a few casualties, he says. 'It's those legal highs. No one knows what's in them. As soon as one ingredient gets banned, they'll put in something else without having any idea what the effect will be. We had one guy sprawled out here and had to call in an ambulance. A policeman came too and said to the guy, "I can't condone it officially, but you'd be better off smoking grass than taking that stuff. At least you'd know what you were getting." Glasgae police, eh?!'

A post-gig van ride can only mean one thing: a few beers and talking bollox for a while. Olga doesn't drink when he's on tour but to show willing he has a banana and gamely clinks our bottles with it, not that a banana really clinks. Soon we are not only talking bollox but also singing bollox as we make up a few spur of the moment songs—though most, such as the appallingly bad-taste potential disco classic 'A Nudge In The Wrong Direction', would be best forgotten. When the beer has gone there's no option but to crack open the bottle of champagne that has been sitting around for a few days, rescued from a backstage fridge somewhere, and pass that around. This is the nearest I will ever get to being on tour with Guns'n'Roses.

Though probably Guns'n'Roses don't stay in hotels where the thermostat defaults to 16.5 degrees centigrade as soon as you take your hand off it.

## 4th November BIRMINGHAM

Halfway down the motorway we stop for a lunch break and I go into M&S and buy a takeaway pot of healthy-looking Nutty Grain and Vegetable Salad, but while I'm queuing up to pay I notice the sign saying, '*Food bought here is sold as a takeaway product and it is forbidden to consume it on the premises.*'

I go back to the restaurant area and take the spare chair at the table with Olga, Merten and Koan, who have all got plates of canteen-style hot food that look like school dinners. I surreptitiously rip the top of my illegal container and pour over the soy and ginger dressing.

Olga puts down his fork with a frown and regards his plate. 'It would have been nice if they could have just made each item taste a little bit different from the others.'

By the time we've negotiated the Birmingham one-way system and road blockages it's late afternoon when we get to the venue. Not much is going on. There's plenty of time to soundcheck and set up a good looking and still-fragrant merch stand at the back of the hall, then we wait it out in the backstage room until doors open. There's wi fi so in theory we can all catch up on emails, but when we try the code written up on the wall no one succeeds in connecting. 'I've got that *Safari Cannot Open Page* page again,' I mention. 'I get that a lot.'

'Me too,' says Tom. 'It's one of my favourites. I've bookmarked it!'

There's plenty of food and drink though. Perhaps Guns'n'Roses get more than Tortilla chips, hummus, salsa and guacamole on their rider: I don't know. This will do for me. But there are no spoons. And the washbasin in the backstage toilet is blocked so after I've had my fill of chips and dips I have to resort to the emergency Wet Wipes from Hammersmith via Russia to get my hands clean.

Even though it's Monday night and not sold out, people start to stream in as soon as the doors open and by the time I start my set there are around four hundred in and it's another great gig. There's some interest at the merch stand afterwards, and I spend the rest of the evening there—apart from my three minutes on stage for Gary Gilmore's Eyes—and am able to watch the Toy Dolls set all the way through for the first time this tour. A fitting way to end the first leg of it. Tomorrow is a day off—I'll take the train home to where the thermostat stays where you set it and I can open the windows just as wide as I want.

## 6th November BRIGHTON

In a way it's harder to have a day off at home than just to carry on. You lose the rhythm of the tour and find yourself trapped into doing everyday things. The idea of just getting into the van and being driven to the next place seemed particularly appealing yesterday morning when I found myself on a crammed platform at New Street station with a platform change announced just as the train pulled in, meaning that I had to take my guitar and suitcase and shuffle along with two hundred other people trying to hoist their luggage up one set of steps and down another. The station imps DELIBERATELY chose the platforms without escalators. When I got home I was confronted with orders for the new CD and book that had stacked up while I'd been away so I spent the rest of the day stuffing jiffy bags, writing out addresses, and cycling to the post office and back. But at least I was able to wash my clothes in the machine and get them dry in the tumbler—I had visions of the band struggling to get their laundry done in the Travelodge sink and drying them on the lone radiator in the room. The heated towel rails in Travelodges were all disconnected some years ago, as the sign in the bathroom says, *'for your own safety.'*

When I get to the venue in Brighton I find that the band had it worse than me: they drove down from Birmingham through heavy traffic and arrived at one in the morning, but the van was too tall to fit into the multi-storey car park and they spent two and a half hours trying to find somewhere to leave it. When they finally got into the hotel, Duncan was given a room with four beds but no towels. He only found out about the lack of towels when he got out of the shower, so had to dry himself off with the duvet from one of the spare beds.

To make it worse, they arrived in the club today to find that the PA wasn't working properly. Everyone is looking strained at soundcheck, and the dressing room is a cramped affair upstairs so there's not even anywhere to go to relax. Happily the club fills up quickly when the doors open and everyday worries are soon cast aside when we get to play. I watch the Toy Dolls set from a spot up in the balcony reserved for guests where I get an excellent view and the sound is actually very good. The more I see the band the more I like them. When it's time for Gary Gilmore's Eyes I leave the balcony and head for the stage with a big smile on my face.

Outside the wind is blowing in from the sea at storm force, so strong that it's difficult to stand up. Rather than brave the atrocious weather looking for somewhere to have a drink in the town we decide to sit in the haven of the Travelodge bar instead. I travel up in the lift with the band to drop off our bags first and when I get to my room I'm quite shocked to see that's it's only eleven o'clock. This is possibly the earliest I've ever been back in the hotel after a gig. Then I meet the rest down in the bar for beer club while the wind hurls the litter around outside and soon it's much later.

## 7th November BRISTOL

I like this venue a lot, and when I walk in I get a welcome from the manager and soundman who remember me from when I played here with the Valentines a few years ago, one of the best gigs on the tour. Tonight has been sold out for quite a while and I'm looking forward to playing. The only thing is, it's another thirty minute set, frustratingly short, and due to start a whole hour after the club opens at 7:30. After soundcheck I have a word with soundman Richard and tentatively suggest that *maybe*—if people come in early—*maybe* I could go on a bit earlier and play a bit longer?

His face lights up. 'Great!' he says. 'How early do you want to start?'

People do arrive early and the place is packed by eight. I'm planning to start fifteen minutes early and on the way to the stage with my guitar divert to the sound desk to make sure Richard is ready. He is chatting with someone, and as I walk up breaks out into a big yawn.

'Just let me know if I'm keeping you up.' I say.

He apologises, introduces me to his girlfriend, then tells me that he's tired because he had to take his horse to the vet this morning for a scan on its leg. 'It wasn't easy but finally they were able to manage it with a hand-held scanner meant for dogs,' he says. It turned out that the horse has an injury on its knee and one of two operations are available. He explains them both to me in some detail. I glance at my watch and see my fifteen minutes extra time is almost over.

'Well, I suppose I should go and play…'

Great gig, but in the end only the advertised thirty minutes.

After the show we drive to a Travelodge on a service station on the M4, which gets us out of town and on the way to London ready for the gig tomorrow. In the room I find the interesting conundrum of a dish containing sachets of instant coffee and teabags yet no kettle. I go back to Reception and ask the man there if there is a spare one. He considers the question for a while.

'We have a problem with the kettles,' he says finally.

*Yes. The problem is, you don't have enough of them.*

'So there isn't a spare one?'

There is another Pinter-esque pause. 'I could double check?' he suggests, with a faraway tone in his voice.

I look at the two shelves behind him holding three irons and some towels and say, 'I'll come back in the morning.'

## 8th November LONDON

On the way in to London we drive within half a mile of my home but there's no time to stop. It's an eleven hundred capacity venue tonight, nearly sold out already, and we need to be there early. Everything looks set fair: great stage, PA, and lights, a big merchandising area so Koan and I can set out everything we have left with lots of space around us. In the dressing room there is a better than average selection of food and drink, and a wi fi connection that works.

As we settle in there I mention the lack of kettle in my room last night and Olga tells me the same thing happened to him. He went back to the lobby to ask for one and the guy said, 'I'm not sure if we have one that doesn't explode…'

Not what you want when you're making your cocoa.

Tom's room had a bath but didn't have a plug.

'Don't you bring your own?' I ask.

'You take your own plug?'

'Of course!'

'How can it fit all the different size holes?' says Merten.

I get the emergency travel sink plug out of my suitcase and show them.

'Cor!' says Tom. 'I'm going to get one of them!'

Often London gigs can be the worst on a tour, but tonight is a triumph, everything right—except for the fact that for some reason a fight breaks out during my set while

I'm singing '*Xmas Bloody Xmas*' and someone gets thrown out. But then, that is the true spirit of Christmas.

Once again, to save my hotel costs I'll be going home tonight then getting an advance cheap train ticket to the last gig in Nottingham tomorrow. The band will drive some of the way tonight and stay at another Travelodge on the motorway. Gaye comes up to the dressing room to say hello to the band, who are packing up in a hurry ready for the journey.

'I learn so much from his books,' says Tom, gesturing at me as he hurries around gathering his things. 'He is the master and I am his pupil.' He goes to the fridge and brings out a plastic bag. 'Look, it's my emergency sandwich for tonight!'

When the band have gone Gaye and I salvage the leftovers from the rider and stuff it all in my suitcase. Possibly a first: I'm taking an emergency sandwich even though I'm going home.

## 9th November NOTTINGHAM

When I arrive at the venue in Nottingham I'm greeted by the always-unwelcome sight of the local soundman on his knees in front of the PA system with a screwdriver in his hand. Merten tells me that he started soundcheck and then found that the speakers were out of phase, which means it sounds terrible. Apparently no one who's played here before had noticed. Happily it's all soon fixed and although the outfront sound is still a little underpowered it's not bad for the room, which is small compared to many of the rest on the tour and has been sold out since soon after the gig was announced. It should be an exciting finish when this place is packed.

After soundcheck I go back to the furnace-like dressing room to sit it out until the club opens. Not long to wait though: once again I'm on only thirty minutes after doors open but most people get in early and I recognise quite a few of the crowd from previous gigs on the tour and notice that they are singing along to the songs now they've heard them a few times. It's a great feeling and reminds me how worthwhile this tour has been, not just because I've had fun and been treated decently and eaten and slept well, but also all-importantly because I have won a lot of new fans along the way.

After the show we all go for a final drink in a bar around the corner before the drive to tonight's Travelodge, which turns out to be in another service station. Not next to it – actually in it. And so it is that we drink the remaining bottles of cava and champagne purloined from dressing rooms sitting in plastic chairs next to the plastic palms flanked by the shutters of closed branches of Burger King and Costa. It's only after we've been sitting there for a while and the booze is nearly gone that Olga mentions that tomorrow Merten will be driving the van back to Germany, dropping off Koan and Johan in Belgium on the way, so we should leave at eight in the morning.

Just a few hours away.

*Oh Olga, I cannot!*

## 10th November LONDON

But I do. And the reward is a sparkling crisp sunny morning. The roads are clear and we reach the outskirts of London by eleven and drive to Duncan's place to transfer the gear out of the hire van into Merten's van, which has been parked here during the tour. When we get out of the van we see that during the tight parking manoeuvre into the only space available we have run over a sensationally huge log of dog excrement which is now spread across the road in tyre-circumference-length splodges that we have to take great care to avoid as we carry the equipment from one van to the next. 'I'm having a word with that dog,' says Keith.

What a tour! Shit at the beginning. Shit at the end. Great in the middle.

## 15th November DERBY

While using the loo at St. Pancras station I notice a sign that says the baby changing facilities are closed 'for security reasons.' I feel safer now.

Train up to Derby for a gig at the Victoria Inn, once one of my regular venues. Kev the soundman, who I remember because his friendly old dog always used to plod up on to the stage during soundcheck, says, 'It's been a while since you've played here, hasn't it?'

'It certainly has,' I agree, then ask brightly. 'How's your dog?'

'Oh...he died two years ago.'

We're off to a good start.

Soundcheck is fine though, and soon done. In the dressing room I find the support band The Standby Setting, who I first became aware of when their singer Jake recorded a cover of my song Together Alone. He is regarding the two small bowls of broken up tortilla chips on the table with an amused air. 'We were just wondering if they crushed them to fit the bowls?' he says.

'I think they're the sweepings,' I reply.

'I've read all your tour diaries, and they are always full of funny food,' he says, 'I was so pleased to finally get to play a gig with you and come into your dressing room and find that there is funny food here.'

In just over a month I will get to the end of this year's tour diary, and by then it will just be about itself, and then I will stop.

By the time I get onstage there's a good-sized crowd in, and more TUTS than I've seen at one gig for a long time, certainly more than managed to get to Germany for the official fan club gig last month. After the short sets on the Toy Dolls tour it's great to stretch out with a nearly-two hour performance, and the presence of the TUTS singing along to almost every number is infectious: by the end everyone is joining in and there's a great atmosphere in the room.

After I've packed everything away I leave the venue with two TUTS, TJ and Smit, who are staying at a hotel next to mine. 'Do you want me to help carry anything?' asks TJ, watching me struggle with the guitar and bag of merch,

'Nooo,' I say, trying to get everything in balance. 'I'm used to this. This is what I do.'

'Yes, I know,' says TJ. 'I saw the documentary.'

## 16th November NORWICH

A long train journey cross country to Norwich, enlivened by the fact I've never taken this route before and watch the fens go by with some interest. There's a very different atmosphere here than anywhere else in Britain. The vast flat peaty-black fields have been ploughed and lie ready for spring planting, here and there an outcrop of trees standing proud above them. Narrow ditches run arrow-straight to the misty horizon. A grey lake washes up against an earth dyke which drops steeply to the flatlands below; a road without traffic, a solitary house. In other circumstances I would be tempted to get out and look around picturesque Ely with its solemn lump of a cathedral on a low hill brooding over the town, interlaced with canals. But I've got a gig to get to.

I check in to the Travelodge and pack the merch bag, then walk down to the venue, where I'll be supporting my old mates the UK Subs tonight. I've arranged to meet a guy called Mathew there to have a chat about punk for a university thesis he is writing. He's waiting outside and walks into the venue, The Waterfront, with me. It's quite a few years since I last played here. I'm surprised to see that there is no gear on the stage and no sign of the Subs either, but then Mathew mentions that there's a second live room upstairs. That turns out to be where we are playing. While the Subs do their soundcheck Mathew and I wander back downstairs and sit outside where it's quiet and we can have a chat without being disturbed. After that I go back up to the venue and have a quick soundcheck myself then set up my merch next to Yuko, which takes considerably longer. I show her my new orange gaffa tape. 'Feel the tack on that,' I say. I can tell she's impressed.

The dressing room is all the way back down the stairs. I gather in there with the band and we spend some time catching up. We're all a bit surprised that although there is plenty of beer and wine on the rider, there is no food. Jamie hasn't eaten all day and spends some time on the internet trying to find somewhere to deliver some food, but the best he can find is a pizza place who estimate getting it to him by 8:30, half an hour before the Subs play. I haven't eaten either, but doors are just about to open and I need to go and man the merch.

A local band are on first, and by the time they are finished the room is quite full and I have a good forty minute set, interrupted only by a string breaking, something that's been happening a lot lately. Wish I'd never bought those more expensive strings, I'm going back to the cheap ones.

It's eight months since I was on tour with the Subs and I enjoy watching their set again from my position by the merch, where I have a few beers stashed and chat with a few familiar faces as they go past, sell a few things and sign a few autographs. Someone I've not met before comes up and tells me how much he enjoyed the gig. He tells me he's studying mathematics at the same university as Mathew and apologises for the fact he is very drunk.

'Maybe sometime – I don't know how – we could work together on something?' he suggests. I'm sure I don't know how either. I am really not sure where the meeting point between punk and mathematics would lie.

Another guy comes up and says, 'My mate tells me it was you singing on 'Gary Gilmore's Eyes'. Is that true?'

I tell him it is. He looks doubtful. 'I always thought it was Gaye Advert singing,' he says. 'Are you sure?'

I tell him I am sure, and he says, 'I'm going to have to go back and listen again.'

Afterwards I pack away to the punk disco, enjoying the classic songs as I fold up the T-shirts and put the CDs back in the boxes. The wife of one of the musicians in the support band is packing away their stuff beside me. She says, 'I saw you at Rebellion in the Summer and you were skinny then, but now you're even skinnier. Eat, my lover.'

I take my merch and guitar downstairs to the dressing room, where the Subs and I indulge in a fairly lengthy wine club, along with a few fans who have found their way down there and the promoter. The promotor pays me the fee, which I'd forgotten about, then when he asks me to put my name on the receipt I accidentally sign my autograph, force of habit. We both laugh when I realise what I've done, but the promoter actually writes the date below the autograph and says he's going to get it framed.

Then it's time to head off to the Travelodges, mine just a fifteen minute stagger away, the one for the Subs an hour away in the van. We say our goodbyes until the mammoth European tour starts again in a couple of months. I'm afraid, dear diary, you won't be there to join me for that one. As we clear the dressing room Yuko hands me the remains of a bottle of white wine we haven't managed to finish. 'Nightcap,' she says. 'For Traverrodge.'

Good idea. It's going to be lonely in there without the Subs around. I put the bottle in my bag.

Just the small matter of food to sort out now, but on the walk back I pass an all-night petrol station which has some snacks in it, including one vegetarian option: a cheese sandwich. Correct.

Back in the Travelodge with the heater switched up to maximum, in my familiar environment—the regulation five coat hooks, the two sachets each of instant coffee and de-caf, the two tea bags and four sugars, the window opening restricted for my own safety—I pour out some Pinot Grigio into the flimsy plastic glass and pull off the cellophane coating of the emergency cheese sandwich. The planets are in alignment and everything is in balance.

## 21st November LONDON

Paul picks me up in the van early afternoon. I'd been wondering what he'd hire for the tour and it looks like a standard Ford Transit, but when I open the back doors to put in my merch boxes I see that there is a fold-down wheelchair ramp—not something you usually find in a band van. I raise an eyebrow. 'Don't ask,' says Paul.

We beat the London rush hour traffic and are in Dover by evening, early enough to catch the ferry before the one we're booked on. It will be good to arrive in our hotel in France early as we have a long day tomorrow: we'll be picking up the Bored Teenagers from Dusseldorf airport and then driving on to an already sold out gig in the Sonic Ballroom in Cologne.

A *Formule 1* hotel somewhere off the motorway near Dunkirk might not be the most salubrious location to start the tour, but the reception area is still open when we arrive and they even provide cutlery for the pizza we've picked up on the way. Paul and I go over the tour itinerary together while we eat then head up to our very basic rooms—bathroom and toilet down the hall, small washbasin in the room but no plug. It's an early outing for the emergency travel sink plug from Exeter.

# 22nd November COLOGNE

We're on the road through Belgium, and the many horses grazing in the fields around us have led to a discussion between Paul and I about why the British are so squeamish about eating horse meat when they are quite happy to eat most other animals. 'They don't seem to mind in the rest of Europe,' I say.

Just at that moment I spot a horsebox parked by the side of the road with an advert for Burger King on the side. A bit blatant.

It's a good time to teach Paul my favourite road game, Horsebox. The rules go like this: when you see a horsebox you have to say 'Horsebox!' before anyone else in the vehicle. That's it. It has to be an actual horsebox trailer though, with the pointy front and little windows, towed by another vehicle. Livestock trailers and lorries with *Horses* written on the side don't count. If you call 'Horsebox!' to something in the distance and it turns out not to be one as you get nearer there is no specific forfeit, but great shame will fall upon you and there will be much muttering. In theory the last person to spot a horsebox before arriving at the venue (or other destination) wins, but it's not really about the winning and anyway, contestants rarely cling on that long. I was taught it by Duncan from the Toy Dolls, who claims it was invented by Frankie from Leatherface, and it was a constant feature of the tour I did with the Toy Dolls five years ago. I'd been looking forward to sharpening my Horsebox skills when I toured with them again recently but Duncan and I both had backward-facing seats, which does make it difficult, unless you get overtaken by a horsebox. Unlikely. Now I'm in the front passenger seat next to Paul and it's game on.

Belgium is pretty much horsebox country, and we spot quite a few as we motor through it, then we're on into Holland, then Germany, and get to Dusseldorf an hour before the flight arrives at three, so drop in to visit Vom who lives close by the airport. There we have a nice cup of tea, and he tells us he will be coming to the gig tonight, and hopefully the next day in Karlsruhe too. In fact, can he sleep in the band room above the venue and travel down there with us if there's space in the van?

What a professional! He's finally got some time off from playing with Die Toten Hosen, so what does he do? He goes to gigs!

The flight is a bit delayed, but after we've picked up Jonathan, Mateo and Marky from the airport, traffic is unexpectedly light on the way to Cologne and we're at the venue right on time for soundcheck at six.

The Sonic is a fairly small club, holding around 150 but has been sold out since yesterday, so this is going to be quite a kick-start to the tour. All goes well in soundcheck and the excitement starts to build.

Paul and I set up the merch in a covered area just outside the entrance hallway, which has recently been extended to give people somewhere to smoke. It soon becomes apparent that this is not an ideal spot because as soon as the club opens people congregate around us, smoking and drinking, and lean against the table which swings back threatening to spill everything off it. 'That table has seen some wild evenings,' says the doorman. 'It's had people up on it dancing many times.'

He also tells me that he saw me the first time I played in the Sonic Ballroom, more than ten years ago. He was intending to have a few drinks with some mates and leave the car outside the club for the night, but not many of his friends turned up and he ran out of money so couldn't drink much anyway and decided to drive home after all. Unfortunately it was the night the German drink driving limit was lowered from 0.08% to 0.05%. He was stopped by the police and found to have 0.06%, which would have been acceptable the day before but now resulted in a ban and a hefty fine.

'Do you want me to pay you now?' I ask.

Soon after doors open the place is already half full. 'Usually there are only five people in by now,' says the promoter.

'No pressure,' I tell the band.

It turns out to be a storming gig, as we'd hoped. From the stage I can feel the thrill rising in the audience when after two or three songs they realise we *really are* going to play the entire set without any breaks.

Afterwards, as the people thin out, I pack my stuff away and leave with my friend Sebastian to stay the night at his place. It's been a long while since I've visited him and his girlfriend Claudia; so long that they now have a fifteen month old baby I've never even met, and it occurs to me that as I play more and more gigs around the world I make more and more friends but see them less often.

It's the first night of the tour and I suppose I should try and get a reasonably early night, but we have to make up for lost time so Sebastian and I sit around the kitchen table with a couple of bottles of wine—along with the neighbour, who sees the lights on and comes to join in—until four. So much for Plan A.

## 23rd November KARLSRUHE

Sebastian conjures up a great vegetarian breakfast, and I finally get to meet the toddler, who grins at me a lot. He's called Henry Tim, after Henry Miller and, well, I don't like to ask.

At around two, Sebastian's brother Stephan and his girlfriend come over to drive me and Sebastian down to Karlsruhe. They plan to come to the gig tonight, stay in a hotel, then go to the match tomorrow: the team from their home town of Dresden are playing. We head off out of Cologne onto the *autobahn* and Stephan puts on some speed. I'm having a long discussion with Sebastian in the back of the car when something on the opposite side of the road catches my eye. 'Horsebox,' I mention in mid-sentence.

'Pardon?'

Sebastian doesn't know about Horsebox, so I teach him. It's a Saturday, a classic Horsebox day, and soon we are spotting them all over the place. I call one on the road up ahead, and then realise what I'm actually looking at—one horsebox following right behind another, a two box convoy. We overtake them and they slip behind us before I have a chance to take a photo, but Stephan has obviously been listening in on our conversation because without a word he pulls into the next lay-by and we wait there for the horseboxes to pass so I can snap them.

We get to the hotel in Karlsruhe with twenty minutes to spare before I have to meet with Paul and the band in the lobby to go to soundcheck. I show them my horsebox photo. I can tell they're impressed.

Another sold out show, and we play even better than last night as the band settles in and we get back into our stride after the couple of months away. I'm proud of them. A second encore is demanded and we play two post-Adverts songs that we haven't tried outside of the rehearsal room so far and they're the highlight of the night.

Back at the hotel, we gather in the empty lobby for a final drink. Vom and I end up last men standing—so much for Plan A—and say goodnight with a tinge of regret: tomorrow he'll be heading back home to Dusseldorf and I won't see him again until I'm passing through on the UK Subs tour next February.

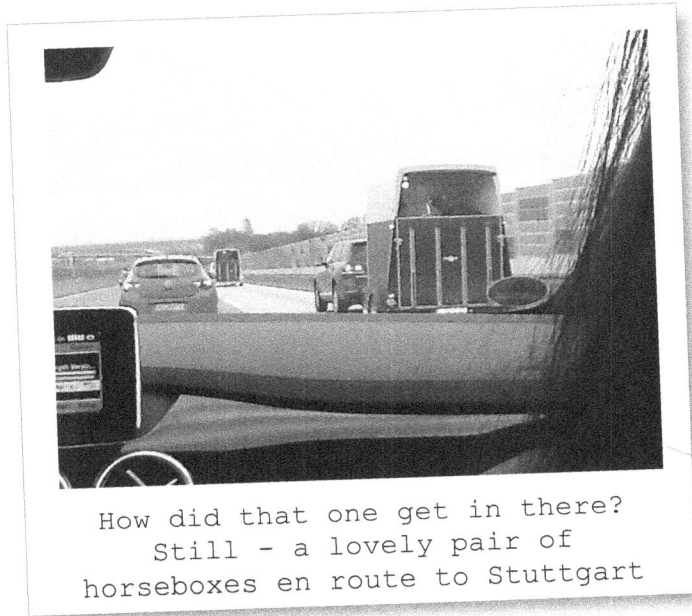

How did that one get in there?
Still - a lovely pair of
horseboxes en route to Stuttgart

## 24th November LUZERN

On to Switzerland, and another of my regular venues, the Sedel in Luzern.

It's a good job I've been here before because the Sat Nav is intent on directing us somewhere else completely. The Sedel is an imposing former prison commanding the hill over the town and even when it's in sight the Sat Nav won't have it. Paul switches it off with a sigh.

Club owner Gössi rarely puts on gigs on a Sunday, so he has made this one an early start for the people who have to go to work the next day. But early really means early: soundcheck time is three and the club opens at five. We'd all been a bit worried that no one would turn up *that* early so as I stand at the spacious merch table with Paul it's a relief to see people starting to arrive. Things are slow for a while though. As I'm hanging around behind the table I absent-mindedly tuck in my shirt and notice something hanging from it—a small plastic bag with a couple of plastic tags in it. 'I've washed this loads of times and never even noticed that,' I say to Paul. 'Must be lapel stiffeners. How are you supposed to use them?'

Paul takes the two pieces of flimsy plastic from me and examines them for a moment. 'Let me help you,' he says, and flings them across the table onto the floor.

We both laugh, but then I start to think—they must be useful for something.

'Actually, you could be right,' says Paul. 'They'd make ideal little price tags.'

I do need price tags for some of the CDs… I get my torch out and go on to the dance floor and hunt around. Luckily there still aren't too many people in and I soon find the lapel stiffeners. I come back to the merch table and show them to Paul. 'This is possibly the most futile and ridiculous thing I've ever done before a gig,' I say. 'You couldn't write this.'

Paul point out the display of tour diaries on the table in front of us. 'Tim, you do.'

Just before the support band starts my friends René and Mariann arrive and I take them backstage to deliver some CDs they have had stored at their place, but then we all find ourselves trapped there until the band finishes as the only way out is back over the stage.

I've travelled to many gigs with René and Mariann, and taught them Horsebox a long time ago, so now seems a good time to show off my picture of the horsebox convoy from yesterday.

'Wait a minute though,' says René, and starts scrolling through the photos on his phone. 'How about this!'

It's a photo of a lorry, but not just any old lorry: it's a car transporter loaded with twelve horseboxes. I am suitably impressed. 'The family horsebox.' René says. 'I had to overtake it then pull up in a lay-by to get the shot.'

## 25th November MUNICH

We have a long drive to Munich, made longer when the Sat-Nav decides to take us the picturesque route along the shore of Lake Luzern despite the sign almost directly outside the hotel pointing to the *autobahn* in the opposite direction. We eventually battle our way back to the major roads but the machine insists on trying to take us off again at every exit. We cross into Austria for a few minutes just before the German border, and here—where we need to stick to the small roads because we don't have a *vignette* giving us permission to use the Austrian *autobahn*—the Sat-Nav perversely sends us up a narrow single-track country road edged by steep ditches directly back to the toll road.

The Orangehouse is one club in a complex of venues under the name of *Feierwerk*. I've played in nearly all of them many times and it's good to be back. We're soon set up, the sound is great, and there's plenty of room to build up a good merch table by the side of the stage. There is one problem though—outside it's snowing.

'Do we have winter tyres?' I ask Paul.

'We have a brand new set of tyres, we'll be fine.'

'But are they *winter tyres*?'

Most people in England have never heard of winter tyres, but it's common practice in the rest of Europe to change over to them at this time of year. The issue becomes more serious when PamP arrives for his soundcheck—he's playing a solo support set— and his girlfriend Verena tells me that since the new German government came into power this year they've made it illegal to drive without winter tyres from November 2nd. 'It's even worse in Austria,' she says. 'They stop you on the motorways all the time there, and there's a five thousand euro fine if you haven't got them.'

We're going to Austria tomorrow.

Outside the snow is bucketing down.

Instead of the pre-gig contemplation I might have liked to enjoy, I find myself in the dressing room checking stockists and prices for winter tyres on the internet. I deliver the bad news to Paul out at the merch. It looks like a full set for the van could cost around eight hundred euros, a serious chunk out of the tour profits. It's a tricky one: Paul feels confident that the new tyres we already have will do the job unless the weather gets seriously bad, and in a week the van goes back to the hire company and we would be spending all that money for nothing. On the other hand: a potential five thousand euro fine if we get stopped.

Another problem is that we have a long drive to Vienna tomorrow and the prospect of wasting hours in the morning looking for a garage and getting a new set of tyres fitted doesn't seem nearly as attractive as getting some extra sleep.

For now we put these thoughts aside. PamP gets on stage and plays his solo set to a good-sized appreciative crowd, then the band and I take over. It's another killer show.

Paul's been phoning around some other people who work with bands and the general opinion is that we're very unlikely to get hit with the full fine even if we get stopped, and meanwhile the snow has eased off and the forecast is for improving conditions so we decide to risk it.

I leave the band to pack away and go off to their hotel. Meanwhile I jump in PamP's van, and we head out to the countryside and his village home for a pleasant few hours chatting over a meal and a couple of bottles of *Weizen*. It's getting on for four by the time we call it a night. Just like the old days! I'm struck by how long it is since PamP and I had a chance to do this. Since I was last here he has acquired a new girlfriend and two dogs.

More friends, less time.

## 26th November VIENNA

Knowing we had a ten o'clock start this morning I woke up two hours earlier than I needed to, then couldn't get back to sleep because I was worried about waking up again.

PamP drives me back into Munich and I meet up with the band in the hotel lobby. They're looking a bit the worse for wear as when they got back last night the bar was still open and they 'went for it.'

Good to know they're having fun. The snow has stopped in town, but as soon as we get on the road there are worryingly frequent wintry showers and it's with some relief that many hours later when we finally near Vienna the weather dries up.

The Chelsea club lies under the railway running down the middle of a busy six lane ring road. It's nestled under the arches, and the only way to get to it is to make some illegal manoeuvres and dip down a small service road. I've been there many a time and not once has a driver found a way in without going round the one-way system a few times. Experience pays off, and this time we get it on only the second round, but promoter David tells Paul that the police get upset if vans are left here all evening. Upsetting the police is not something we want to do with the prospect of a five thousand euro fine hanging over our heads, so after we've unloaded Paul dutifully moves the van back out and eventually finds a parking space on the side of the ring road.

The show is sensational, lots of people in the club, the whole crowd buzzing, and I leave the stage exhausted. I go over to the merch table and spend a couple of hours there chatting to people, then sneak up to the tiny upstairs dressing room to wind down as the band pack away. Considering how good the gig was I'm surprised that Paul is looking so irritated as he comes up the stairs. He tells me that he just went to fetch the van and found that while it had been parked a passing car had hit the left hand wing mirror and broken it completely off. No small problem when you have a right hand drive car and are driving on the right.

This is really not the news we need right now. We've had a seven hour drive, set everything up, played the gig...we're all tired and now we're faced with the prospect of finding a Ford Transit wing mirror in Vienna at two in the morning. We have found a couple of possible 24 hour garages on the internet but—realistically—what are the chances?

Jonathan, who is used to tour managing and driving bands in Spain, steps up to the frame. 'The rest of you go and get some sleep at the hotel,' he says. 'I'll see if I can find a garage with Paul.'

I can't think of anything I'd rather hear right now than the instruction to go to sleep.

So I get in the back with Mateo and Marky, and Jonathan takes the front passenger seat, his head out of the window warning Paul about any traffic coming up on his left. They drop us at the hotel and drive off into the night.

Just before I go to bed I have a quick check of my emails and find one from Gaye saying that the sink plunger plug in our bathroom has broken. She's having to use the spare emergency travel sink plug!

The tour never ends, not even at home.

## 27th November DRESDEN—28th November BERLIN

Marky is coming out of the breakfast room as I go in and he tells me he's just seen Jonathan. Last night they couldn't find a garage with a wing mirror, but while they were driving around looking they got stopped twice by the police. Luckily they didn't check the tyres. This morning he and Paul set off at 8:30 and found a garage with a similar mirror, which they managed to adapt so that it works as well as the original.

In the van I notice they've used a nice black gaffa to stick the mirror on to the remains of the smashed frame, you can hardly notice it's a repair job. On the way to Munich, Paul tells me they were getting so frustrated at not being able to find the right part that they were seriously thinking of buying a dressing table mirror from a junk shop and cutting it up.

Although the routing on the tour has been quite good, today is a real punisher: from Vienna to Dresden, which requires traveling the length of the Czech Republic. The road isn't all motorway, and even when it is it's the *clunk-clunk-clunk* variety, bumpy and worn from years of cross-Europe heavy goods traffic. By the time we get to Germany it has been dark for hours and we are all deeply tired. Within a couple of kilometres of the border a car pulls up alongside us in the fast lane and the passenger shines a torch through the window at us. *Polizei*.

At a dark and deserted rest station, the police wander around the van, look in the back and ask a few cursory questions. They don't seem all that interested in us but perk up a bit when they realise we are musicians. As they let us drive on, one of them says, 'What kind of music do you play?'

'Punk rock,' says Paul. 'Sorry.'

Not too lengthy an inconvenience in the end, and at least they didn't check our tyres, but all the same an unwelcome delay after eight hours on the road. To make it worse, none of us thought to bring any Czech currency with us so the only thing we've had to eat all day is the emergency sandwich we bought with us from the hotel breakfast. By the time we pull into the yard of the Chemiefabrik we're hungry, thirsty and tired. It's a late gig tonight so before we can find the strength to unload the van we devour the vegan snacks that club owners Mario and Andy have put out on the bar.

Then it's down to the business of soundcheck and waiting it out for show time. The band and Paul will be sleeping in a band flat, I have a hotel a ten minute walk away so I go over there now to turn the heaters up and dump some of my baggage. I stay in the room a while, trying to shrug off the tiredness that seems to be settling over me, then make my way back to the club, somehow not really looking forward to another night of crowds and noise.

The club is reasonably full for a Wednesday and the gig starts off well, but as it goes on I find myself increasingly concerned about my lack of energy. I'm pushing and pushing but can't seem to nudge my performance up a gear, and to make it worse I'm starting to feel rather queasy. By the end I'm struggling for breath and abort the second encore. I make my way through the audience towards the merch table in the bar feeling disorientated and dizzy while people slap me on the back as I pass and say how much they enjoyed the show.

At the merch, Paul eyes me with concern. 'Okay?'

'I need somewhere to sit down.'

I've started shaking. There's no backstage and nowhere to get away from the crowds who are now swarming around the table and asking for autographs and photos.

'Mario's office…' says Paul.

I stumble off towards the toilets, where an unmarked door along the way leads to the drinks storage room and a makeshift office in the narrow back room. Unfortunately the temperature there is quite a few degrees lower than in the club. I feel the sweat chilling on my skin. Andy is in the office going through tonight's figures. He sits me down and finds an electric heater which he sets in front of me. I huddle in front of it shivering uncontrollable.

'Tim, I feel so bad about this,' he apologises. 'The heating broke down in here.'

'D-d-don't w-worry. I'l be f-f-f-fine.'

But I don't feel fine and at the first opportunity I get out of there and head back to the hotel, where the room has become super-heated since I switched all the radiators up earlier, exactly what I need right now.

I swoon into an hour's sleep, then wake up with a sudden shock and straight away realise what is going to happen. I make it to the bathroom just in time and double up over the toilet. What follows throughout the course of the night I can only describe as 'a complete purge.'

As the first grey light of morning tinges the sky I realise any hope of sleep tonight is gone. The bedsheets are soaked with sweat, my stomach is cramped, but the shakes and purging seem to be over, at least for now. There's nothing left in me to come out.

I pack my bags and walk heavy-footed and light-headed back to the club, where the rest are waiting and we set off for Berlin.

Berlin, Wild At Heart. Always hot, crowded, exciting, usually a gig here is one of the high points of any tour. But tonight it's something I'm dreading in the way a mountaineer eyes up the brutal sheer face of the distant peak he is going to have to climb. The stage is at the far end of the club, nowhere to escape, the dressing room at the opposite end by the entrance. When the place is full it can take a good ten minutes to push through the crowd to it. Once I get on stage there will be no going back. I can only hope my stomach is as empty as it feels.

We get into Berlin at around two. Jonathan is keen to show Mateo and Marky around the city but I need to rest. On the way to unload the gear at the club Paul drops me off at the hotel, where I switch the radiators up and crawl under the bedsheets with all my clothes on, instantly plunging into a deep sleep. Two hours later I wake up to a noise, which I gradually realise is my phone ringing in one of my pockets somewhere. Not knowing what time it is, and suddenly panicking that I might have missed my own gig I hunt frantically around for it and find it just as the ringing stops. A text message comes through: it's a journalist asking if I'm in Berlin already and shall we do the interview now?

Completely forgot. I text back that we can do it after soundcheck, then realise that I need to leave for to the venue now if I'm going to be there in time for it.

It's a relief that as always the sound in the Wild At Heart is excellent. Soundman Uli gets it all set up in just a few seconds, and I can hear my vocals loud and clear over the band without having to strain. If I can just get some energy everything should be fine. Energy could be a problem though: I haven't eaten anything since the snacks when we walked into the Chemiefabrik more than twenty-four hours ago. My stomach is crawling with hunger but I don't dare put anything in it.

I go next door to the Tikki bar, also owned by the Wild At Heart team, to meet the journalist. Bartender Nic sympathises with my condition and brings me over a mug of Yogi tea then I do the interview in a voice so soft I fear the recorder can't possibly be picking it up. The band come over from the club, sit at a neighbouring table and get stuck in to some of the items on the menu. I don't think I'll be having the 'Lemmyburger' myself, or even my usual—the sensationally tasty tofu stir fry.

'I have just the thing for you,' says club owner Lea, and presents me with a bowl of light soup, some simple boiled root vegetables in it. 'East German worker's soup,' she says. 'They would just put a hunk of *Würst* in there and it would be the perfect meal.'

It's the perfect meal for me too. I risk a few spoonfuls and almost immediately feel a little spark of energy course through me. Even more importantly the soup stays down. What a place: the finest small rock'n'roll club in one of the finest rock'n'roll cities in the world—the tattooed staff look like a bunch of ex-bikers who would tear your head off with chains if your crossed them—yet they are some of the kindest most considerate people you could ever hope to meet. These people are what doing this is all about: community spirit and friendship.

Back in the club Texas Terri arrives with photographer Spunge. I tell Tex about the previous night, and Spunge says, 'Hey, you need electrolytes!' and rushes out of the door, coming back a few minutes later with a bulging plastic bag. 'Here you are,' he says, pulling out a few bottles of sports drinks, '…and this is really good for sickness— Ginger Ale.'

It does feel odd drinking Powerade before a gig instead of my normal beer—but it seems to work. By showtime I push my way towards the stage through the packed crowd fairly confident I can do the gig, and it turns into a classic Wild At Heart stormer. Afterwards I still can't handle the idea of beer, but I celebrate a triumphant night with a vodka and orange in the dressing room—strictly medicinal—then get back out into the club to work the merch.

It's two in the morning before we get out of there. We leave the van and go by foot to where we're sleeping, with the plan to stop off for something to eat on the way. The band are all hungry and I'm feeling a stirring of hunger again myself. Paul knows a great fast food place where they cook the food just as you order it, but when we get in there I have second thoughts about risking eating just yet and while the rest wait for their food I head off to the hotel instead. If I can get through a gig in a packed Wild At Heart I'm sure I can get through the final two gigs but I don't want to do anything that might endanger my recovery. I sink into sleep with an overwhelming sense of relief, reasonably confident that the worst is over.

## 29th November HANNOVER

It's another potential six hour drive to the penultimate gig in Hannover, and the numbing rhythm of the road is all too familiar as we set off at eleven. In theory, we're in good time for soundcheck but Uli's warnings that there will be a two hour traffic jam as we pass Braunschweig—'there always is!'—are uppermost in our thoughts. It's already dark by the time we get past the danger area without incident and Paul and I are just discussing the ups and downs of touring and how surely our run of bad luck has finished now when he suddenly glances at the dashboard and says, 'It's not over yet.'

He slows the van to a crawl and glances at the sign for a rest station a couple of kilometres ahead. 'Temperature gauge just shot up to full,' he says, and turns all the heating controls up and the fans to maximum to to try and cool the engine down. Fearing a leaking radiator or a total engine breakdown or both—just one of them would be enough to stop us getting to tonight's gig and eat all the tour profits—we limp up to the pumps and park under the canopy to protect us from the freezing rain as we check the engine.

'Be careful, don't get your hand near it!' shouts Jonathan, as Paul goes to check the radiator.

'But...it's not even hot,' says Paul, puzzled.

Back in the van, he turns the ignition key and the temperature gauge has dropped back to normal. If the engine had really been overheating there is no way it could have cooled down so quickly. Jonathan and Paul both phone up mechanics they know and both come back with the same explanation: short circuit on the temperature gauge. We have been spared.

We arrive in Hannover only half an hour late for soundcheck and with plenty of time before the club opens. It takes a while to find the Glocksee as it's tucked away in a cobbled courtyard behind a large complex of buildings, and we try a lot of doors—among them the Glocksee Youth Club and the Glocksee Theatre—before we are finally directed to the Glocksee music club. We pull up outside and Paul and I wait in the van while the band go in to make sure we are in the right place. Jonathan comes back with a thumbs up sign, then circles his hand to show Paul should turn the van around for load in.

'How am I doing on your side?' Paul asks as he edges the steering wheel round. He's missing the couple of large rocks next to the path, but just behind them there is a man-sized wrought iron sculpture of a dinosaur.

'You're fine,' I say. 'Just mind the dinosaur.'

He hesitates, then looks into the gaffa-taped wing mirror, sees what I am talking about and bursts into laughter. He can't drive for a couple of minutes as he's giggling too much. I join in. I think we may be hysterical.

What a great club! You know it as soon as you walk in: a good looking stage and P.A., plenty of space, a warm welcome from the people running it and a big spread of food laid out along the bar for us. I've had only a half a bowl of soup in the last 48 hours and am feeling desperately hungry but, fearful of unexpected consequences if I put anything in my stomach now, I make an emergency cheese sandwich and wrap it up for after the gig.

After soundcheck, promoter Marc walks me over to my hotel. I tell him that I can find it myself, but he insists. He's interested to see the protests, he says, and explains that there's a Swiss 'grey area' band playing in a big venue across the river. They have dubious politics with pop star stylings and are drawing in a lot of young people, so the anti-fascist campaigners have organised a demo outside the concert—just down the road from the hotel. Despite the pouring rain and the cold there is a good turnout for the protest, and my one hour rest in my room is accompanied by the sound of amplified speeches, chanting and firecrackers. I am a noise attractor.

Back at the venue, the first of the audience are coming in and there's a buzz in the air. I spend some time at the merch with Paul, where people are quite interested in what's on sale. One guy points at everything on the table and says he wants one of each. As he walks off with his haul, Paul looks on approvingly and under his breath says, 'Nice tickle.'

About ninety minutes before showtime I step across the stage, the only way in to the dressing room, and a girl in the audience screams excitedly assuming the show is about to start. In the backstage, Jonathan says drily, 'TV, you've still got it.'

Still, there's no backstage toilet so it's going to be embarrassing going back out for the pre-gig pee.

I still can't face the thought of beer, but handily the promoter has left a bottle of good Spanish wine back here, and I find a glass of that slips down a treat and helps get me in the mood for the show. My second ever gig without beer!

I definitely feel like I've lost weight though, my trousers keep threatening to fall down. I fiddle with my belt and grumble to Jonathan, 'I need a hole between *this* one which is too loose and *this* one which is too tight.'

'Now you want a belt roadie?' says Jonathan.

I glance at my watch. Still an hour to go. We who can't wait.

'An hour feels like a long time before a gig,' Jonathan agrees. 'But actually I love this feeling of being trapped, waiting for the cage to open, waiting to spring out, waiting for the circus to start…'

Waiting to fall off the trapeze. Waiting to break your fucking neck.

None of that happens. The gig goes like a dream and it feels good to actually enjoy it, compared to yesterday when I was just hoping I could get through it.

Back at the hotel the emergency sandwich tastes like the best meal I have ever eaten in my entire life.

## 30th November BRUSSELS

The final gig and miraculously we encounter no problems on the way. The fact that it is a Saturday probably contributes to the light traffic, and certainly to my triumphant victory in Horsebox, when I spot them in all the countries we travel through along the route: Germany, Holland and Belgium. Not that it's about the winning. But I am ready to accept my trophy in the Three Countries Horsebox Challenge Cup.

The fast journey means that we are in Brussels early enough to spend an hour in the hotel, but the narrow roads of the city centre are choked with traffic, there is absolutely nowhere to park, and despite the fact it's four in the afternoon two of the rooms aren't ready, so we decide to drive on to the venue. Paul has stayed in this hotel before and found that next morning a lot of the vehicles parked outside had been broken into, so we're going to play it safe and leave the van at the venue tonight, which is out of the centre opposite a police station.

The unassuming Excelsior Café conceals a surprise: you walk through the bar through a set of double doors to find a massive hall and high stage. I'm slightly worried about our ability to fill this place, and promoter Jean Claude has his concerns too. 'We have only sold about seventy tickets in advance,' he apologises.

'Oh dear,' I say, while secretly thinking, *Seventy? Yesss!!*

It's an old-fashioned concert hall, the wooden boards making up the floor of the high stage worn into ridges through heavy use. Soundcheck goes as good as can be expected in a place this size, then it's time to wait.

Jean Claude takes the band and Paul out to a restaurant he highly recommends, but I still can't risk eating before the gig and go upstairs to the large dressing room and make up an emergency baguette for later from the spread laid out on the table there. I tentatively open a bottle of beer but it still tastes disgusting. The red wine on the other hand tastes good. My third ever gig without beer.

I take the time alone to put on my stage clothes, somewhat more elaborate than for my solo gigs. I'm getting into my shirt when I hear the door open behind me. I button up and just as I am turning around to see who came in I hear the click of the door closing again and then the sound of footsteps gently retreating. I realise I have put on the shirt with the slogan 'LOOK AWAY!' on the back.

'You should try this wine,' I say to Jonathan when the band comes back in.

'Man, we just had the best wine and the best steak *ever!*' he exclaims, and collapses into a chair with a sigh of satisfaction. Touring is hell.

Paul storms in and eyes up the snacks on the table. He grabs a melon. 'These are the *devil's dumplings!*' he says. I guess he doesn't like melons.

Downstairs I'm delighted to see that the hall is filling up nicely. As it gets near showtime Jon and Sophie arrive. Next week I'll be playing their send-off party in London, just before they go back to live in Florida, but they've still come all the way over from the UK to Belgium to see the show here tonight. And have a little holiday, of course. 'We went to this amusement park today, TV,' says Jon. 'It had some nice little old-fashioned merry-go-rounds, but the best things was a journey through the inside of a dinosaur. You walk in through the mouth, then you make your way down the throat and the stomach to the intestines, then finally you get farted out the end!'

Unmissable, but sadly we will have to leave for our ferry tomorrow before I get the chance to get farted out of a dinosaur's arse. Something to look forward to next time perhaps.

Koan and Johan, two of the crew from the Toy Dolls arrive. There's Iain and Gerti, whose wedding I played last year in Belgium, and lots of other people who I don't know but who tell me how much they are looking forward to this evening. This is going to be one hell of a show.

Afterwards, Jean Claude tells me: 'You are welcome any time. Next time, I won't call you—you just tell me when you want to come.'

The band intend to stay and party and celebrate the last night of the tour, but Paul and I have a long drive back home tomorrow and we take a taxi back to the hotel at three.

In the hotel bathroom there is a sign that informs me:

*Using of the dusty room:*
*The dusty room takes place at level -1, when you get out the elevator, it's on your right.*
*You can throw your bin at every moment in the day.*

I bet you can. But right now I'm going to sleep.


## 1st December DOVER

The band have been dropped off at Brussels airport, we've made good time and caught our ferry, and are now sitting in the van among all the other vehicles at Dover waiting to drive off the ramp and back onto UK shores. The man in the hi-vis jacket gives a sign and we all start to edge forward.

'Eyes left, Paul!' I say.

There, just drawing out from behind a lorry and pulling up beside us, near enough to touch, a lovely…

'Horsebox!'

What a grand way to end a tour.

## 6th December LONDON

Back at the 12 Bar, for my second show this year here. A couple have come down from Sunderland to see the gig and find me at the merch: 'You were right when you said it's small!' they exclaim. Last time they saw me was at the one thousand capacity gig with the Toy Dolls in their home town. They want to know if it's best to watch from downstairs or from the balcony.

'Try and get in the front row downstairs,' I suggest. The up-the-nostrils view.

With fifty people in, the place is heaving. There's a great atmosphere and it's a pleasure to play—though after the Bored Teenagers tour I do find it slightly tricky to be playing guitar again and every now and then my fingers go off on a little unplanned journey of their own.

Afterwards I find Richie Rocker—a friend of mine from Liverpool and guitarist for support band The Crows—sitting at my merch stall. 'Looka tha',' he says. 'You left a scouser in charge of the merch and it's all still here!'

I expected to find the table up on bricks.

Cheers!
(At the merch table, 12 Bar, London)

# 7th December SOUTHEND-ON-SEA

My third gig in The Railway in Southend, one of my favourite music pubs in Britain. I try to get here once a year, and something unexpected always seems to happen when I do. The first time I played they had set up a makeshift stage in the downstairs bar and one of the speaker columns toppled over during the gig into the crush of people— luckily it wasn't too heavy. The second time I played in the upstairs room where there's a proper stage and there was a stage invasion at the end: all good fun, but then in the excitement a girl dived into the crowd and a couple of people got hurt when she landed on them. It's a health and safety nightmare.

I walk in to find what I presume is the support band setting up on a stage at the end of the downstairs bar and set my stuff down next to theirs, but they tell me I'm actually playing upstairs. I didn't realise there were going to be two gigs on at the same time. It's virtually a festival. Upstairs I find another band setting up called Eight Rounds Rapid. It turns out they are my support band for tonight and their guitarist is Wilko Johnson's son. Should be good. Even better, there's one overhead spotlight. Last time the only lighting was from a bank of floor lights at the front of the stage which did the dual job of making me look like I was in a scene from the Addams Family, and also blinding me every time I looked down at the guitar.

The adjoining upstairs bar isn't in use tonight but they open it up for me so I can set up my merch in there. Sometimes I'm fighting for table space but tonight I've got an entire room! Steve, one of the co-promoters, buys me a drink and as I start setting out what I have to sell we reminisce about the previous times I've been here. He gestures at the books I'm laying out. 'I'm almost thinking of making some terrible cock-up with the promoting tonight just so I'll get in your next diary!' he says.

'I'll tell you what, Steve,' I say, 'Don't bother. I'll put you in anyway.'

The audience start to arrive, and I notice Wilko has slipped in and is having a sit down on the other side of the room so I go over and have a chat. I have a huge amount of respect for the way he has handled his cancer diagnosis, always positive and celebrating life as long as he has it. Most people thought he'd be long gone ages ago. He set up his 'final tour' and when he'd finished that he was still going strong so he's put in some more gigs. 'It's getting embarrassing now,' he admits, and adds with a wry smile, 'I can't really plan too far ahead though.'

There's a good mix of old and new faces coming up the stairs, quite a few I recognise from the previous times I was here. One girl leaning on the bar where I have the merch set up tells me, 'I was knocked out last time you played.'

'Great!' I say, 'thank you!'

'No—I was actually knocked out. When that girl landed on me.'

That girl is here again tonight, and gets up on stage again, but perhaps armed with the knowledge of what happened last time, no one gets up to join her so she tires after a while and we get through the gig without any injuries. Dave, another of the co-promotors, told me before I started that the sound man Duncan has an 'operatic voice' and that it might be fun to invite him up to sing with me, so for the final song that's what I do. It not only makes a good finish to the two hour set, but also—when he's made his way through the crowd and is up beside me—gives me the chance to indulge in a favourite Harry Hill-ism and say into the microphone, 'But Duncan, if you're up here with me…*who's minding the sound desk?!*'

Afterwards I'm back behind the merch table, and my friend fanzine writer Andy P comes to say goodbye and give me a copy of the latest issue of 'Fear'n'Loathing,' in which he's generously given over the full back page to an advert for my solo album.

His girlfriend Karen is still in the gig room. He tells me, 'She said, "Where's Tim?" and I said, "He'll be in the other room on his merch." She thought about it for a moment and then said, "On his *perch?*"'

Yes, as always after a gig. Running from side to side a bit. Pecking at my mirror.

## 13th December MAIDSTONE

My third gig this year in the Style & Winch pub in Maidstone. I don't think I've played any other venue three times in a year. It's not that there's anything particularly special about it—a simple room at the back of the pub, no stage, free entry, small fee—but there's a regular bunch of locals who turn up, the atmosphere is always friendly, the sound is good, and organiser Clive keeps inviting me back.

Even better, I got an advance room for £29 in the brand new Premier Inn, just a stone's throw from the railway station. It's only a fifteen minute walk to the venue, across the river and into the town, which is festooned in Christmas lights, traffic clogging the streets as people do their last minute panic shopping. I feel a bit out of place trudging through the drizzle with my guitar case and bag of merch.

At the pub I find support act, my old mate Steven Cooper, already there along with his wife Fiona and the guy who's playing guitar for him. 'We saw you from the taxi, just by the station,' says Steven. 'We thought about stopping to give you a lift, but didn't. I poked my head out of the window and shouted 'Oi Tim, fuck off you wanker!' but by then we were already well past and I found I was shouting it at some random stranger."

Cheers.

I get the feeling that the numbers are down a bit for the gig compared to previous times, probably because everyone is in Christmas hysteria and out shopping or at home saving their money, but as it's a small room it still looks pretty full and it's a nice intimate gig.

Afterwards I stay on for a drink at the bar, then Clive and his girlfriend say they'll walk some of the way back towards the hotel with me as they're heading in the same direction. As we get outside the pub, Clive's girlfriend points at the funeral parlour across the road. There is a white Christmas tree in the window with sparkly lights. 'That's nice,' she says. 'Usually it's a coffin.'

They leave me at the end of the road and I walk on through the town centre. The mean streets of Maidstone are not a nice place to be two Fridays before Christmas. As I walk past a fried chicken takeaway shop a young lad is staggering out of it, eyes glazed, and suddenly throws up copiously in the doorway. His mate comes out and grabs him by the arm. 'Not there!' he says, and leads him into the next doorway, a gaming arcade, where he starts puking again to the resounding drunken cheers of people passing by.

It's enough to put me off my emergency sandwich.

## 14th December UXBRIDGE

Just a few miles down the road to tonight's gig. Jon and Sophie, who have been to many of my gigs over the last few years, are relocating back to the States in January, and have asked me to come and play their leaving party in a pub in Uxbridge. There will be plenty of people they have met at my gigs coming, as well as some of their work colleagues who they have harassed constantly over the past two years trying to convince them how good I am. If they don't like me, there's the buffet.

Jon and Sophie have booked a taxi to take me at 6:45, but at 7:00 it hasn't turned up and when I phone up the office there's no reply. I try that a few more times then ring Jon to tell him the situation. A few minutes later Sophie rings back to say I should try and get another cab. I'm just looking for a number when I get a call from an unknown number: it turns out to be Jon saying their phone just died so he's borrowing this one, and to let me know that if I'm having trouble finding a taxi Sophie could come and pick me up. If traffic is bad the round trip could take an hour so I tell him to hang on in case I can find a taxi. For a moment I consider simply getting on a bus, but it's just started raining, and I'm carrying a microphone and stand in addition to the merch and guitar because the PA in the venue is very basic. I'm looking through taxi numbers on the internet when I get another call from the unknown number, and it's Sophie saying she found a cab company and they are on their way. Twenty minutes later I get another call just as the doorbell goes. It's Sophie: 'They're ringing your bell now.'

I load my gear into the car and we set off, on the very first corner almost getting sideswiped by another car as my driver doesn't bother looking left as he pulls out of the junction. That keeps me on my toes for the twenty minute journey. By the time I walk into the pub it's getting on for 8:30, most of the guests are in and the buffet has had a good going over. 'I don't know what happened with the taxi,' says Jon. 'Somebody said they saw one hanging around outside here earlier so maybe they got it the wrong way around.'

A good number of TUTS are in the pub, as well as plenty of Jon and Sophie's workmates who have mainly staked out the tables running up the length of the room and look quite settled in. My friends The Phobics, whose gigs Jon and Sophie have also often attended, are standing at the back of the pub with their gear half set up on the floor around them, looking a bit bemused by it all.

Before I start attempting a soundcheck I go to wind down with a beer from the free bar, and I'm having a chat with a few TUTS when something occurs to me: there's no P.A. 'I thought this was going to be an easy one,' I sigh to no one in particular. I ask the pub landlord and he says that someone came in with a PA, but then saw the band setting up their equipment and thought it wasn't needed.

Luckily it hasn't gone far. A couple of speaker boxes and a mixer are carried back in and dumped on the table and the Phobics and I set about trying to wire it up. I hold my torch in my mouth and twiddle the knobs on the mixer while the Phobics try a soundcheck and we all agree it's as good as it's going to get.

I attempt to clear away some space on a table to set up some merch. I'm pretty certain no one here will be interested, but then some members of the Phobics come over and buy a couple of things, which is pleasing but slightly embarrassing. Singer Tom buys the latest diary and asks if I have another one on the way. I tell him about my project to write up every gig this year, and he says, 'So if we fuck up tonight we might end up in it...' He turns to his band mates. 'I hope you're listening.'

Soon it's time for them to start and as they have a couple of stand-ins and ex-members for this one-off gig, they play a few punk standards by Tom's favourites The New York Dolls and Dead Boys as well as their own songs. It's all good garage-y fun and Jon and Sophie's workmates clap politely. I imagine most of them have never heard of the Dead Boys.

Then it's time for me, and I have no idea what reaction I'm going to get but it seems like the workplace brainwashing has worked because everyone seems to get it. After the show a few people come up to the merch table to say how impressed they were, and one couple tell me, 'In future we are going to be the new Jon and Sophie and come to all your gigs.'

No sign of my lift home at 12:30 but at 1:00 a.m. a taxi arrives for the barmaid and the driver agrees to take me on to my place. It's sad to say goodbye to Jon and Sophie for the time being but they're already talking about coming back for Rebellion next August. I've got friends in London I see less often than that.

## 15th December LONDON

At 6:30 the phone rings. 'This is your driver. I'm on the way but traffic's bad so I might be a bit late.'

'Take your time,' I say. 'You're twenty-four hours late already.'

## 20th December KIRKCALDY

Black Friday. Not only the shortest day of the year but the final Friday before Christmas. Those who aren't out shopping seem to be travelling to Scotland, judging by the crush of people trying to get on the train. I get to my carriage just in time to grab the final free luggage spaces for my suitcase and guitar then settle in for the long journey. As we get further North the skies darken and the rain starts to hammer down, the trees whipping around in the strengthening wind. The forecast storm is coming, and after I've changed onto the branch line in Edinburgh it's a relief to safely get over the Forth Bridge, which was closed during the last big winter storm which brewed up a couple of weeks ago. At least I'll get to tonight's gig. Tomorrow may be a different story—I have to travel even further North to Aberdeen, which will involve going over the Tay rail bridge, also prone to bad weather closures, and the worst of the storm is supposed to be blowing in overnight.

By the time I get to Kirkcaldy station the rain has stopped. That's good news, because I can't see any sign of promoter Vonnie at either of the station exits so set off for the venue on foot. I'm about half way there when I get a call from my mate Jock, who is co-promoting the gig, to ask where I am because Vonnie is at the station in her car and can't find me. I turn around and head back, and over the blustery wind I hear someone calling my name. In the distance by the station I see a figure waving.

During the drive Vonnie says she has to tell me something: 'when I heard you were a vegan I didn't know what to get you to eat. I walked around the supermarket for half an hour and the only thing I could think of to get was a baguette and some salad.'

'That's fine,' I say, 'but I'm vegetarian not vegan. Would be great if you could find some cheese to go in it as well.' I'm not sure an emergency salad sandwich will be quite what I'm hungering for at the end of the night.

We park around the back of the rather seedy-looking Windsor Hotel, and go through the fire doors to find a surprisingly smart and well-equipped music room: large stage, wooden dance floor, the sound man just in the final process of setting up the more-than-adequate P.A. system. I get my soundcheck over quickly and make way for the other four acts who will be on tonight, then go and have a chat with Jock. He and Vonnie have been running this venue for a while now and have been trying to get me up here for ages. He tells me how well it's been going, and points out the table reserved for me to set up my merch, and the nails dotted around the wall that previous bands have used to hang up their T-shirts. The nail above where I've spread out the CDs and books comes out of the wall when I put a coat hanger on it, so I pull out a bigger nail from further along the wall and try and push it into the hole above my table, but it won't go. Luckily a guy I know called Larry, from Scottish band the Square Peg, has just turned up and tells me he has a hammer in his van. He brings it in for me and with a couple of hits the nail goes in nicely and I can hang the shirt up. I put the hammer down on the table and Larry looks at the display of books next to it. 'Will that get me a mention in the next volume?' he asks.

'It will,' I tell him.

While he's not looking I make up a sign saying *Hammer £10*, and put it on the table too.

Q: How do you fit a square peg in a round hole.

A: You whack it in with Larry's hammer.

Larry's not actually playing tonight, but some of the bands who are have arrived and started setting their equipment up on the stage. While they get ready for their soundchecks Jock gives me a key to one of the rooms upstairs where I'll be sleeping tonight and I go to put my suitcase in there and see what it's like. As I walk out I see that a few drops of water are dripping through the ceiling and some of the bar staff are hurrying to get buckets underneath to catch it. Doesn't bode well for my room.

Well, half a room. The ornamental plaster moulding on the edge of the ceiling stops suddenly where the once-spacious room has been divided, and the wall takes a sudden turn at one end to fit the window in. There's no bathroom either, and it's freezing cold. The thin radiator is barely working and there's a cable coming out of the back of the seventies-era TV that runs along the floor and out of the window so that it won't shut all the way. The gale is howling in so I try stuffing a towel into the gap. It also covers up some of the mildew.

Downstairs there's a solo singer-songwriter called Mark Ayling having a soundcheck, and a few more buckets have been set up under the leaks, which appear to have grown in number since I left. Vonnie and the pub manager are looking up at them with worried expressions, and a member of staff rushes in with a tall waste bin and replaces one of the overflowing smaller buckets with it. Jock and Larry are up on the roof trying to improvise a tarpaulin over the area, but come back to report that it's impossible as the roof is sloping and the rain is running down underneath the tarpaulin.

This is not good at all. Yesterday in London part of the ceiling of a West End theatre fell down after rain-damage injuring seventy-nine people and if the leak here doesn't stop soon we could be putting our audience at risk too. Vonnie points at the area of ceiling around the leaks, which are now starting to pour in over one of the light fittings. 'Does tha' look like it's *bulging* to you?'

It does. Suddenly a couple more staff run in and erect a portable barrier around the leaking area along with a yellow plastic prop-up 'DANGER! WET FLOOR!' sign, while others mop frantically and put down towels. Members of the audience who have turned up early watch from the bar area in fascination. One of the company who had been laying the new roof earlier today arrives and explains that the adhesive seals didn't have time to set before the rain started. Someone gets up on a stool and starts to cut away at the plasterboard with a knife to relieve the water pressure from above, then two metal posts are brought in from a lorry parked at the back and winched up to support the wettest section of the ceiling. Vonnie taps my arm. 'Tim—a word in the other room please.'

The word is, we have to cancel.

All this distance, my one hundred and twenty-first—and next-to-last—gig of the year scuppered by a leaking roof. 'We'll pay your train fare of course, and you can still sleep upstairs the night—and there's a case of beer for you!—but we can't go ahead with the roof like that,' says Vonnie. 'I'm going to have to go and tell the other bands to pack their stuff away.'

The venue manager also apologises. Exactly one year ago today, he confides, he held a Christmas party in another club in the town. During the evening an elderly woman slipped over, broke a collar bone and subsequently died. I can see why he's nervous about this. Black Friday.

Of course it's an annoyance to not get paid for tonight but what really bothers me is that some of the early arrivals I've been speaking to have travelled quite some distance for the gig. They're going to be even more disappointed than me. As I go back into the venue I notice a door off the corridor marked 'Restaurant' and poke my head in to have a look. There are just a few tables in there which could easily be pushed to one side. If they were out of the way there would be room for thirty or forty people at a squeeze. I have my guitar and can play without a PA system. It might just work.

How they hold the roof up
in Kirkcaldy

I talk it over with Vonnie, and she agrees it could be done. She offers one of the bedrooms upstairs to Mark so he doesn't have to drive back home tonight, and he agrees to play an acoustic set too. We'll let the people in for free so at least there will be some kind of event for them. It's disappointing for the other bands who now have to pack away, but for the rest of us—we have a gig!

While the tables are cleared to the sides of the room in the restaurant I go over to my merch table and start putting the CDs back into their boxes and take the T-shirts off the wall. I look sadly at the nail I went to so much trouble to organise. 'You'll best be taking that with you,' says Jock, 'You may be needing that in Aberdeen.'

'Has it really got that bad in Scotland?' I ask him. 'You have to bring your own nail?'

When I've nearly finished packing away I notice my friends Steven and Fiona hurrying through the rain outside to the open back doors. I go out to meet them. I saw them last at the Maidstone gig a couple of weekends ago and they're now up here visiting friends. I tell them the situation: 'We've had to cancel! The roof's leaking, there's water pouring in everywhere.' At that moment Jock rushes past with the waste bin that has been under the biggest leak and throws the contents out into the yard. 'There goes some of it now!'

I explain that I'll play an acoustic gig in another room. Steven and Fi come in and admire the scaffolding around the leaking roof then go up to the bar and get themselves something to drink. I carry my merch over to the restaurant and am quite surprised to see that Mark has already started. The light in there is so bright that the room has the ambience of a hospital, and the twelve people in there are pressed against the walls, understandably reluctant to stand in the middle. I go back out to the venue, where a lot more than twelve people are standing around in the bar enjoying a few drinks and watching the water gush down from the ceiling with rapt interest. I find Vonnie. 'We have to do something about the lights,' I tell her. 'It's horrible in there.'

'We could take in one of the stage lights,' she suggests.

'What colour are they?'

'Let's have a look...' She takes one of the boxes over to the electrical socket and plugs it in.

'Green! That's even worse!'

'Let's try the other one.'

The other one doesn't work at all.

'We could just unscrew some of the bulbs? At least then it won't be so bright.'

Vonnie goes to have a look and comes back smiling. 'There was a dimmer switch!'

I go back to the restaurant and catch Mark's last few songs. By the time he finishes there are around twenty people in the room and I tell them I'll start in a quarter of an hour. Most of them then go back out to the bar to get a drink and watch the progress of the leaks. Meanwhile I get Jock to help me up-end a few of the tables on to other ones to create some more space and set out a few chairs to try and draw people in to the middle of the room away from the sanctuary of the walls. Then I set up the merch again on a table next to where I will play, grab a few beers from the case, tune up, and strip down to my stage vest. The little room is crammed by the start and I play for an hour, receiving heartfelt applause at the end of each song. It's a very special gig, even though there are a few people who have had too much to drink and don't seem to realise that when they chatter away to each other they are louder than me. This draws a lot of annoyed comments from the rest of the crowd who are trying to listen. 'Can ye noa just *leave*?' says Jock, who is standing on a chair at the back of the room, exasperatedly to them.

Far from leaving, the two loudest girls make their way to the front and sit down on the sofa right next to me just as I get to the last song. When I finish they complain, 'C'mon, we've just go'a seat. Play sam moah!'

It's the right time to stop though, and now there's a crowd around the merch table so I go and deal with them. Many of them tell me it was the best gig they've seen all year. One guy says, 'I'm so glad I caught it. I came in and heard the gig was cancelled. One of the bar staff told me, "There's just going to be someone playing acoustic in the other room instead,' so I started home. On the way, I started to think, *It wouldn't be TV would it?* and came back…"

Soon the room starts to empty. I notice that it's now only 11:15, a quarter of an hour before my planned start time in the other room. Although Jock had been intending to stay the night upstairs he now tells me that he and girlfriend Carol have decided to drive home to Leven after all. 'That's a shame, would have been nice to sit and have a drink with you,' I say. 'But if you are going…could I have your room? Mine's bloody freezing!'

'Ach, I've already handed the key in,' says Jock. 'You could go and get it from behind the bar,' he adds, 'but, you know, our room was pretty cold too…and there was a *smell* in it…'

Okay then. Maybe stick with what I've got.

Vonnie comes to tell me she's leaving too. She apologises for the way things have turned out but promises to invite me back next year, and reminds me that there's still the rest of the case of beer for me in the other room behind the sound desk, and there's that baguette in the fridge behind the bar when I want it. Then everyone leaves and I quietly start packing away. A guy who is obviously quite drunk comes in and I recognise him as one of the talkers who was having a lively conversation with the two girls during the gig. 'Wheer ah yew frum?' he asks.

'London,' I say.

'So yer noa fram Norwich?'

'No. Why do you ask?'

He shows me his forearms, both of which have the word 'NORWICH' tattooed on them. 'Ah thought yew wiz fram Norwich,' he says forlornly. He spots the tour diary books I am just putting into my bag. 'I want one o' them!' he exclaims, and rummages around in his pockets, coming up with a crumpled tenner. He sits down at a table with the book and his pint and chats away while I pack the rest of my stuff. I hear a burp and a quick slosh of liquid. 'Aah, ah just pished up a bit there,' he apologises.

Well, time to go and put my things in my room, which it turns out hasn't warmed up any.

Back downstairs there's a grotesque karaoke in the front bar, so I go back to the music room, where the leak has finally stopped and it's mercifully peaceful. Mark and his girlfriend Morag are sitting quietly at a table and I go over to join them. 'I've heard you're getting the train up to Aberdeen tomorrow,' says Mark. 'We live twenty minutes north of there—we could give you a lift if you like.'

Great! Not only do I save the price of the ticket, I'll have some company and also avoid the risk of the rail bridge being shut. We sit amiably chatting for a while, but it doesn't take long for the drunk guy to find us. He plonks the book and a fresh beer down on the table. After a while he pishes up a bit again and some of it lands on the book. Shortly afterwards he staggers out and doesn't return. Out in the corridor the two drunk girls are arguing loudly with the security guys on the door. Wafting in from the front bar come the strains of the most appalling karaoke version of 'A Fairytale In New York' that I have ever heard. After the dreadful duo attempting it have finished, the DJ puts on the original version, just to remind everyone what it's supposed to sound like.

I suddenly realise that I am now very hungry and remember the sandwich that was supposed to have been put in the fridge behind the bar for me. I go and ask the barmaid if it's still there and she looks doubtful. 'I'll just double check,' she says.

That doesn't sound very promising. But in fact a few minutes late she turns up with it. Some cheese has apparently been found—I can see it in there amongst the salad. A whole baguette is more than I can eat, and Morag and Mark say they are hungry too so I split it with them then tell them I'm going to go and eat in my room, away from the terrible karaoke and the water-splattered floor and the puke-stained book, which the guy has left behind. 'I don't think I'll be able to re-sell that on the merch,' I say. We arrange to meet up tomorrow for the ride up to Aberdeen, then I head upstairs where I eat the emergency sandwich using a tourist brochure titled *Welcome To The Kingdom Of Fife* as a plate.

Just before I go to sleep I notice the hotel fire instructions posted on the back of the door. They are going to be difficult to follow:

*ON HEARING THE ALARM BY NIGHT: -*

*1. Put on your dressing gown and shoes.*
I don't have a dressing gown.

*2. Awaken other occupants of the room.*
No other occupants!

*3. Close all windows.*
One word: 'Cable.'

*4. Go directly to the assembly place.*

But where is the assembly place?!?

*5. Close the room door.*

Just a minute—according to number four I'm already at the assembly place, wherever it is, so that would mean I have to come back into the burning building just to close the room door...

It's so cold I sleep in my clothes.


## 21st December ABERDEEN

I wake up early to find the the sun shining in through the window. Outside I can hear the gentle *whoosh* of roofers heating tar somewhere nearby. The shower room is occupied when I first try it, but ten minutes later on the second attempt it's free, and I'm relieved to find it's still clean too. There's no plug in the washbasin though. O, emergency travel sink plug from Exeter—I call upon your services for probably the final time this year.

Once I've showered and dressed I text Mark to tell him I'm ready to leave if he is, and he replies saying let's meet downstairs in five minutes. As he and Morag get into the car I notice an advertising hoarding for the hotel on the wall outside with a photo of a spacious and light bay-windowed room with a double bed and a single bed in it. 'Was yours anything like that?' I ask.

'No,' Mark replies. 'It smelled of onion and garlic and there was only a single bed for the two of us. I really should have checked it first.'

As we drive off he tells me that last night after I'd gone upstairs he found someone who wanted the book. 'Didn't he mind the puke stain?' I ask.

'No, he thought it made it more *punk*.'

Before heading to Aberdeen we drive down to Kirkcaldy seafront to see what it's like. Put it this way, I won't be making any new holiday plans.

Mark gets a bit confused finding the way to the motorway from the seafront and we are soon heading South, which as he points out, is extremely picturesque with spectacular views across the Firth—but the wrong direction. Morag says from the back seat that we need to be following the signs for Perth, but there are none. We head inland along some B-roads through assorted small towns, hoping we will at some point hit a major route. While Morag attempts to pick up a GPS signal on her phone, Mark turns to me and says, 'I suppose we will be in your next book now, for offering you a lift and getting lost.'

'You will be in it for being kind enough to give me a lift,' I assure him. 'I'm enjoying going the pretty route.'

Morag pipes up from the back, 'I've found Perth. But it's Perth, Australia.'

Soon enough we hit an A-road, then a dual carriageway, and then we are on the motorway heading North. It doesn't take long before the sun disappears behind the clouds and the rain starts to hammer down again. The car is rocking in the crosswind. 'I don't think that repair job they were doing on the roof stands much of a chance of holding,' I point out.

By the time we get to Aberdeen at midday it's as dark as evening, and we pull up outside tonight's gig, The Moorings, down on the harbour to find that, alas, it is closed. Soundcheck isn't until six. I'm supposed to sleep in a room above the venue tonight, and now Mark and Morag have to drive on to their home so I am effectively stranded. There's a gale ripping off the North Sea and the rain hits like icy bullets so I hole up in a café for a few hours where I get a late breakfast and am able to log on to wi fi and check my emails. It's nearly three in the afternoon when I happen to look at the Moorings website and find that their weekend opening hours are one until three, so I gulp down the rest of my coffee and hurry back down there to catch them before they close up again.

In fact they don't close in the afternoon at all, the barmaid tells me—they're now open until three *tomorrow morning*. She rings up Flash, the owner of the venue, and he comes in and takes me upstairs. All the bar staff stay in apartments in the building, with one reserved for the bands, comprising the office, kitchen, bathroom and bedroom— three bunk beds in it. As I'm on my own that's spacious enough, if somewhat cold. The first thing I do is go around plugging in all the heaters and switching them up to full.

With a few hours to kill and unencumbered by my luggage and guitar it occurs to me that this is the last chance I will have to get anyone any Christmas presents so I head into the centre to see if inspiration strikes. For God's sake, you'd think there'd be some little independent shop selling some traditional Scottish shortbread—at least it would be a token gift—but no, I soon find myself wondering helplessly around a clone town mall full of the same brand names you see everywhere and despairingly realise that this year there will be no presents for anyone I know. Unless it's packs of mini shortbreads with *Network Rail* stamped on them. And if I *ever* hear that song that goes, '*You should never dance a tango with an eskimo—no, no, no—no, no, no,*' again I may have to kill someone, possibly myself.

Back at the apartment it's a relief to sit in silence only interrupted by the occasional twang of my guitar strings as I put on a new set. Promoter Hen turns up and busies himself in the office. He warns me that Flash doesn't usually pay the bands until next morning. 'Probably because they're sleeping here: insurance in case there's any damage I suppose. There's probably nothing going to get destroyed with you here on your own though, eh?' he says.

'I'm more likely to tidy the place up,' I admit.

Hen tells me that there's no food here and gives me some money to go out and buy something, so I slip back outside and skirt round the Christmas consumerism nightmare to the nearest corner shop and buy an emergency cheese sandwich for after the gig. It's chilly and dark out there, but the rain has stopped and the skies are clearing to reveal twinkling stars. The longest night is over. We're on the way to Summer.

At six I take my guitar downstairs for soundcheck. The soundman cranks a chain behind a door on the back wall and a metal grille slides up to reveal a fully equipped stage behind it, drum kit and amps ready set up for bands, and even a couple of D.I. Boxes attached to the drum riser where they can't get kicked about and their cables damaged. Consequently my soundcheck takes no time at all, and support act Fred Wilkinson from local legends Toxik Ephex is able to get on stage after a few minutes and set his stuff up. He'll be playing some solo songs, then the rest of his set with a new band he's trying out for the first time.

Refreshingly, the club has a huge selection of real ales, and I settle on the lightest one I can find—a local, specially brewed Christmas ale. That's the nearest I'll get to celebrating the festive season. The place soon starts to fill. A lot of people have travelled long distances: I recognise a couple from Bacup—that's a six hour drive. The last time I saw them they'd driven down to a gig in Devon. I still can't quite believe that people like what I'm doing enough to do that.

Fred gets on stage and starts his set with some excellent politically-charged solo songs with a folk feel to them, then invites the three other members up and it sounds even better. After he finishes I tell him, 'That mandolin was sounding really nice.'

'That's a bazouki,' he says.

We chat a bit about the state of music and how the good stuff doesn't seem to get through. 'All the business is interested in is celebrity,' I say. 'It's much easier to manipulate than talent.'

'And as soon as people get famous they lose the talent.'

'Usually,' I agree.

'Success is like the Bermuda Triangle,' says Fred. 'You slip into it and you disappear.'

I get on stage and play for my life, taking a lot of unexpected requests from the crowd and making the most of my last gig of the year. The Aberdeen audience rewards me with a treat: towards the end three guys crouch in front of the stage, two more hop on top, then finally a sixth jumps on their shoulders and they serenade the final song of the set with a human pyramid, the guy at the top punching his fists in the air. Then the pyramid collapses and a conga starts up to the encore, Runaway Train Driver—all these tough-looking punk rockers running up and down the pub having a whale of a time doing a train impression.

You just never know what will happen.

## 22nd December ABERDEEN—LONDON

Under an hour to go before my train to London leaves, and I'm getting a bit nervous about getting the fee—two in a row without getting paid would be a less than ideal way to end the year—when I hear Flash coming into the apartment. I'm somewhat surprised to see he has a large brightly-coloured parrot on his shoulder. I manage to stop myself checking to see if he has acquired a wooden leg to go with it. I follow him into the office and the parrot hops up onto the top of the door while Flash gets out the money.

'That is a beautiful bird. How long have you had her?' I ask.

'Seven years,' says Flash, reaching up and chucking the parrot under the throat affectionately. 'She should live a long time too. Unfortunately she's ill at the moment.'

'Really? She looks healthy...'

'That's the trouble—parrots don't show it when they're sick. The only way I can tell is that her voice is a bit croaky. It could potentially be life-threatening and and I can't get a vet this close to Christmas. I might have to start medicating her myself and hope for the best.'

It's just a short walk up to Aberdeen rail station, my luggage mercifully light after good merch sales over the last two nights. A seven hour journey ahead of me so I settle back into my seat and I start writing this.

From Kings Cross it's the Hammersmith and City line to Shepherds Bush Market tube station, then a chilly wait for the 207 bus and a walk down the road. I'm home by 8:30 in the evening. Open a Christmas card. Get a paper cut.

www.ingramcontent.com/pod-product-compliance
Lightning Source LLC
Chambersburg PA
CBHW080513090426
42734CB00015B/3043